Create detailed, annotated maps to enl
and illustrate your data.

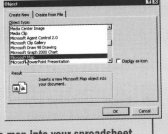

Insert a map into your spreadsheet as you would any object.

Create headings, titles, and borders to help distinguish and clarify your data segments.

	Stores	Sales (Thousands)
Austria	4	$ 6,000.00
France	4	$ 6,400.00
German	10	$ 14,000.00
Ireland	5	$ 8,500.00
Italy	6	$ 6,000.00
Poland	1	$ 1,100.00
Spain	8	$ 15,200.00
Sweden	8	$ 16,000.00
Switzerland	3	$ 4,800.00
UK	8	$ 13,600.00

Excel maps automatically produce legends, color-code countries, and zoom in on and display population centers.

Office 2000's Microsoft Maps not only provide pictorial map data; they also show relative distances and customized location settings.

BLUEPRINTS *for Busy People*

Create a spreadsheet that includes all the variables needed to figure out your retirement savings needs.

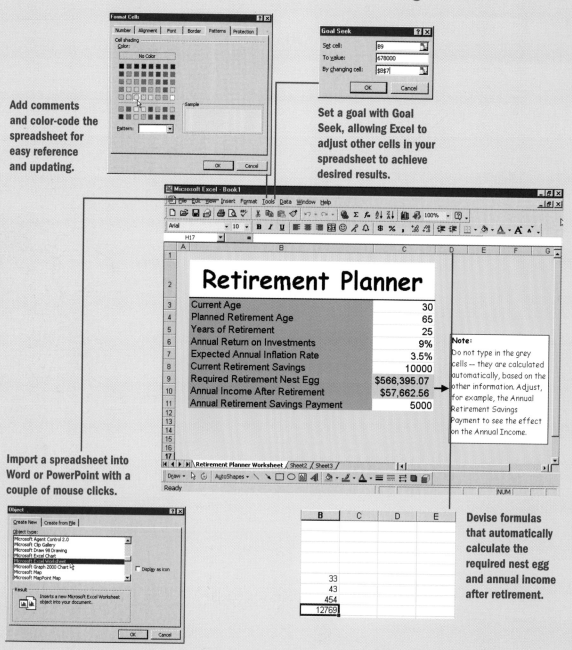

Add comments and color-code the spreadsheet for easy reference and updating.

Set a goal with Goal Seek, allowing Excel to adjust other cells in your spreadsheet to achieve desired results.

Import a spreadsheet into Word or PowerPoint with a couple of mouse clicks.

Devise formulas that automatically calculate the required nest egg and annual income after retirement.

Retirement Planner

Current Age	30
Planned Retirement Age	65
Years of Retirement	25
Annual Return on Investments	9%
Expected Annual Inflation Rate	3.5%
Current Retirement Savings	10000
Required Retirement Nest Egg	$566,395.07
Annual Income After Retirement	$57,662.56
Annual Retirement Savings Payment	5000

Note: Do not type in the grey cells -- they are calculated automatically, based on the other information. Adjust, for example, the Annual Retirement Savings Payment to see the effect on the Annual Income.

Excel 2000

for Busy People

BLUEPRINTS *for Busy People*

Create brochures and flyers that entertain as well as inform with Excel's drawing, formatting and artistic tools.

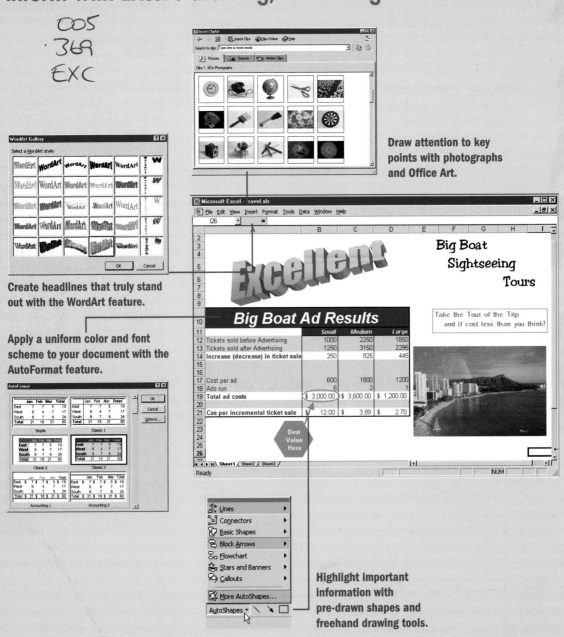

Draw attention to key points with photographs and Office Art.

Create headlines that truly stand out with the WordArt feature.

Apply a uniform color and font scheme to your document with the AutoFormat feature.

Highlight important information with pre-drawn shapes and freehand drawing tools.

Big Boat Ad Results

	Small	Medium	Large
Tickets sold before Advertising	1000	2250	1850
Tickets sold after Advertising	1250	3150	2295
Increase (decrease) in ticket sale	250	925	445
Cost per ad	600	1800	1200
Ads run	6	2	1
Total ad costs	$ 3,000.00	$ 3,600.00	$ 1,200.00
Cos per incremental ticket sale	$ 12.00	$ 3.89	$ 2.70

Big Boat
Sightseeing
Tours

Take the Tour of the Trip
and if cost less than you think!

Best
Value
Here

Analyze credit card, mortgage, and other loan data by calculating interest owed and number of months to pay off.

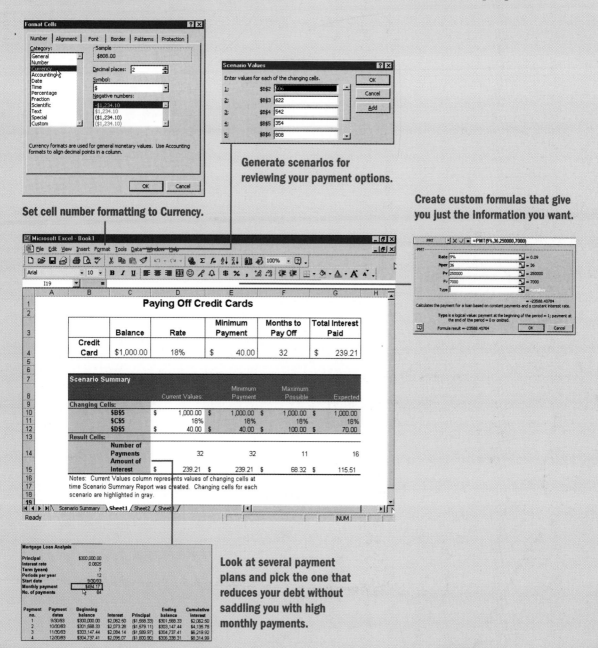

Set cell number formatting to Currency.

Generate scenarios for reviewing your payment options.

Create custom formulas that give you just the information you want.

Look at several payment plans and pick the one that reduces your debt without saddling you with high monthly payments.

Create a Billing spreadsheet that automatically includes price information when you type a billable item.

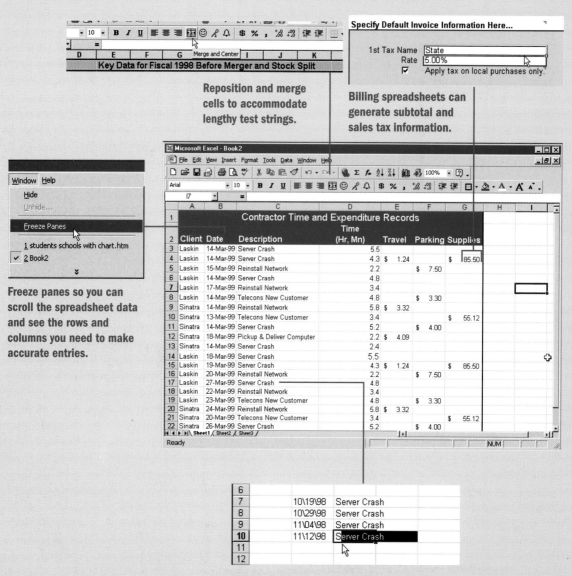

Reposition and merge cells to accommodate lengthy test strings.

Billing spreadsheets can generate subtotal and sales tax information.

Specify Default Invoice Information Here...

1st Tax Name State
Rate 5.00%
☑ Apply tax on local purchases only.

Key Data for Fiscal 1998 Before Merger and Stock Split

Window Help
Hide
Unhide...
Freeze Panes
1 students schools with chart.htm
✓ 2 Book2

Freeze panes so you can scroll the spreadsheet data and see the rows and columns you need to make accurate entries.

Microsoft Excel - Book2

Contractor Time and Expenditure Records

	Client	Date	Description	Time (Hr, Mn)	Travel	Parking	Supplies
3	Laskin	14-Mar-99	Server Crash	5.5			
4	Laskin	14-Mar-99	Server Crash	4.3	$ 1.24		$ 85.50
5	Laskin	15-Mar-99	Reinstall Network	2.2		$ 7.50	
6	Laskin	14-Mar-99	Server Crash	4.8			
7	Laskin	17-Mar-99	Reinstall Network	3.4			
8	Laskin	14-Mar-99	Telecons New Customer	4.8		$ 3.30	
9	Sinatra	14-Mar-99	Reinstall Network	5.8	$ 3.32		
10	Sinatra	13-Mar-99	Telecons New Customer	3.4			$ 55.12
11	Sinatra	14-Mar-99	Server Crash	5.2		$ 4.00	
12	Sinatra	18-Mar-99	Pickup & Deliver Computer	2.2	$ 4.09		
13	Sinatra	14-Mar-99	Server Crash	2.4			
14	Laskin	18-Mar-99	Server Crash	5.5			
15	Laskin	19-Mar-99	Server Crash	4.3	$ 1.24		$ 85.50
16	Laskin	20-Mar-99	Reinstall Network	2.2		$ 7.50	
17	Laskin	27-Mar-99	Server Crash	4.8			
18	Laskin	22-Mar-99	Reinstall Network	3.4			
19	Laskin	23-Mar-99	Telecons New Customer	4.8		$ 3.30	
20	Sinatra	24-Mar-99	Reinstall Network	5.8	$ 3.32		
21	Sinatra	20-Mar-99	Telecons New Customer	3.4			$ 55.12
22	Sinatra	26-Mar-99	Server Crash	5.2		$ 4.00	

6			
7	10\19\98	Server Crash	
8	10\29\98	Server Crash	
9	11\04\98	Server Crash	
10	11\12\98	Server Crash	
11			
12			

If you've previously typed a phrase or number, Excel remembers it, finishing your typing as soon as you begin.

Save time and energy by using Excel's expense template with its built-in formatting and formulas.

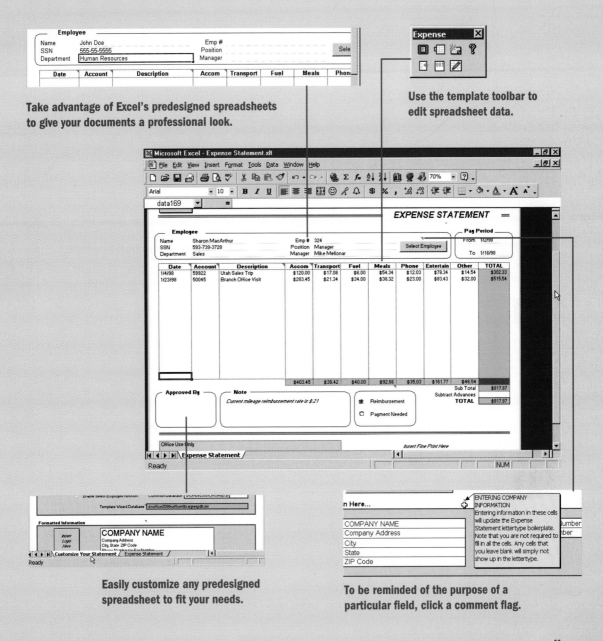

Take advantage of Excel's predesigned spreadsheets to give your documents a professional look.

Use the template toolbar to edit spreadsheet data.

Easily customize any predesigned spreadsheet to fit your needs.

To be reminded of the purpose of a particular field, click a comment flag.

Create spreadsheets like this College Expense table to calculate variables and provide muliple solutions based on your choices.

Clarify content by using different colors to highlight changes in the data category.

Use functions to create projections that reflect real-world changes in your financial picture.

Create font and cell styles that can be applied to any spreadsheet as needed.

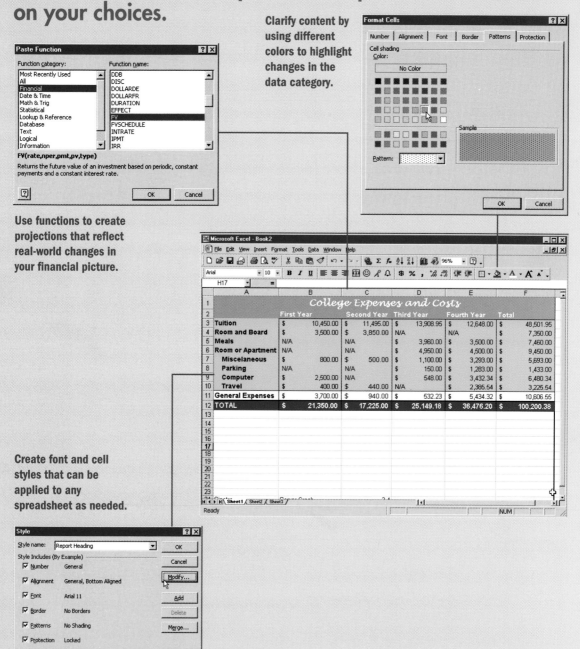

Instantly turn your data into fully labeled charts, complete with legends and scalable data ranges.

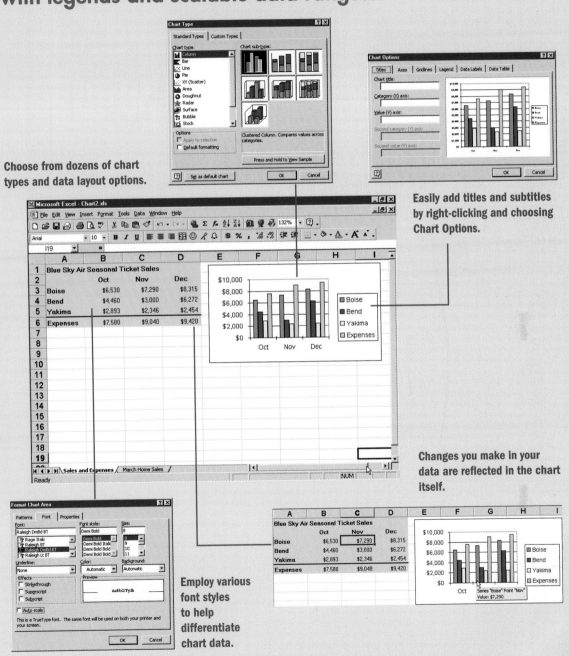

Choose from dozens of chart types and data layout options.

Easily add titles and subtitles by right-clicking and choosing Chart Options.

Changes you make in your data are reflected in the chart itself.

Employ various font styles to help differentiate chart data.

Instantly create Web pages from Excel spreadsheets. Your spreadsheet will appear just as it does in Excel, and it can be edited online without downloading.

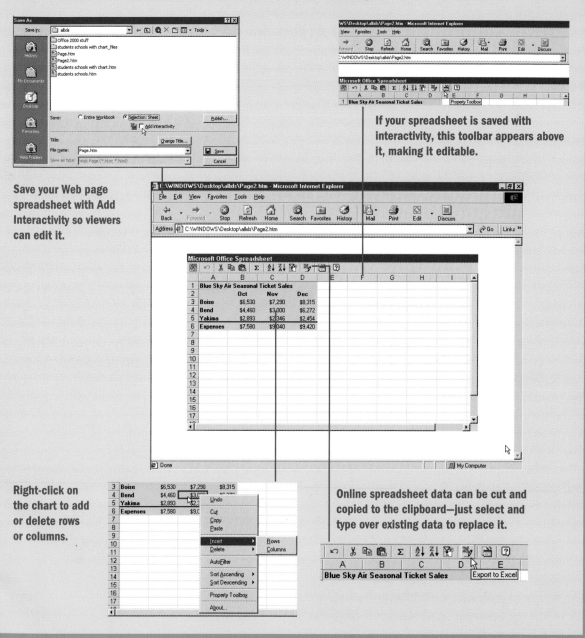

If your spreadsheet is saved with interactivity, this toolbar appears above it, making it editable.

Save your Web page spreadsheet with Add Interactivity so viewers can edit it.

Right-click on the chart to add or delete rows or columns.

Online spreadsheet data can be cut and copied to the clipboard—just select and type over existing data to replace it.

Excel 2000

for Busy People

The Book to Use When There's No Time to Lose!

Ron Mansfield

OSBORNE

Osborne/McGraw-Hill

Berkeley / New York / St. Louis / San Francisco / Auckland / Bogotá
Hamburg / London / Madrid / Mexico City / Milan / Montreal / New Delhi
Panama City / Paris / São Paulo / Singapore / Sydney / Tokyo / Toronto

A Division of The **McGraw·Hill** *Companies*

Osborne/**McGraw-Hill**
2600 Tenth Street
Berkeley, California 94710
U.S.A.

For information on translations or book distributors outside the U.S.A., or to arrange bulk
purchase discounts for sales promotions, premiums, or fund-raisers, please contact
Osborne/**McGraw-Hill** at the above address.

Excel 2000 for Busy People

1234567890 DOC DOC 90198765432109

ISBN 0-07-211988-8

Contributing author on this book was Winston Steward.

Publisher   Brandon A. Nordin
Associate Publisher and Editor-in-Chief   Scott Rogers
Acquisitions Editor   Joanne Cuthbertson
Project Editor   Jennifer Wenzel
Editorial Assistant   Stephane Thomas
Technical Editor   Bryan Sennigan
Copy Editor   Judy Ziajka
Proofreader   Rhonda Holmes
Indexer   Valerie Robbins
Graphic Artist   Robert Hansen, Beth Young, Brian Wells
Computer Designers   Michelle Galicia, Roberta Steele, Gary Corrigan
Series Designer   Jil Weil
Cover Design   Damore Johann Design, Inc.
Cover Illustration/Chapter Opener Illustration   Robert deMichiell

This book was composed with Corel VENTURA.

Not everybody remembers the first time they opened up a spreadsheet on their computer, fighting off a gnawing sense of incomprehension that gradually gave way to panic. This book is for you. Keep reading. It will get better.

About the Authors

Ron Mansfield is a microcomputer consultant and a critically-acclaimed author. He has written more than a dozen best-selling computer books with over 2,000,000 copies in print. Ron is a frequent lecturer at national computer seminars and has written hundreds of articles for industry magazines and newsletters.

Contributing author, Winston Steward, has written or co-written nearly a dozen books on computer graphic design, word processing, desktop publishing, web design, personal finance and business management software. He lives with his family in Los Angeles, California.

CONTENTS AT A GLANCE

1   Getting Started   1

2   Stuff to Do Once to Make Your Life Easier   27

3   Rearranging Your Worksheets   53

4   The Basics of Numbers and Formulas   71

5   Formatting Tricks   103

6   Managing Large Projects   129

7   An Introduction to Functions   155

8   Charts   175

9   Graphics   201

10 Introduction to Macros   231

11 Automating What-If Projects   245

12 Excel, the Internet and Intranets   265

    Index   289

CONTENTS

Acknowledgments, xxv
Introduction, xxvii

1 Getting Started **1**
Getting Familiar with Excel 4
   Cells and Worksheets 4
   Sheets and Workbooks 5
   How Cells are Organized 6
Starting Excel 9
   Opening an Existing Worksheet 10
   Getting To Know Excel 12
Selecting Cells 13
   Selecting Cells with a Mouse 13
   Selecting Cells with Your Keyboard 15
   Moving to a New Cell 16
Navigating in Excel 16
   Navigating with the Keyboard 17
   Navigating with the Edit Menu 17
Entering Text and Numbers 19
   How Excel Automatically Fills Cells 19
Saving Worksheets 21
Protecting Your Work from Prying Eyes
   and Flying Fingers 22
   Protecting Your Files 23
   Protecting Your Workbooks, Worksheets,
      and Cells 23
Quitting Excel 24
Checkpoint 25

2   Stuff to Do Once to Make Your Life Easier   27

Using an Excel Template   30

Features Common to Most Excel Templates   32

Locating and Opening a Template   34

Locating Additional Templates   35

Working with an Excel Template   39

Exploring a Template Example   41

Exploring Other Types of Templates   46

Customizing Toolbars and Menus   47

Customizing Toolbar   48

Customizing Menus   51

Checkpoint   52

3   Rearranging Your Worksheets   53

Moving Data from Place to Place on Your Worksheet . . .   56

Fearless Updating   56

More Than Just Copying   56

Selecting Cells   57

Selecting Multiple Cells   57

Moving Cells, Rows, and Columns   57

Moving Cells   58

Using the Cut-and-Paste Feature   58

Sorting Cells, Rows, and Columns   62

Adding New Cells, Rows, and Columns   63

Inserting Cells   64

Inserting Rows and Columns   65

Removing Information from Your Worksheet   65

Clearing Cell Contents   65

Expert Selecting   66

Selecting New Cells and Adding Content
Simultaneously   66

Using Excel's Add-and-Repeat Labels Feature   67

Creating Data and Label Patterns 68

Avoiding Data Growth in a List 69

Checkpoint 70

4   The Basics of Numbers and Formulas 71

Working with Numbers 77

Understanding Number Formats 78

Formatting Number Cells 78

Working with Formulas 80

Creating Formulas 81

The Order of Operations in Formulas, or Operation
Precedence 82

Applying Formulas to New Cells 83

Moving Formulas Simultaneously 84

Excel's Formula Operators 85

Arithmetic Operators 85

Comparison Operators 86

Text Operator 86

Reference Operators 86

Referencing Cells in Your Formulas 86

Advanced Formula Techniques 89

Triggering an Action with a Text Entry 89

Putting a Formula to Work 90

Instant Calculations 94

Excel's Automatic Recalculation Feature 98

Using Relative, Absolute, and Mixed Cell
References 98

Formula References and Moving Cells 100

Checkpoint 101

5   Formatting Tricks 103

What Formatting Accomplishes 108

Examples of Formatting 108

"Automagically" Formatting Your Worksheets 112
    Using Excel's AutoFormat Feature 112
    Using Styles 114
    Using Format Painter 116
Creating Formats 117
    Modifying Rows and Columns 117
    Formatting Your Text 119
    Formatting Numbers 123
    Borders, Colors, Images, and Page Breaks 124
Removing Formatting 128
Checkpoint 128

6   **Managing Large Projects** **129**
Understanding Named Cell Ranges 133
Creating and Applying Range Names 133
    Creating Formulas
      with Your Named Groups 137
Expanding and Collapsing Worksheet Segments 141
    Using the Collapse/Expand Feature 143
    Using Filters to View Specific Data 143
Freezing Rows and Columns 147
Working with Multiple Worksheets 149
    Naming Your Worksheets 149
    Moving and Copying Worksheets 150
Checkpoint 153

7   **An Introduction to Functions** **155**
Using Worksheet Functions 158
    Understanding the Parts of a Function 159
    Pasting Functions 161
    Dealing with Error Messages 163
    Using Functions That Require Excel Add-Ins 165

Types of Functions 166
    Date and Time Functions 166
    Database Functions 167
    Engineering Functions 167
    Financial Functions 168
    Information Functions 170
    Logical Functions 170
    Lookup and Reference Functions 171
    Math and Trigonometry Functions 172
    Statistical Functions 172
    Text Functions 173
Checkpoint 173

8 Charts **175**
Understanding Chart Terminology 179
    Axes 179
    Tick Marks and Grid Lines 181
    Chart Text 181
    Chart Data Series 181
    Chart Data Series Ranges 181
    Chart Data Series Names 181
    Category Names 182
    Chart Data Series Markers 182
Creating Charts 182
Modifying Charts 184
    Editing Chart Elements 185
    Resizing and Moving Charts 186
    Adding Text Boxes 187
    Drawing Arrows 189
    Creating Trendlines 191
    Adding Overlay Charts 192

Changing Chart Defaults 193
    Changing the Axis Default 193
    Changing the Chart Type Default 194
Using Microsoft Map 195
    Editing Maps 196
    Using Demographic Information 197
Printing Charts 197
Deleting Charts 198
Publishing Charts on the Internet 198
Checkpoint 198

9   Graphics 201
Showing Restraint: How to Employ Spreadsheet
   Graphics 205
Types of Graphics 206
    Clipart 206
    Simple Drawings 207
    Word Art 207
    Flow Chart Tools 208
    Imported Pictures 208
Adding Graphics to Your Spreadsheet 209
    Creating Callouts, Starbursts,
      and Complex Shapes 211
    Creating Text Boxes 215
    Creating Word Art 216
    Adding Clipart to Your Spreadsheet 217
    Inserting Images from Other Sources 219
Editing Graphics 220
    Moving, Nudging, and Aligning Images 220
    Grouping and Layering Images 223
    Cutting, Copying, and Pasting Images 225

Changing a Picture's Color Depth 226
Graphic Insertion Methods 227
Checkpoint 229

10 Introduction to Macros **231**
Understanding Macros 234
Recording Your Own Macros 235
Creating a Sample Macro 237
Running a Macro 237
Using Menus and Toolbars
to Run Your Macros 238
Assigning a Macro to a Toolbar Button 238
Assigning Macros to Graphic Objects 241
Deleting Macros 243
Displaying Your Personal Macro Workbook 243
Checkpoint 244

11 Automating What-If Projects **245**
Keeping Track of Changing Variables 248
What Is a Scenario? 248
What Is Scenario Manager? 249
How Scenarios Work 249
Starting with Good Data 249
Creating a Scenario 250
Viewing Scenarios 254
Creating Scenario Summaries 254
Creating Scenario Pivot Tables 255
Changing Scenarios 256
Protecting Scenarios 256
Using Solver 257
Installing and Loading Solver 257

Solving What-If Problems 258

Checkpoint 263

12   Excel, the Internet and Intranets **265**

Create Editable Online Spreadsheets 269

Deciding to Use Excel with Networks 270

Differences Between the Internet and Intranets 270

Adding Internet and Intranet Tools 271

Publishing Your Worksheets on a Web 273

Step 1: Prepare Worksheets 274

Adding Links to Your Worksheets 275

Step 2: Save Worksheets 278

Step 3: Testing Worksheets 281

Step 4: Publish Worksheets 281

Sharing Documents on the Internet 286

Sharing Worksheets with People Who Don't
Have Excel 286

Checkpoint 288

Index **289**

Acknowledgments

Special thanks to Joanne Cuthbertson, Stephane Thomas, Jennifer Wenzel, and Nancy McLaughlin at Osborne for all their patience and thoughtful editing, guiding this project through thick and thin, and Margot Maley Hutchison at Waterside Productions, for always coming through.

Introduction

It's not necessary to love spreadsheets in order to use them. Nor must you know all there is to know about Excel to do a job with it. Perhaps you've bought this book because your career requires a working knowledge of Excel, or the organizational demands of your small business are beyond what you can keep track of on paper. Or perhaps you have an idea for your financial future and you want to see if the numbers justify it. In any event, you are here to learn to make sense of numbers. Numbers do tell a story, and Excel makes that story clear.

Numbers also change. Sales volumes fluctuate, laboratory results vary from week to week, populations grow and shrink, and Excel takes that entire jumble of data and distills it to patterns that make sense to you, and those who read your work. With Excel, you type in numbers, the "how many?" "how far?" "how long?" and walk away with colorful charts and tables, with all the important stuff highlighted, ready for you to make the most of. Excel puts the data at your service.

This book brings you essential Excel knowledge in a hurry. I remember quite well the frustration of trying to learn a complex program in a night or two, dearly wishing I could sleep with a book under my pillow and wake up knowing it all. In any tricky program, you sense a division between the important stuff—the features you need to know right now—and the more esoteric functions that you won't have time to cover any time soon.

Yes, and wouldn't it be nice to have the basics of a program clearly laid out at your fingertips? Excel for Busy People does just that. It is with those needs in mind that this book was written. So, very soon from now, if someone says: "Fax me that budget," or "E-mail me those statistics," you'll have it done quickly.

I Know You're in a Hurry, So ...

Lets cut to the chase. I suggest cruising Chapter 1 and reading Chapter 2 first, but you'll be fine no matter how much you bounce around. In a remarkably short period of time, you'll be able to:

- Start and quit Excel
- Create great looking workbooks and worksheets
- Use and create templates
- Rearrange and reformat worksheets
- Deal with printing and font issues
- Personalize the look, feel, and sound of Excel
- Organize large spreadsheet projects
- Use Excel's built-in functions for complex computations
- Display numbers in powerful, convincing graphs, and even create maps
- Harness macros to speed repetitive tasks
- Use Excel in conjunction with the Internet or intranet
- Take care of all of those one-time-only tweaks that make working with Excel more productive and enjoyable
- Audit, troubleshoot, protect, and share your worksheets

Remember, though, just because you can do something with Excel doesn't mean that you should. Simple is often best, particularly when you are busy. We'll try to remind you of that from time to time.

Excel 2000 for Windows 98/2000: The Next Generation

With Excel 2000, creating a Web page from your spreadsheet is almost instantaneous. Excel 2000 also brings new graphic, chart and mapping tools to the table, and more convenient menu options. There are more formulas, and more powerful table options than previous versions, as well as other subtle improvements that you'll enjoy.

Excel 2000 also integrates seamlessly with other Office and Windows 2000 applications, allowing you to think more about the content and "look" of your document, rather than what program you are working in. It's easier than ever to incorporate elements of Word, PowerPoint, Access and Excel into one informative and entertaining presentation. You can post it online, too. In Excel 2000, what you put on the Web will look exactly like what you originally created.

Things You Might Want to Know About This Book

You can read this book more or less in any order. Use the book as a reference, or read it cover to cover. Here's a quick run-down of the important elements you'll encounter as you go:

Blueprints

At the beginning of the book, you'll find blueprints highlighting some of the most dynamic ways of using Excel 2000. Use each as a visual guide for designing impressive spreadsheets and making maps for your information. Reference the page numbers provided for specific information.

Fast Forward

Each chapter begins with a section called Fast Forward. These sections may offer all the instruction you need. If all you want in a lesson is a single example with the barest of explanations, the Fast Forwards may suffice. Fast Forwards are, in effect, a book within a book, a built-in quick reference guide summarizing the key tasks explained in each chapter. Written step-by-step, Fast Forwards also include illustrations and page references to guide you to the more complete information later in the chapter.

Expert Advice

Don't overlook the Expert Advice notes. These short paragraphs suggest timesaving tips and techniques. These tidbits of advice also give you the big picture and help you plan ahead. Expert Advice notes often provide a deeper and more detailed explanation of a procedure or technique.

EXPERT ADVICE

Look here for helpful hints and additional in-depth explanations!

Shortcuts

Shortcuts are designed with the busy person in mind. When there's a way to do something that may not be as fancy as the material in the text, but is faster, it will be described in the margin and highlighted by a special Shortcut icon.

Cautions

Sometimes it's just too easy to plunge ahead, fall down a rabbit hole, and spend hours of extra time finding your way back to where you were before you went astray. The Caution boxes in the margins will warn you before you commit potentially time-consuming mistakes.

CAUTION

Watch for these warnings!

Definitions

Usually, I'll explain computer jargon in the text when the techno-babble first occurs, but occasionally, I'll call out definitions in the margin. Most of the time these definitions are informal and often a little playful.

DEFINITION

Jargon: Technical terminology to be aware of.

Margin Notes

Throughout the book, these asides appear in the margin.

Look for these in the margin.

Checkpoints

The Checkpoints provide a brief summary of the information covered in a chapter as well as a look ahead at what's to come. These will help you keep your place and perspective as you work through this book.

Let's Do It!

Ready? Hang out the Do Not Disturb sign, open that Jolt cola, and lets dig into Excel 2000. Incidentally, I'm always happy to hear your reactions to this or any of my other books. You can reach me through the publisher or on the Internet at rmansfield@aol.com. Winston Steward can be reached at wish4time@aol.com.

Excel 2000

for Busy People

CHAPTER 1

Getting Started

INCLUDES

- Starting Excel
- Selecting cells
- Entering and editing your data
- Undoing and redoing actions
- Navigating in Excel
- Saving your worksheets
- Protecting files, workbooks, worksheets, and cells
- Quitting Excel

Start Excel ➡ pp. 9–12

- Start Excel by clicking the New Office Document option on the Start Menu. Below New Office Document is the option for opening an existing Office document.
- You can also launch Excel by double-clicking any spreadsheet file that is Excel-compatible (assuming that you've associated the file type with Excel).
- Once Excel starts, use the full-featured Open menu to locate exactly the kind of file you need.

Select Cells ➡ pp. 13–16

- Click a cell to make it the active cell.
- Click and drag to select a range of cells.
- Click row or column headings to select entire rows or columns.
- Click the Select All button to select all cells.

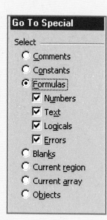

Navigate in Excel ➡ pp. 16–18

- To navigate using your mouse, just point and click.
- Use the navigational keys (PAGE UP, PAGE DOWN, and so on) to navigate via the keyboard.
- Use the Find or Replace command on the Edit menu (or press CTRL-F or CTRL-H, respectively) to search for text strings, formulas, and other items of interest. (The Replace command then lets you replace these with the word(s) or value(s) of your choice.)
- Use the Go To command on the Edit menu (or press CTRL-G) to reach specific, named items.
- Use the Special button in the Go To dialog box to find specific elements (notes, formulas, and so on).

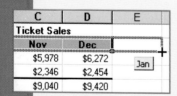

Enter Data ➡ pp. 19–21

1. Select the cell (point to it and click) in which you want to place the information, and begin typing.
2. To accept the entry, just press ENTER or click outside the cell, anywhere on your worksheet. To cancel it, click the Cancel (X) button on the formula bar or press ESC.
3. To allow Excel to automatically add data to adjacent cells, drag downward or to the right on the cell's right lower corner.

Undo and Redo Actions ➡ p. 21

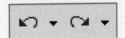

- Using the drop-down Undo list on the standard toolbar, you can choose to undo one or several recent actions.
- Using the drop-down Redo list on the standard toolbar, you can choose to redo one or several recent actions.

Save Workbooks ➡ pp. 21–22

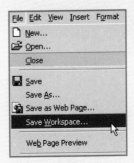

- The Save and Save As options on the File menu are the same as those used in other Windows applications.
- Click Save as Web Page for fully functional online viewing and editing. Your Excel workbook can move seamlessly between HTML and normal formatting.
- The Save Workspace option on the File menu saves information about all open workbooks, including the location, window size, and screen position.

Protect Your Files, Workbooks, Worksheets, and Cells ➡ pp. 22–24

- You can protect your Excel workbooks by using the Options button in the Save As dialog box.
- You can assign various levels of protection to workbooks, worksheets, and cells by selecting Tools | Protection and choosing what you want to protect from the submenu.
- To unprotect a workbook, worksheet, or cell, choose Tools | Protection and select what you want to unprotect from the submenu.

Quit Excel ➡ p. 24

- Use the Exit command on the File menu, or click the Close box at the top-right corner of your screen. You'll be prompted to save any unsaved work.

In this chapter, you'll learn some of the basic functions of Excel, along with some essential terminology. Specifically, you'll learn how to start Excel, enter data into cells, navigate around the screen, save and protect your files, and exit Excel.

Excel spreadsheets are more than just lists. You'll not only be typing numeric data, but labels, headings, and formulas (which are used to perform calculations on the numbers you enter). Just knowing the basics of cell and data entry will greatly reduce the mystery of this program.

Getting Familiar with Excel

Looking at a blank spreadsheet for the first time, it may appear as an endless sea of cells spreading, ad infinitum, in all directions. You'll soon learn how adaptable this layout is to your needs. Cells will automatically resize to accommodate all kinds of information. Numbers, formulas, and even paragraphs of text all can go inside cells. The spreadsheets you create need not look like intimidating boxes that only a mathematician could love.

Cells and Worksheets

The basic rectangular unit you type into is called a *cell*. The page of cells you build one cell at a time is called a *sheet*, or a *worksheet*. At times, the term *worksheet* is used interchangeably with *spreadsheet*.

When you start Excel, the program assumes that one page of cells may not be enough. That's why, if you look at the bottom left of the screen, you'll see three tabs named: Sheet 1, Sheet 2, and Sheet 3.

When you start Excel, it opens to Sheet 1. On Sheet 1, you can fill as many cells as you like. You may never need to move on to Sheet 2 or 3. But should you want to (imagine that you are keeping track of the scores of three seasons of little league, and one sheet holds the scores of all teams for an entire season), just click the tab labeled Sheet 2 or Sheet 3, and that sheet will open with a blank page of cells, ready for you to add data. You can add as many sheets as you like; you are not limited to just Sheets 1 through 3. To add a sheet, right-click any sheet's tab (at the bottom of the screen) and select Insert.

Sheets and Workbooks

The Excel file that you open and save each time you use the program is called a *workbook*. A workbook holds your sheets. Even if you type data into only one sheet, Excel will save your data as a workbook. When you open or create an Excel file, you are opening or creating a workbook.

Do not worry that your Excel sheets will run out of room. Don't think you have to use a new sheet because you created so many cells that they are disappearing off the edges of your screen (we'll soon discuss how to navigate the Excel screen). A single Excel sheet can accommodate 65,536 rows and 256 columns.

When would you create a new sheet? If, for example, you are using Excel to track the mileage and repair data for two cars, you may want to use two sheets: one for each car.

When would you create a new workbook? If you use Excel for two unrelated purposes—for example, to manage household matters and to track work or business—you can use one Excel workbook for each.

Clicking the New icon on the standard toolbar creates a new Excel workbook.

How Cells are Organized

How are cells organized on a spreadsheet? By rows and columns.

- A *row* is a single line of cells arranged horizontally. Think of rows of seats at a concert or baseball game. When you go to find your seat, you start by looking for a certain row number. Accordingly, the top row of cells in Excel is called row 1. The numbers increase as you move farther down the page.

- In Excel, you spend lots of time pinpointing specific cells, and to do so, you also need to organize them vertically. A single line of cells aligned one on top of the other is called a *column*. Think of the columns holding up an ancient Greek temple, and you'll remember that columns go up and down.

To identify a particular cell, indicate both its column and its row. For example, B4 would be the fourth cell down in the second column from the left of a worksheet. B4 is the *cell address*. The cell address appears in the upper-left part of the spreadsheet, in an area called the Name Box, as shown in Figure 1.1. The column is always identified first, followed by the row. Therefore, the cell at the upper left of a spreadsheet is referred to as A1.

What Gets Typed into Worksheets

A worksheet accepts three types of information:

- **Numeric data**   Numeric data consists of numbers that have to be calculated. This could be stock market prices, baseball scores, the number of anions in an atom, or any set of numbers that require some sort of mathematical crunching.

- **Formulas**   Formulas are instructions for performing operations on numbers. A formula can be a simple command to add all the numbers in a certain row, or it can direct the program to apply the cumulative beta probability of all cells returning a mean of less than 50 joules of heat loss.

Even though a formula may affect many cells, it can fit into one tiny corner of your spreadsheet. Like everything else on your worksheet, formulas are squeezed into cells and can work their magic on cells anywhere on your page.

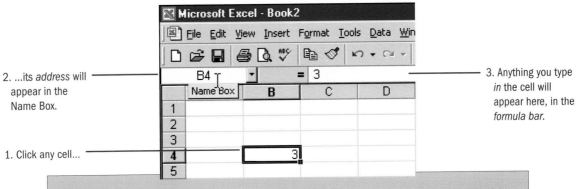

2. ...its *address* will appear in the Name Box.

3. Anything you type *in the cell will appear here, in the formula bar.*

1. Click any cell...

Figure 1.1:   The currently active cell is B4. This cell address appears in the upper left of the screen, in the Name Box. In the cell address, the row (in this case, B) is always listed first, followed by the column (in this case, 4).

Figure 1.2 shows a formula that instructs cell B4 to multiply the sum of cells B2 and B3 by 6. Look at the numbers in cells B2 and B3 and add them together; their sum is 7. Thus, the formula yields a result of 42.

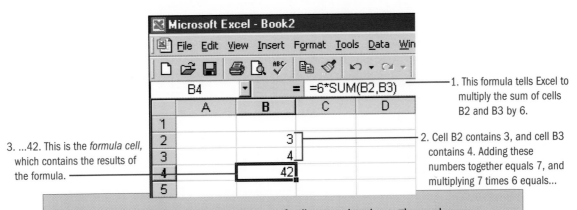

1. This formula tells Excel to multiply the sum of cells B2 and B3 by 6.

2. Cell B2 contains 3, and cell B3 contains 4. Adding these numbers together equals 7, and multiplying 7 times 6 equals...

3. ...42. This is the *formula cell,* which contains the results of the formula.

Figure 1.2:   This formula multiplies the sum of cells B2 and B3 by 6. The results are displayed in the cell that contains the formula: in this case, B4.

- **Text** A spreadsheet requires that you label the columns and rows of cells, making it clear what you are measuring. However, you can also type entire paragraphs of text into a cell if you like. After typing text, you can double-click the right border of the head of the column you just typed into, and the cell will automatically expand to accommodate the words you typed.

TIP

When creating spreadsheets, make sure you set aside room for labels (usually row 1 and column A).

Interpreting Cell Contents

Once you grasp the concept explained in this section, you'll be more than halfway to understanding Excel.

Figure 1.3 shows three cells: D3, D4, and D5.

- D3 and D4 contain numbers, or numeric data, and cell D5 contains a formula.
- Cell D5 contains instructions to display the sum of the numbers found in cells D3 and D4.
- After the formula is entered, the formula cell displays the results. In this example, the formula is simple: D3+D4.

Figure 1.3: The formula displays simple instructions to add the numbers found in cells D3 and D4. In this case, the sum is 5. Change the numbers in cell D3 or D4, and the resulting sum in cell D5 will change also.

EXPERT ADVICE

You need not fill every cell in your spreadsheet. Cells that contain no data are simply ignored. Also, don't think your final spreadsheet needs to resemble an endless screen of rectangles. You'll learn how to change the color, border thickness, and text size of your cells to give your spreadsheets a unique appearance.

Peeking Ahead at the Formula Bar

In Figure 1.3, how is it that cell D5 displays the sum of the other two numbered cells? Where did it receive instructions to do that?

The answer lies a little higher up in the figure: in the *formula bar.* Cell D5, the cell with the sum in it, does not really contain numbers. Although cell D5 *displays* numbers, it actually *contains* a formula. As you'll learn later, when you click a cell and then click the equal sign on the formula bar, Excel knows that you want to type a formula, not a regular number

Later in this book, you'll learn all about formulas and how they affect other cells. For now, simply remember that cells can contain numeric data, text, and formulas.

Starting Excel

To Create an Excel worksheet from scratch, do one of the following:

- Choose Excel from the Programs submenu of the Start menu.
- Click the Excel icon on the Office shortcut bar if you installed Excel as part of Microsoft Office.
- Click New Office Document on the Start menu. When the New Office Document dialog box appears, click Blank Workbook (Figure 1.4).

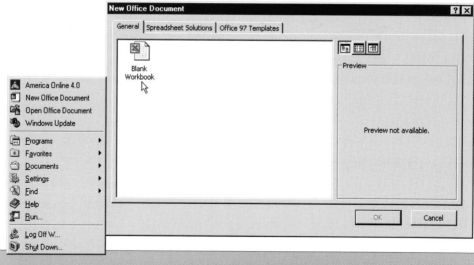

Figure 1.4: To start Excel, click New Office Document from the Start menu and then select the Blank Workbook icon.

When Excel saves a worksheet you've been working on, it automatically places it in the My Documents folder. To open any document found there, click the Windows Start menu and select Documents. Then scroll up and select the My Documents icon. Unless you told Excel to save your files elsewhere, all your worksheets will be found here. Just click any worksheet icon to open it.

Opening an Existing Worksheet

Just like all Office documents, a worksheet is represented by an icon. When you click a worksheet's icon, it will open, with Excel up and running. So to open an existing worksheet, do one of the following:

- Click a spreadsheet icon in the Documents list on the Windows Start menu. This list remembers the last 15 documents you worked on.
- From within Excel, click the Open icon at the upper left of the screen.

After you click Open, and the Open dialog box appears (Figure 1.5), you'll see many options for locating the Excel file you have in mind. Having so many ways to track down a particular file may not seem so important to you—until you've created dozens of spreadsheets. Here are two methods for locating the file you need:

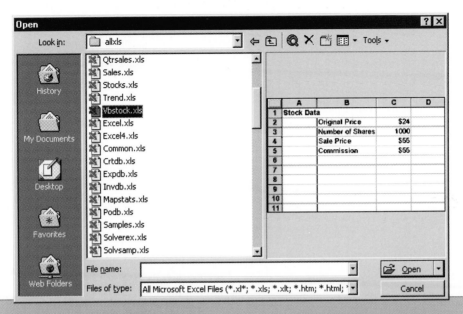

Figure 1.5: The Open dialog box lets you sort Excel spreadsheet icons before you open a document, helping you to positively identify a worksheet even while it appears in a list.

- View the most recent workbooks, which could help you determine the most current of two identically named files.
- View a miniature display of a workbook before opening it.

For a look at the most recent past, do the following:

1. In the Open dialog box, click the History button.

The main screen shows the most recently modified workbooks.

2. Double-click the icon of any document to open it.

To see a small preview of an Excel workbook before you open it, do this:

1. Select the Views button at the upper right of the Open dialog box and click Preview.

Each time you click an Excel document icon, a small preview will fill the right half of the screen.

2. Double-click a document's icon to open it.

Now you've learned two ways of starting Excel: opening to a blank spreadsheet and opening an existing spreadsheet.

Getting To Know Excel

Some example worksheets are provided with Office 2000. The best way for a busy person to learn Excel is to see a spreadsheet in action. Click around and see what the different cells contain. To do this, place the Office 2000 CD in the CD-ROM drive, open Windows Explorer, and click the CD-ROM icon. Then open the Samples folder. Click any spreadsheet icon and it will open in Excel. Click some cells. You'll notice that some of the cells contain numbers. Now click some of the cells at the bottom of a column. Keep your eye on the formula bar; you'll see that some cells, though appearing to contain numbers, actually contain formulas. Formula cells are often

At times, you'll need to select cells that are not right next to each other. Also, you'll need to know how to move and reposition cells once you've selected them. These operations are explored in Chapter 3.

at the bottom of a column because they perform some sort of calculation involving the cells above.

Selecting Cells

Before you can enter text or formulas, you have to know how to select cells. You can select a single cell or a range of cells. The following sections describe ways that you can select cells using either your mouse or your keyboard.

Selecting Cells with a Mouse

To select a single cell, simply point to it and click your left mouse button. The techniques shown in Figures 1.6 through 1.9 are for selecting rows, columns, and ranges.

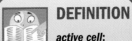

DEFINITION

active cell:
The cell you are currently typing in. Click a cell with your mouse, and it becomes active. You'll recognize the active cell because it has a thick black border. When you use the keyboard or the mouse to move from one cell to another, you are changing the active cell.

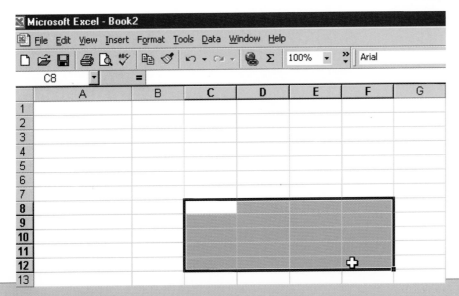

Figure 1.6: To select a simple, square *range* of multiple cells, simply click any corner in the desired range and drag your mouse pointer to the diagonally opposite corner.

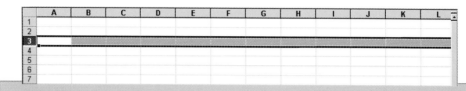

Figure 1.7:   To select a single row of cells, click the *row header*, which is the number at the far left of the row.

To select multiple columns or rows, click the first row number or column heading in the group and drag your mouse pointer across all the numbers or headings for the items you wish to include. To select cells in different parts of your spreadsheet, hold down the CTRL key

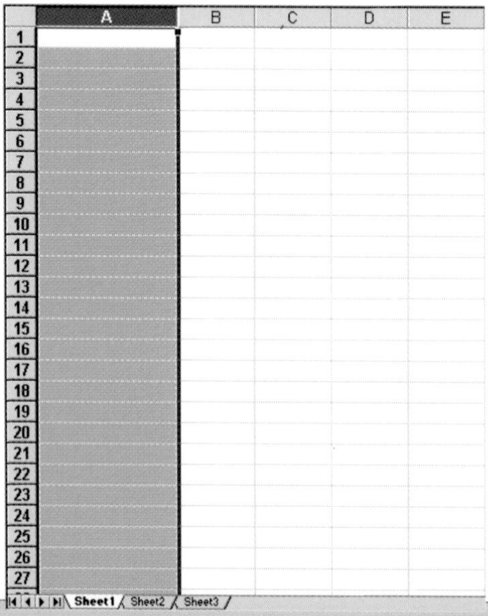

Figure 1.8:   To select a single column of cells, click the *column header*, which is the letter at the top of the column.

and select anywhere you like. For example, here's how you would select rows 2 and 4 without selecting row 3:

1. Click the heading for row 2.
2. Press (and hold) CTRL.
3. Click the heading for row 4.

Selecting Cells with Your Keyboard

While you will probably want to use your mouse for most selections (it's quicker), you can use many keyboard selection tricks:

SHIFT-SPACEBAR selects the entire row or rows in which the cells are located (if you've already selected a range of cells).

CTRL-SPACEBAR selects an entire column.

CTRL-SHIFT-SPACEBAR selects the entire worksheet.

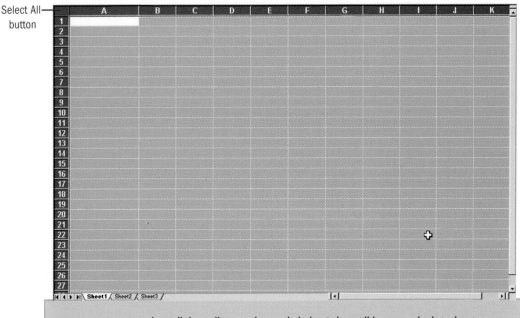

Figure 1.9: To select all the cells in a sheet, click the Select All button, which is the tiny rectangle at the top of the screen where row 1 and column A intersect.

To extend selections in any direction, hold down the SHIFT key and press the appropriate arrow key (up, down, left, right) on the number pad. The other navigational keys also can be used to extend selections. For instance, CTRL-SHIFT-END extends the selection to the end of your worksheet.

Moving to a New Cell

It is important to note that, when you are entering data into cells, you need not pick up the mouse and click a new cell in order to move to it. Using the mouse to relocate your cursor, putting it down, and then typing again is a real time-waster. Here's how to move from one cell to another with as few steps as possible:

- If you are typing into a row of cells from right to left, just enter your data and then press the TAB key; the cell to the right will become active. Each time you press the TAB key, you'll move one cell to the right.

- After typing, press ENTER, and you'll move down one cell. To move down several cells, keep pressing ENTER.

- Use arrow keys to move up, down, right, or left in relation to the current cell. You can use the number pad arrow keys (with NUM LOCK off) or the standard set of arrow keys.

- You can use the mouse to click any cell to make it active.

Navigating in Excel

Getting around in Excel is pretty easy. Click one of the worksheet tabs at the bottom center of the screen to bring a worksheet forward. Use the scroll bars at the right edge and bottom of your screen to scroll within Excel worksheets.

The following two sections describe how to navigate using your keyboard and the Edit menu.

Navigating with the Keyboard

Most Windows keyboard navigational tools work in Excel. For example, you can scroll with the scroll bars; use PAGE UP, HOME, and related keys; or use the arrow keys. These techniques are described in Table 1.1.

Navigating with the Edit Menu

Once you get started using Excel, you're likely to build some long workbooks and worksheets. The Edit menu offers three ways to help you locate information quickly and easily:

- *Find* allows you to search for text strings, formulas, and other items of interest.
- *Replace* allows you to search for text strings, formulas, and other items of interest and lets you replace these with the words or values of your choice.

Key	Action
HOME	Moves to the leftmost column (column A).
PAGE UP or PAGE DOWN	Moves up or down by the height of your computer screen.
ALT-PAGE UP or ALT-PAGE DOWN	Moves right or left by the width of your computer screen.
CTRL-PAGE UP or CTRL-PAGE DOWN	Moves right or left by one sheet.
UP, DOWN, RIGHT, or LEFT ARROW	Moves in the direction of the arrow by one cell.
END-ARROW	Moves in the direction of the arrow to the last occupied cell of the data region.

Table 1.1:   Navigation Keys

- *Go To* allows you to find areas you've named or to go to a specific cell address. You can click the Special button in the Go To dialog box to find specific elements such as notes or formulas.

Accessing and using these menu features is easy:

1. From the Edit menu, choose Find, Replace, or Go To. Alternatively, press CTRL-F (Find), CTRL-H (Replace), or CTRL-G (Go To).

2. In the dialog box that appears, enter the words or values you're looking for.

3. If you're using the Find or Replace command, click Find (or Find Next); then click OK when you're done. If you're using the Go To command (Figure 1.10), click OK.

Figure 1.10:   To see a list of the most recent active cells, choose Go To from the Edit menu.

Entering Text and Numbers

To enter text and numbers in your worksheets, select the cell where you want the information to appear (point to it and click) and then begin typing. The numbers, formula, or text you type will appear in the cell itself and in the formula bar (at the top center of the screen, next to the equal sign).

There are a few points to keep in mind when typing something in a cell:

- Don't think that because a cell is small, you can type only a few characters in it. If your typing starts to fill the next cell, click the right border of the top cell in that column.

- When you type, you need not add dollar signs, phone number hyphens or most other kinds of number formatting. Later, after you have created your long list of numbers, Excel can apply any type of formatting you want, all with a couple of mouse clicks.

How Excel Automatically Fills Cells

Based on what you are typing at the moment, Excel will always make a guess at what you will do next. With very little prompting, Excel will fill in the cells for you. Here's how:

- If you type a date in a cell and then drag the lower-right corner of the cell downward or across, Excel will insert the subsequent dates in the cells you touch while dragging.

- If you type a number in a cell, press CTRL, and then drag downward on the right border of the cell, the subsequent numbers will fill the cells you touch while dragging.

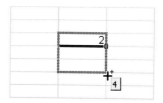

- If you type a word in a cell and drag the bottom border toward new cells, the cells will fill with that word. If you type a word and then move to a new cell and begin typing the same word, Excel will finish the word for you.
- If you type a number in a cell and all the numbers in the cells above it are percentages, Excel will assume that this new number you are typing is also a percentage. Likewise, if you type a number in a cell and the cells in the same column are dollars and cents, Excel will convert the numbers you are typing to currency also.

Why are these features important to you? Because when you have to create a spreadsheet in a hurry, it's nice to know that Excel will take over some of the redundant typing. Just remember this: If you find that you are repeating actions, Excel probably has a way for you to automate them. You'll learn many such techniques later in this book.

Erasing Cell Data

What if you type something in a cell and you want to erase it and type something else? Simply press the ESC key and then type something new. Excel automatically deletes what you typed the first time and replaces it with your new entry. To erase only part of what you've typed, use the BACKSPACE key.

To undo any action, you can use the Undo arrow at the top of the screen. You can undo over 100 previous actions, if you like. Next to the Undo arrow is a drop-down menu that lists your previous actions. Use this menu to identify a recent action you want to pinpoint for undoing.

If you undo an action and then decide that you want to *keep the original edit after all,* click the Redo arrow, which is to the right of the Undo arrow. (Note that the Redo arrow will appear to the right of the Undo arrow only *after* the first time you use Undo. If you've never used the Undo arrow, you'll have to click the More Buttons arrow, found on the standard toolbar, to access the Redo arrow.)

Saving Worksheets

Excel provides four save options, located on the File menu: Save, Save As, Save as HTML, and Save Workspace.

The *Save* and *Save As* options are the same ones you've used in other Windows applications. Figure 1.11 shows the Save As dialog box. When it's time to save your work, you'll probably want to save your most recent changes over the previous version of the same file. To do this, choose the Save option. When you want to save your old version of a file *and* keep new changes in a different file, choose Save As. You can then give the file a new name and still have the older version as well.

The *Save as Web Page* option lets you save your Excel files as HTML Web pages (see Chapter 12). With very little ado, Office 2000 seamlessly converts your files to HTML, but if you want to actually

> **CAUTION**
>
> Once you save your worksheet, you cannot undo any action that occurred before you saved it. Saving breaks your link to all past actions. Also after saving, the Redo arrow is not available, and the Undo drop-down list is cleared until you again take some action that can be undone.

> **EXPERT ADVICE**
>
> By default, Excel prompts you to save your workbook every 10 minutes. To turn off or to change this option to a less frequent reminder, click AutoSave on the Tools menu. The AutoSave dialog box appears. Make adjustments and click OK. (If AutoSave does not appear on the Tools menu, you may have to install it as an add-in. Installing additional Excel Options is discussed in Chapter 7.)

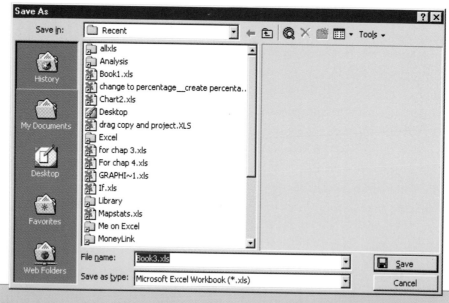

Figure 1.11:   When you select Save As, you can choose among several save options, including online locations, your desktop, and your favorites list.

publish your files to the Web at this time, simply click the Publish button at the lower right of the Save As dialog box.

The *Save Workspace* option saves information about all open workbooks, such as their locations, window sizes, and screen positions. Then, when you want to open these files again, all you have to do is open the workspace file, and your files will open.

Protecting Your Work from Prying Eyes and Flying Fingers

At some point in your Excel career, you'll probably work on projects that you'll want to keep confidential—or prepare information that you want people to read but not change. Excel gives you the option of protecting entire files as well as workbooks, worksheets, and cells.

Protecting Your Files

Using Excel, you can prevent other people from viewing or tinkering with your files:

- You can assign a password to a file so that others will not be able to open it unless they know the password.
- You can assign a password so that others can open and view a file but can not modify it without entering the password.
- You can instruct Excel to display a message requesting that the viewer not make any changes.

To activate any or all of these measures, click the Options button in the Save As dialog box and select the level of protection you want.

Protecting Your Workbooks, Worksheets, and Cells

In addition to protecting files, you can also protect individual worksheets or cells. This is particularly useful when others use your worksheets, but "I", not "we", for one, protect a lot of my personal files to safeguard myself from myself. (Or is that my evil twin who's always replacing formulas with numbers?)

Here's how to protect a workbook or worksheet:

1. Choose Tools | Protection.
2. Select Protect Sheet or Protect Workbook from the submenu. Protect Workbook only keeps people from changing the workbook structure—it does not protect each individual sheet in the workbook.
3. Select the level of protection you want from the Protect Sheet dialog box.

If at any time you want to remove protection, just go to Tools | Protection and then choose either Unprotect Sheet or Unprotect Workbook from the submenu.

Here's how to protect individual cells in your worksheet:

1. Select the cells you want to protect (places where you want to enter variables—numbers, names, and so on).

2. Choose Cells from the Format menu.

3. Click the Protection tab in the Format Cells dialog box.

4. Uncheck the Locked box and click OK.

5. Go to Tools | Protection and choose Protect Sheet to protect only the current sheet.

6. In the dialog box that appears, select the items that you want to protect. When in doubt, protect everything—select Contents, Objects, and Scenarios.

7. Enter a password, if you want. Then reenter the password to prove that you were paying attention the first time (capitalization counts) and click OK.

To unprotect your work, use the Unprotect commands on the Tools | Protection menu. You'll need to provide the correct password.

Quitting Excel

To quit Excel, do one of the following:

• Choose Exit from the File menu.

• Click the Close box (the little X) in the top-right corner of your screen.

• Press ALT-F4. This method is good for closing a program if, for some reason, your mouse becomes unavailable.

The above methods close any open files and exits Excel. Excel reminds you to save any unsaved work before it closes your files.

Checkpoint

Well, busy person, now you know enough to be dangerous. You've learned how to get around in Excel, and you've learned the basic terminology that will get you through the rest of this book—pretty big accomplishment so far!

The next several chapters build on the skills you have just learned. Chapter 2, for instance, will tell you how to get help as you're learning different Excel techniques. Then, in Chapter 3, you'll learn to rearrange your worksheets. In Chapter 4, you'll learn the basics of working with numbers and formulas—the heart of Excel.

Stuff to Do Once to Make Your Life Easier

INCLUDES

- Customizing toolbars and menus
- Creating or editing a template
- Starting Excel with a document already open

Obtaining Additional Templates ➤ pp. 35–36

1. Use the additional templates found on your Office 2000 CD. They are located in the be Valupack\Templates\Excel folder of the CD

2. Download Excel templates free of charge from Osborne/McGraw- Hill's Web site (http://www.osborne.com/busy/of97temp.htm). These would include credit card balance planners, future college expense planners, and many others.

   Download templates from Microsoft, at http://officeupdate.microsoft.com/index.htm#Exceldownloads.

Minimize Your Work by Using a Template ➤ p. 41

1. Open the Template folder (Usually C:\Office 2000\Templates\ Spreadsheet Solutions)

2. Choose the template you want to work with.

3. Notice how the template contains "placeholder" data that you replace with your own numbers.

4. Replace the "dummy" information with your own information, including addresses, budget or purchases or other pertinent data.

5. Save the Template as an Excel Document.

6. Next time you need to create a similar document, simply replace the data you've already added. There's no need to start from scratch.

Personalizing a Template ➤ pp. 42–43

1. Most templates include graphics and logos that you can replace with something pertinent to your spreadsheet. On the template, click the graphic you want to replace and, from the Excel menu, click a new one.

2. Type in information that will not change from project to project, like company name and address.

3. Change the look of the company name by changing the font type, size and style.

4. Hold your mouse over a red corner to see what type of information should be typed into a certain field.

5. Once you are happy with your template customization, lock in your changes with the Lock/Save Sheet button.

Customize Toolbars ➡ pp. 48–50

1. Right-click any portion of any toolbar.
2. Choose Customize from the resulting shortcut menu.
3. Click the Commands tab.
4. Make a selection from the Categories list box.
5. Click the displayed buttons and see their descriptions.
6. Drag the desired button to the toolbar and release the mouse button.

Customize Menu Options ➡ p. 51

1. Choose Customize from the Tools menu.
2. Click the Commands tab.
3. Make a selection from the Categories list box.
4. Click the displayed buttons and see their descriptions.
5. Drag the desired command to the menu and release the mouse button.

In this chapter, you'll explore how to change the appearance of the Excel screen when the program first opens. You'll learn how to open Excel with a particular document already up and running. This can be helpful if you find that there are really only a handful of spreadsheets that you ever use. You'll learn how to set up your own working preferences, and spend less time hunting for a particular option. You'll see how easy it is to customize Excel to suit your own needs.

Using an Excel Template

If you've wandered around in Excel a bit and have felt somewhat mystified at its operations, the idea of creating a document from scratch in this unfamiliar program may seem farfetched. It turns out that you may not have to. If time constraints require that you be up and running with Excel in a matter of a week or so, you can use a template.

A template is a document that's all ready to go; you simply fill in the blanks. Excel comes with many such templates. These are fully formatted documents that require you to only type in your own contact information, personal data, and the numbers relevant for each project. Excel has created the formulas, the structure, and the look and design of the document. Once you've chosen a template, you can use it again and again for many projects. Here are some templates included with Excel:

- Lease agreements
- Loan documents
- Time cards
- Time tracking data sheets

- Sales quotation forms
- Complete budget analysis worksheets (like the one you see here):

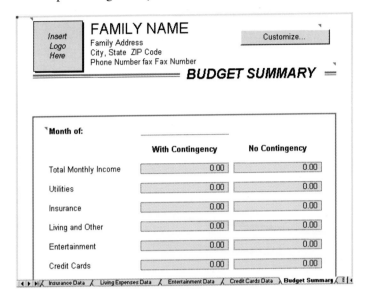

- Project planners
- Asset charts
- Invoices
- Purchase orders
- Expense statements

Osborne McGraw-Hill has also provided a number of templates free for your use, available for downloading from **http://www.osborne.com/ busy/of97temp.htm**. These templates include the following:

- Credit card balance planners
- Future college expense planners
- Home buying planners
- Life insurance coverage assessment worksheet
- Retirement and general savings planners

And, specifically for business, you can download a very valuable profit-volume-cost worksheet (see Figure 2-1), which gives you an all-important peek at break-even and profitably points in product sales. Also available are 5-year and 12-month business plan packages.

Remember: These templates are free to you!

	A	B	C	D	E	F
1		Month	Month	Month	Month	Month
2	Balance Sheet	0	1	2	3	4
3	Assets					
4	*Current Assets*					
5	Cash & Equivalents	$50,000	$60,832	$71,446	$82,826	$94,198
6	Accounts Receivable	80,000	80,000	80,000	80,000	80,000
7	Inventory	10,000	12,000	14,000	16,000	18,000
8	Other Current Assets	7,000	8,000	9,000	10,000	11,000
9	*Total Current Assets*	147,000	160,832	174,446	188,826	203,198
10	*Plant, Property, & Equipment*	50,000	67,500	85,000	102,500	120,000
11	Less: Accumulated Depreciation	(25,000)	(42,500)	(60,000)	(77,500)	(95,000)
12	*Net Plant, Property, & Equipment*	25,000	25,000	25,000	25,000	25,000
13	*Other Noncurrent Assets*	2,500	2,600	2,700	2,800	2,900
14	Total Assets	$174,500	$188,432	$202,146	$216,626	$231,098
15						
16	Liabilities					
17	*Current Liabilities*					
18	Accounts Payable	$8,000	$8,000	$8,000	$8,000	$8,000
19	Accrued Expenses	10,000	10,192	10,192	10,192	10,192
20	Other Current Liabilities	2,500	2,600	2,500	2,600	2,500
21	*Total Current Liabilities*	20,500	20,792	20,692	20,792	20,692
22	*Noncurrent Liabilities*					

Forecasting Inputs \ **Balance Sheet** \ Common-size Balance Sheet \ Income Statem

Figure 2.1: You can download a number of useful financial templates like this one, available at no charge to you from Osborne/McGraw-Hill.

Microsoft also offers free templates for Excel users, downloadable from **http://officeupdate.microsoft.com/index.htm#Exceldownloads**. Some of these are:

- Business planners
- Car lease advisors
- Loan managers
- Personal budget planners
- Pricing estimate worksheets
- Production tracking worksheets
- Time cards

Features Common to Most Excel Templates

Although Excel templates may look very different from one another, and each performs a unique task, most have the following features in common:

- They are all reusable documents. You can open a blank template, week after week, month after month, and fill it with your data. You can then save this template as your own document. Then, the next time you start a new project, you can again open the same blank template, fill it with your new data, and save it under yet another name.

- They all contain placeholders for your company and personal data. Once you've done your work with the template, it will look like it's entirely your creation. You can customize the templates with your business logo, detailed contact information, and personalized graphics that help convey your message. Figure 2.2 shows an unused template, and Figure 2.3 shows the same template customized with company data.

Each template contains formulas that calculate the numeric data you enter and provides usable and valuable information. Handy templates such as these are often called *spreadsheet solutions* because they go beyond simply being number banks. They are set up so they can immediately be brought into play by your company or institution, and they are designed to provide convenience and speed of implementation for even novice Excel users.

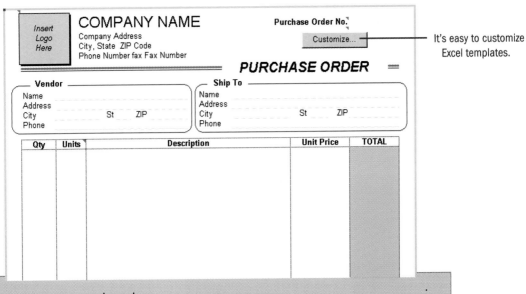

Figure 2.2: An unused template...

Figure 2.3: ...and the same template after company data has been entered.

Locating and Opening a Template

To open a template, choose New from the File menu (selecting the New icon on the toolbar actually opens a different set of options that we don't need at the moment). When the New dialog box appears, click the Spreadsheet Solutions tab. Click any of the available templates to open them.

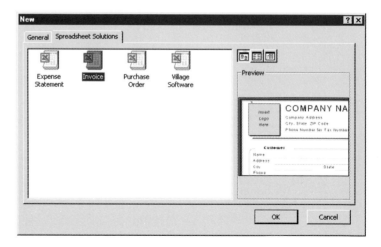

This procedure gives you access to templates that are loaded automatically when you install Excel. If you've chosen a minimal Office 2000 installation, Excel's extra templates may not be available.

Earlier in this chapter, we mentioned templates from three different sources. How do you access them? There are two steps: First you must locate the templates and then you must place them in folders where Excel can automatically access them.

Locating Additional Templates

As mentioned earlier, Excel templates from Osborne/McGraw-Hill (the publisher of this book) are available from **http://www.osborne.com/ busy/of97temp.htm**. Simply download the template package file as instructed; then after they've been downloaded onto your computer, follow the directions for file placement.

Similarly, the Microsoft Excel Web site **http://officeupdate. microsoft.com/index.htm#Exceldownloads** offers templates that you download to your computer and then move to the appropriate folder on your computer.

To download a template, unzip it, and copy it to the correct folder, follow these steps:

1. On the Web page or other source, click the template you want to download.

The Business Templates

There are three business templates: two for forecasting finances over different time periods, and the third to analyze profits vs. costs.

12-month and 5-year Plans

- 12moplan.xls - (download zip file <u>12moplan.zip</u>)
- 5yrplan.xls - (download zip file <u>5yrplan.zip</u>)
  These templates forecast a business's pofits, cash flow, and financial condition over a 12-month or 5-year forecasting horizon. These two templates also provide common-sized income statements and balance sheets, and they

2. You'll be asked where to save the file. Choose the folder Spreadsheet Solutions, found in your Microsoft Office\ Templates folder.

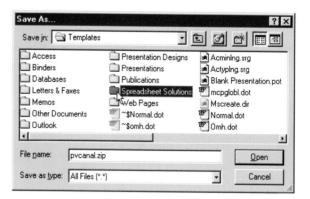

3. Open the Spreadsheet Solutions folder, and you'll see that your new template has been downloaded in the form of a zipped (compressed) file.

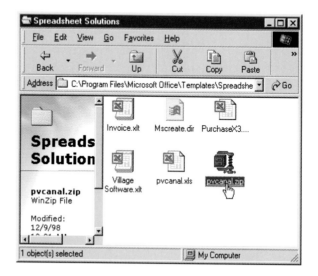

You'll need to use an unzipping program to decompress the file into a usable Excel file.

4. Back in Excel, click New or Open on the File menu. The new spreadsheet will appear as one of the choices.

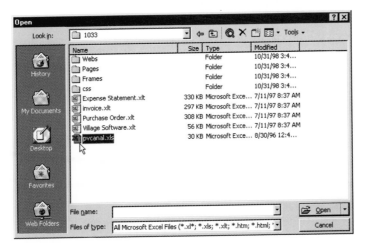

Placing Templates in the Right Folder

Where do templates belong so that you can access them using the method outlined at the beginning of this section? Excel looks for templates following this path: C:\Program Files\Microsoft Office\ Templates\Spreadsheet Solutions. Use Windows Explorer to copy the template from its original location to this folder, as outlined in Figure 2.4. Or, use the Windows Copy command to copy the template to the Windows clipboard and then paste it into the correct folder.

Identifying a Template File

Any file with an .xlt file extension is an Excel template. You can locate Excel templates in any folder by opening My Computer or Windows

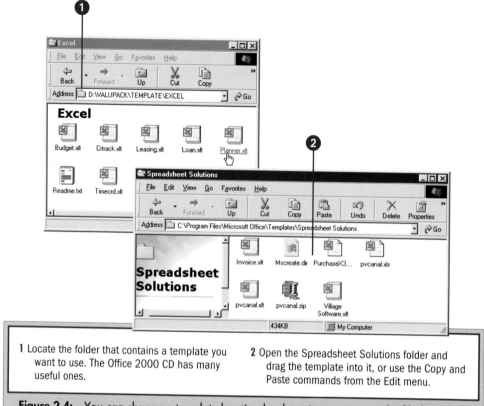

1 Locate the folder that contains a template you want to use. The Office 2000 CD has many useful ones.

2 Open the Spreadsheet Solutions folder and drag the template into it, or use the Copy and Paste commands from the Edit menu.

Figure 2.4: You can change a template location by dragging or copying the file from its source folder to the appropriate target folder.

Explorer, right-clicking, and choosing the Find command. In the Named field, type ***.xlt**, and press ENTER.

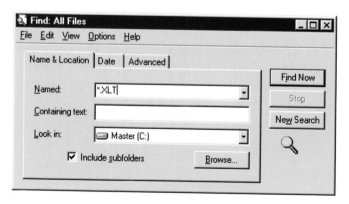

All the Excel templates on your computer will appear in the list. Simply copy or move any additional templates to the Excel template folder, and they'll be available with the others.

Locating Office 2000 CD Templates

Your Office 2000 CD contains Excel templates that are not installed automatically. You can manually copy them to the Excel template folder, and they will always be available when you start the program (later, you'll learn how to open Excel with your selected preferences up and running). Excel template files are found in the ValuPack folder. If your CD-ROM drive is drive D, then the path would be D:\Valupack\Templates\Excel. Simply use one of the methods shown earlier in Figure 2.4.

Working with an Excel Template

There are four steps to working with a template.

1. Learn your way around a little, click in some of the rectangles, and see what type of data they accept. You may be amazed that these handy documents do not even resemble spreadsheets. Learn where the data goes, and where the results will appear on the sheet. If this document will end up as hard copy, get a feel for how it will look printed.

2. Type in your own personal data, name, company name, address, and so on, as well as personalize the template by adding a company logo or an image that represents you. This is called customizing, or personalizing, the template.

3. Begin entering data. Make a practice invoice, budget, expense sheet, or whatever, depending on the type of template you are working with. Practice a little and see how your numbers look plugged into this ready-made document.

4. Determine how to name this document once you've edited it and put your own data into it. You'll probably be either regularly updating this spreadsheet, whatever it turns out to be in your own hands, or creating a new one, perhaps monthly or

If you've installed your Office 2000 files in a customized location (if you did not accept the defaults when you installed the program), then the path listed here will not be exactly where you need to copy your templates. For example, if you installed your Office 2000 files on a different hard drive and folder (let's say E:\Office 2000), then the path where your template files need to be copied would be E:\Office 2000\Templates\Spreadsheet Solutions.

quarterly. You'll need a naming convention for two reasons:

• You need to be able to open this edited version of the spreadsheet and know exactly which volume or edition you have opened.

• You'll need to have a blank version of this template quickly identifiable and ready to open to use for your next related project. Soon, you'll get the hang of simply making the changes related to a particular month's (or quarter's, or week's) data, adding new data, generating necessary reports, and moving on to the next task.

Figure 2.5 shows how to uniquely name a template after you've personalized it and added data to it.

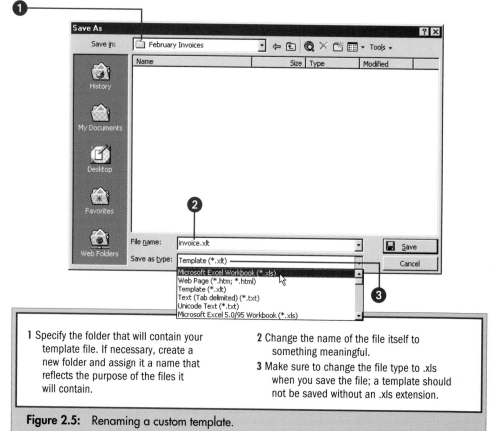

1 Specify the folder that will contain your template file. If necessary, create a new folder and assign it a name that reflects the purpose of the files it will contain.

2 Change the name of the file itself to something meaningful.

3 Make sure to change the file type to .xls when you save the file; a template should not be saved without an .xls extension.

Figure 2.5: Renaming a custom template.

Exploring a Template Example

Using an example of an invoice, we'll take a quick tour to see how such a template works. Then we'll glance at others, just to get a feel for the different ways a template can be constructed and laid out.

Pictured in Figure 2.6 is the Invoice template that comes with Excel. You can use it to bill for services rendered and for the supplies related to those services.

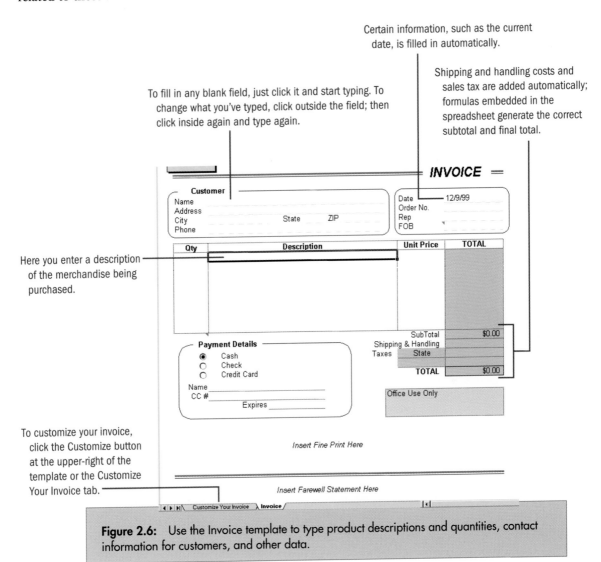

Certain information, such as the current date, is filled in automatically.

To fill in any blank field, just click it and start typing. To change what you've typed, click outside the field; then click inside again and type again.

Shipping and handling costs and sales tax are added automatically; formulas embedded in the spreadsheet generate the correct subtotal and final total.

Here you enter a description of the merchandise being purchased.

To customize your invoice, click the Customize button at the upper-right of the template or the Customize Your Invoice tab.

Figure 2.6: Use the Invoice template to type product descriptions and quantities, contact information for customers, and other data.

Now let's explore this template:

- Click below or to the right of any label (Description, Amount, or Unit Price, for example). These areas are where you can describe the items you are selling or enter data about them.
- Click to the right of Name and Address or other adjacent lines. This area is for contact information.
- Scroll down to the lower portion of the invoice, and you'll see the Total area, where Excel automatically sums the items you record in the Descriptions area. Notice that shipping and handling, as well as sales tax, can be added in automatically.

To read a quick description of some of the main elements of this template, hold the cursor over any of the tiny red triangles. Don't click the mouse; just momentarily pause it over one of the triangles. You'll see a tip describing how to use and personalize that portion of the template.

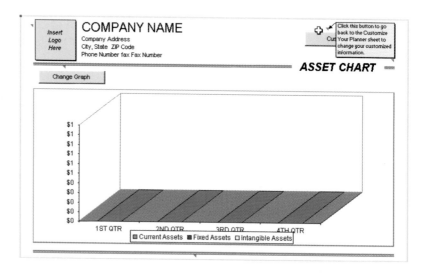

Personalizing the Template

You've just seen how to use this invoice template to record items sold and how much they were sold for. But how do you *personalize* the invoice? You will need to put your return address and company logo in the proper fields. Also, even though this invoice automatically generates sales tax and other extra charges, you'll still need to indicate the appropriate amount for your state.

To personalize your invoice, click the Customize button at the upper right. The invoice changes, and many of the fields become alterable. When using the invoice for day-to-day tasks, you simply enter the data you want; however, customizing a template creates permanent changes that will appear any time you open it (see Figure 2.7). For example, don't use the Customize button to add a client's name, because you undoubtedly have more than one client if you are in business. Use

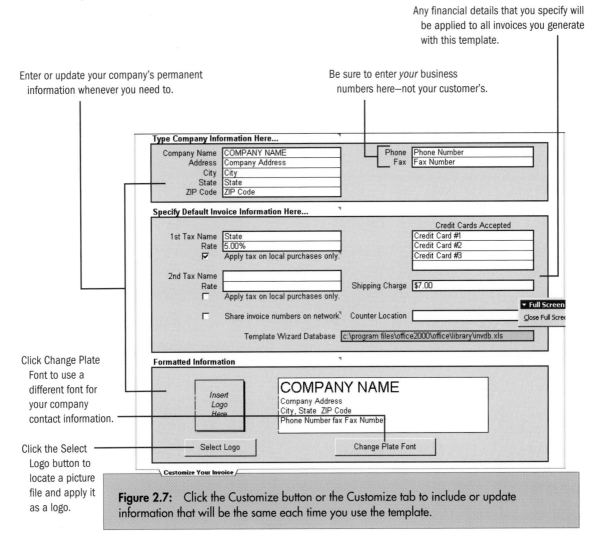

Figure 2.7: Click the Customize button or the Customize tab to include or update information that will be the same each time you use the template.

Customize to add your return address, company logo, and other permanent template features. Here are some tips for customizing your template:

- To change any field, whether it contains numerical data or a label, simply click inside it and start typing. To undo a change, type in the field again, and change it back to the way it was.

- To place a logo on this template, scroll down near the bottom of the template while in the Customize mode and click the Select Logo button on the bottom left. A Browse menu for locating logo artwork on your hard drive or CD-ROM will appear. To change the font used for your company name, click the Change Plate Font button. Again, a menu opens.

- Near the top of the Customize view of the template, click the Lock/Save button to preserve your template changes. When you click this button, a dialog box appears offering you a choice between locking your changes in place without immediately saving the template, or just saving the template right away. When you opt to save, Excel suggests a new name for your customized template, so that you don't save customized changes over the original.

To view your invoice as it would appear when printed, click the Invoice tab at the bottom of the screen.

Using the Invoice Toolbar

This particular template, as well as several others included with Office 2000, provides a toolbar that lets you quickly implement certain key features.

The buttons on the Invoice toolbar help you put your template to practical use almost immediately. Here is what each button does:

The *View button* toggles between Full-Size view and Fit to Screen view. You can display your template at its actual size or, if you need to examine it more closely, just click here and it will enlarge to fill up the whole screen.

The *View Comments button* turns comments on or off. You can either display all the comments in your invoice, or hide them (and remove the red triangles).

The *Insert Comment button* lets you add a comment at any point on your Invoice template.

The *Help button* displays template-related help.

The *Example button* fills the template fields with model text. Click here to view your template fleshed out with an everyday-use example.

The *Assign a Number button* assigns each form a unique ID number. The ability to generate individual ID numbers is very important for tracking invoices and similar documents.

The *Capture Data from a Database button* copies entries from a database into all the invoices that are based on the current template. Click here if you want to create multiple copies of the template and populate each one with data from a database. A dialog box appears, offering to walk you through the process of linking the template to a data bank that you already have up and running.

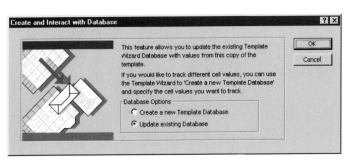

We've explored only one type of template here. Let's look at some features of other types.

Exploring Other Types of Templates

The Invoice template we've been working with has two pages: one for customizing the look of the template, and the other for regular use. The Planner template, included on the Office 2000 CD, has several tabs, as shown in Figure 2.8. Use the planner to chart your income, balance your budget, list assets, or carry out many other tasks simply by clicking the appropriate tab.

The Leasing template is an example of a worksheet that collects data on one page, as shown in Figure 2.9, while compiling and displaying the results on another. Templates that compute amortization and create scenarios for college and life-savings goals often set aside one page for asking many detailed financial questions and display the resulting projections on an entirely different page.

Templates provide a way for you to be up and running with Excel in almost no time at all. If you know the kind of document you will

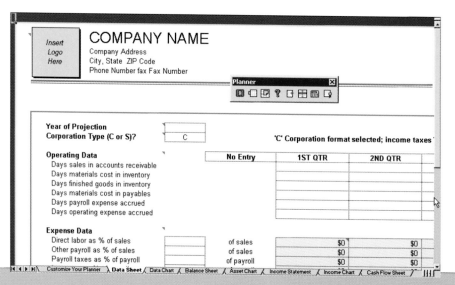

Figure 2.8: The Planner template includes many pages, accessible from the row of tabs at the bottom.

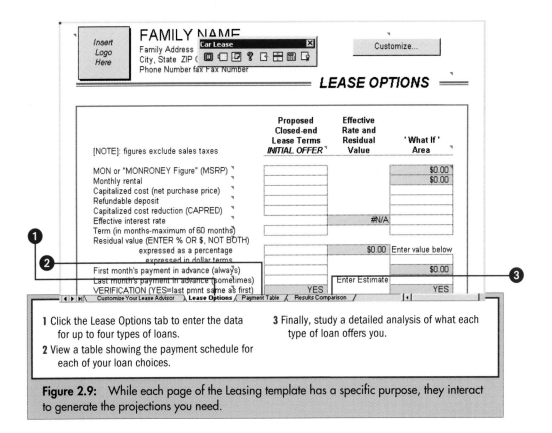

Figure 2.9: While each page of the Leasing template has a specific purpose, they interact to generate the projections you need.

be creating with Excel, it may be worth your time to investigate the template sources suggested earlier and see if you can find a document that, with a little modification, can become your own. If a quick perusal is not fruitful, open any Web browser to locate a search engine, and type **Excel Templates** in the Search field. You're bound to strike gold somewhere.

Customizing Toolbars and Menus

Before adding a new feature to a toolbar or menu, make sure it's something you'll use frequently (remember that in Office 2000, the most frequently used menu options migrate to the top of the window). An overstuffed toolbar or menu is no use to you. When you peruse the buttons and options that Excel allows you to place within reach, ask yourself if such a tool is worth the space it requires. Don't add tools or menu options unless you are clear about what they do. There's no hurry. After you're more acquainted with Excel, you can always come back later and make more adjustments. The next two sections show you how to customize your toolbars and menus.

Customizing Toolbar

Excel lets you add a command button to any toolbar in a single motion. Before you do, you can select a possible command and learn a little about its function by clicking the Description button. Here are the steps for adding a button to a toolbar:

1. Right-click any part of any toolbar.

2. Choose Customize from the shortcut menu. The Toolbars page appears. Toolbars that are currently open are shown in the toolbar list with a check mark next to their names. You can add any new command to any open toolbar, as you'll see in a moment. If you want to add tools to a toolbar that is not visible, just click its check box and it will appear.

    Although the toolbars look the same as before, you can now drag a command to a toolbar and it will stay there, wherever you drop it—even after you close Excel.

3. To access all available commands, click the Commands tab.

You'll see a list of categories on the left; commands within those categories appear on the right.

5. Click a category, and the list of commands on the right changes to reflect your choice. Note that you'll need to use the scroll bars to see the full extent of both lists.

6. Select a command on the right. Click the Description button to display a summary of its function. Move through as many categories and descriptions as you wish.

7. If you see a command you like that isn't already on one of your toolbars, drag it to the toolbar and release the mouse button. The command button will appear with a + as you drag it.

   The button that you've added will now remain in place along with the other tools on the toolbar.

EXPERT ADVICE

Normally, when you drag a command to a toolbar, an icon appears. If the command does not have an icon next to it, Excel will still add it to the toolbar as a button with a text label. To replace the text label with an icon, right-click the button and choose Default Style. To change the icon, right-click again and choose Change Button Image. Select an icon from the collection that appears. You can also click Edit Button and create your own image from scratch.

Here are some examples of useful toolbar additions:

- Add a Find button to your standard toolbar if you are always looking for lost files. (You'll find Find under the Edit category.)
- Place the Save As command (from the File category) on the toolbar right beside the Save button.
- If you are constantly adding annotations to worksheets, add a Text Box button from the AutoShapes category.

Use the New item in the Customize dialog box to create a new toolbar from scratch featuring all of your most used tools.

TIP

To remove a tool button from a toolbar, even one that you did not place there, simply drag it from the toolbar toward the Customize dialog box. The disposed button will appear with an X as you drag it.

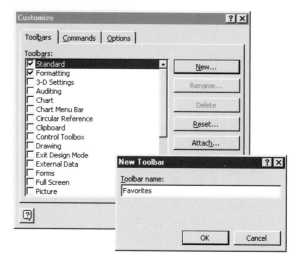

Restoring a Toolbar You've Customized

To restore a toolbar to the way it was before you changed it, locate the name of the toolbar you want to restore on the Toolbars page of the Customize dialog box. Click the Reset button. When prompted to confirm this choice, click Yes. All tool buttons you've added will be removed.

Customizing Menus

Customizing menus involves the same steps as customizing toolbars.
Figure 2.10 illustrates the process in detail.

 TIP

Whenever the Customize dialog box is open, you can drag items onto and off of menus and visible toolbars. Additionally, you can rearrange your menus and toolbars by dragging existing items from their current locations to new locations that are handier for you.

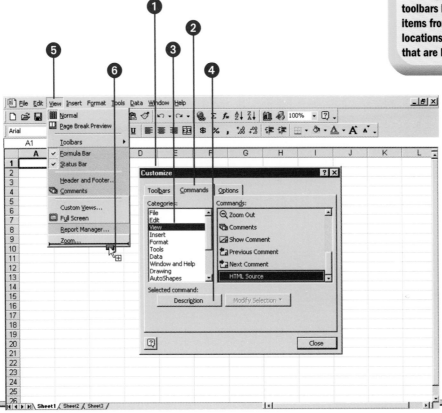

1 Right-click any toolbar and choose Customize. The Customize dialog box appears.

2 Click the Commands tab to view the lists of command categories and commands.

3 Click a category on the left to view the list of commands available within that category.

4 To see a brief summary of any command, select it and then click the Description button.

5 Click the name of the menu where you want the command to appear.

6 Drag your chosen command from the Commands list to the menu you've opened.

Figure 2.10: You can add a command to any Excel menu just by dragging it from the Customize dialog box with your mouse.

Checkpoint

You now know how to use precreated documents (templates) to speed up your work, and even create your own templates to suit your needs. In Chapter 3, you'll learn to rearrange your worksheets—to move cells, rows, and columns around with ease.

CHAPTER 3

Rearranging Your Worksheets

INCLUDES

- Moving and copying cells, rows, and columns

- Sorting cells, rows, and columns to get your data in order

- Inserting new cells, rows, and columns into your worksheets

- Removing information from your worksheets

FAST FORWARD

Copy or Move Cells, Rows, or Columns ➡ pp. 57–62

1. Select the cells, rows, or columns.
2. Right-click the cells and choose Cut or Copy.
3. Click the new target cell. This is the cell that you now want to contain the data.
4. Press ENTER or choose Paste from the Edit menu.

Sort Cells, Rows, or Columns ➡ pp. 62–63

1. Select the cells, rows, or columns you want to sort, or the whole worksheet.
2. Choose Sort from the Data menu.
3. Choose up to three criteria for sorting.
4. If your list has a row heading for each column, click a header row option. Choose other sorting criteria if necessary.
5. When you've set up the sorting specifications, click OK.

Insert Cells ➡ pp. 63–65

1. Highlight the area where you want to insert a new, blank cell, right-click, and choose Insert.
2. In the dialog box that appears, choose whether you want the existing cells to shift right or down.
3. Click OK.

Delete Cells, Rows, or Columns ➡ pp. 65–66

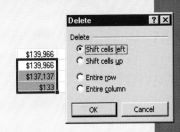

1. Select the unwanted elements.
2. To just clear the cell contents, simply press the DELETE key. To remove cell data and shift the neighboring cells as well, right-click the selection and choose Delete from the shortcut menu.
3. Use the Delete dialog box to specify how to reposition the surrounding cells.

Select New Cells and Add Content
Simultaneously ➡ pp. 66–67

To create a column or row with a simple numerical sequence, do the following:

1. Type the number you want to start with into a cell. If you like, type two cells of data, to establish a pattern.
2. Place the cursor over the lower-right corner. The cursor turns into a small cross.
3. Press the CTRL key and drag down or to the right to continue the number sequence. Drag up or to the left to create a pattern.

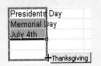

Create Automatic Data Labels ➡ pp. 68–69

1. From the Tools menu, click Options. Then click the Custom Lists tab.
2. In the List Entries panel, type labels for any list that you think you'll be using from time to time, pressing ENTER after you type each line.
3. After typing your list, click the Add button and then click OK.
4. From now on, just type any word from this label list and drag the right corner of the cell; Excel fills subsequent cells with the entries you added and saved, repeating if necessary.

As a new Excel user, you have the double burden of learning a new tool while simultaneously making your numbers look good and worthy of everybody's attention. To this end, learning to quickly reposition cells around your sheet is not just for experts—it's for you, too. Your goal is to let Excel take care of repetitive copying and formatting tasks, freeing you to do the task that the machine cannot: interpret results.

Moving Data from Place to Place on Your Worksheet

Fearless Updating

Most often, Excel updates information immediately. Replace a number in a data cell, and all formulas that refer to that cell will instantly change to reflect the new number. Unless you've gone out of your way to change this automatic feature, you can add and delete data and move columns and rows, and Excel will update all formulas accordingly.

Arranging spreadsheet data requires experimentation. It's my goal to make sure that you feel comfortable rearranging your rows and columns, able to fearlessly add to your existing data without worrying about ruining something. So let's get started learning how to move, copy, and edit cells so you won't have to spend half an afternoon doing something that really could have taken 15 minutes.

More Than Just Copying

Perhaps you've used programs that let you point and click a picture or block of text and move it around the screen. Excel works that way. However, when you move and reposition cells in Excel, you can do a lot more than relocate, copy, and paste them. Right now, we'll learn the difference between simply copying cells to a new location, and *continuing a sequence of cells* (for example, if you type a number and drag downward or across, the new cells will continue the number sequence). You'll also learn how to create an instant link to a cell group, instead of having to manually copy the cells to a new location.

Selecting Cells

To select a single cell, click it. A thick outline surrounds it, indicating that the cell is selected.

Any operation you undertake will apply to this cell; whether you copy or move data, or change the border color or cell pattern, this cell is the target.

Selecting Multiple Cells

You can select more than one cell at a time:

- To select more than one cell, place your mouse within a cell. Then click and drag in any direction. The additional cells you drag over will be selected.

- To select a large part of a row or column, click the cell at one end of the selection you have in mind and press the SHIFT key. Then click at the opposite end of your desired selection. All the cells in between the two cells you clicked will be included in your selection.

- To select cells that are not right next to each other, hold down the CTRL key and then select any cells you want, anywhere on your spreadsheet.

Moving Cells, Rows, and Columns

One easy way to rearrange your worksheet is to move cells, rows, and columns from one place to another.

Moving Cells

To move a single cell or group of cells, place the cursor near the selected cell border, and when the cursor becomes an arrow, click and drag the cell or cell group to a new location (see Figure 3.1). To copy the cells rather than move them, press the CTRL key while you drag.

To move the cells to a new spreadsheet, just select the ones you want to move and drag them downward, over the destination sheet's tab. Press the ALT key while you drag over the tab. Once your cells are over the tab, the new sheet will appear along with the cells. (See Figure 3.2.)

Using the Cut-and-Paste Feature

Perhaps you've used Cut and Paste with Windows programs before, selecting some text or a graphic and cutting or copying it to the temporary storage area known as the clipboard. You then click elsewhere in your document and paste the contents of the clipboard. With Excel, you can select any group of cells, copy or cut them, and paste them elsewhere. The new location can be a different sheet or workbook, if you like.

T**he cells you copy or move do not have to be right next to each other. While pressing the CTRL key, click anywhere, adding to the cells you already selected. In this way, you can build a selection of cells scattered throughout your spreadsheet.**

Cutting and Pasting Data, Graphics, and Labels

Cutting and pasting in Excel is powerful because you can select graphics, labels, rows of cells, address and name fields, or any cell grouping you want, and move or copy the cells to a new location.

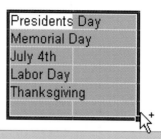

Figure 3.1:   Make sure the mouse cursor is an arrow before you drag cells to a new location. Press and hold CTRL to move a copy of the cells. The plus sign indicates that you are moving a copy.

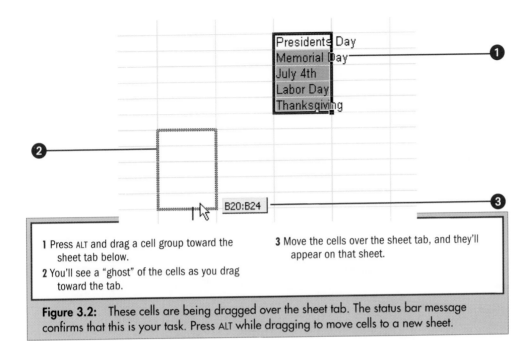

1 Press ALT and drag a cell group toward the sheet tab below.

2 You'll see a "ghost" of the cells as you drag toward the tab.

3 Move the cells over the sheet tab, and they'll appear on that sheet.

Figure 3.2: These cells are being dragged over the sheet tab. The status bar message confirms that this is your task. Press ALT while dragging to move cells to a new sheet.

Using cutting and pasting, you can transfer a major chunk of your existing spreadsheet to a new document, saving yourself the chore of reproducing something that already exists (see Figure 3.3).

Here's how to cut, copy, and paste cells and groups of cells:

1. Select the cells, rows, or columns you want to cut and paste.

2. Right-click and choose Cut or Copy from the shortcut menu. Use cut to move the cells from their current location to a new one. The Copy command leaves the group of cells intact where they are and allows you to paste that group elsewhere.

3. Click the target cell. If you've cut or copied a group of cells, then this single cell you've just clicked will be filled with the upper-left cell of your selection. The rest of your selection will fill downward and to the right. When pasting a group of cells, keep in mind the size of your selection, because when you paste it, any cells in its path will have their contents erased.

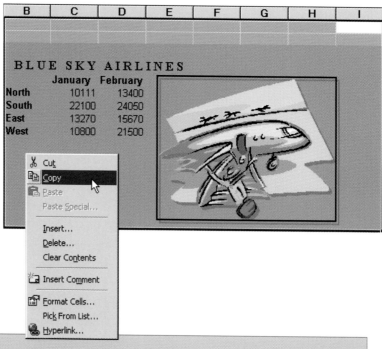

Figure 3.3: This sheet's labels, data cells, and graphic are all being copied at once.

CAUTION

Excel does not warn you if your pasting will overwrite the contents of a cell, so keep your eye on the screen.

4. After you have selected a target cell and are assured that pasting will not erase anything you want to keep, click the clipboard slot that holds the cells you have in mind for this new location. After you do so, the cells will appear there.

Using the Multiple Copy-and-Paste Feature

In Excel 2000, when you copy or cut data to the clipboard and then copy something else, an image of a clipboard appears, showing four slots for storing selections.

After you make a second copy or cut, the pasteboard appears, with the first two slots filled with the cells you just copied or cut. Then, rather than pasting, you can move about and cut another entirely different selection of cells. This new selection will appear in the third slot of the clipboard.

You can use this procedure to store up to 12 temporary selections, ready for you to paste at will. The clipboard shown in Figure 3.4 contains 9 stored selections, all ready to be pasted. They include the airplane picture, some labels, a formula, and some data cells.

Each slot on the clipboard represents a selection of cells you've cut or copied. To paste a selection, click the target location and then click the slot that contains the selection you want to paste. Since all the storage slots look alike, it's easy to forget what you have stored in each.

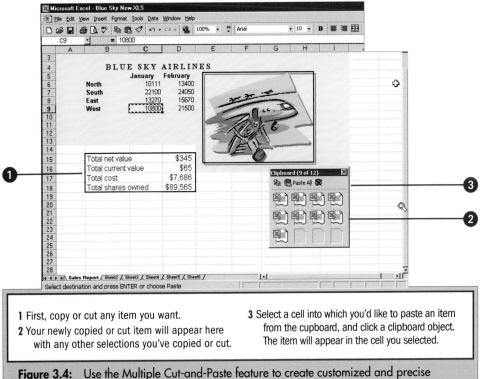

1 First, copy or cut any item you want.

2 Your newly copied or cut item will appear here with any other selections you've copied or cut.

3 Select a cell into which you'd like to paste an item from the cupboard, and click a clipboard object. The item will appear in the cell you selected.

Figure 3.4: Use the Multiple Cut-and-Paste feature to create customized and precise selections from your sheets and paste them elsewhere.

Hold your mouse over any storage slot for a reminder of what's inside. If you paste the wrong group of cells, just click the Undo arrow and try again.

Sorting Cells, Rows, and Columns

Information you need from your cells is not always easy to locate quickly. If you're seeking all cell entries made three months ago, how can you find them if your worksheet is a mile high and just as deep? Excel lets you quickly locate groups of cells according to date, range, and content, bringing only those cells that you are looking for to the front of the screen in an instant. You can even tell Excel to sort based on three different criteria at one time. For instance, if a spreadsheet contains client names, dates, and times, tell Excel to sort by client first, then by date, and then by time. Figure 3.5 shows the setup for this type of sort.

Here's how to sort cells:

1. Select the cells, rows, or columns that you want to sort. Make sure to select all the information you want included.

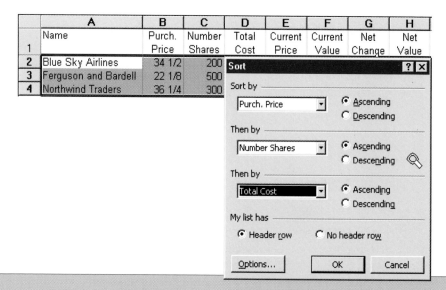

Figure 3.5: A list of stock offerings is shown, sorted according to three criteria.

2. Choose Sort from the Data menu. The Sort dialog box will appear.

3. Click the Options button if you want to sort by columns instead of rows. (Excel sorts by rows unless you tell it otherwise.)

4. Excel assumes that your list has a header row with labels for the data. Check the Header row option in the dialog box, and if Excel has guessed wrong, correct it.

5. Pick the first sort key. If you use headings for keys, you will see them listed in drop-down lists.

6. Tell Excel whether you want the sort to produce ascending or descending results. You can specify a different order for each sort criterion.

   Here's an example of three-criteria sorting:

   - The first criteria applied is alphabetization: You have several lists, one list for all items that pertain to each client, and those lists are *alphabetized*.

   - Within each client group, you want the entries displayed in chronological order. This calls for an *ascending sort by client and date*.

   - At the top of these entries, you want to see the clients you spent the most time with. A *descending sort for time* is used, causing the largest time entries to appear first.

7. When you've set up the sorting specifications, click OK and inspect the results.

Adding New Cells, Rows, and Columns

Now you've learned to rearrange your worksheets by selecting cells, adding to selections, copying and pasting, and sorting information. Next, you'll explore how to insert new rows and columns. This can be important when you realize you've omitted a category or heading from a worksheet.

Inserting Cells

At times you'll need to add an entirely new category or classification of information to your spreadsheet. If you are listing schools within a 20-mile radius of your home, for instance, perhaps you've determined a need to include a student-to-teacher ratio along with your other data. Or perhaps you need to add a new school entry to your list, fitting it in between existing entries.

Figure 3.6 shows a column being inserted between two existing columns. The Entire Column radio button is clicked. Click OK, and the column will move to the right.

The preceding example assumes a need to insert new rows or columns into an existing spreadsheet. Let's now look at how to add single cells; then we'll see how to insert entire rows and columns.

To add a cell, do the following:

1. Highlight the area where you want to insert a new, blank cell.

2. Right-click the selected cells and choose Insert from the shortcut menu. The Insert dialog box appears.

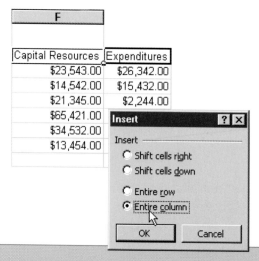

Figure 3.6: To add a column, select the column (or a portion of it) to the right of where you want the new column to appear, right-click, and choose Insert.

3. Specify whether you want the existing cells to shift right or down.

4. Click OK.

Inserting Rows and Columns

Just as you can insert individual cells, you can also insert entire rows and columns. Here's how:

1. Click the row number or column letter where you want the new row or column to appear.

2. Right-click the selected area and choose Insert from the shortcut menu. A new row or column will appear.

When inserting rows and columns, keep the following in mind:

- When you insert rows, the existing rows shift down, and the new rows are inserted where the selected rows used to be.

- When you insert columns, the existing columns shift to the right, and the new columns are inserted where the selected columns used to be.

Removing Information from Your Worksheet

From time to time, you'll probably need to remove information from your worksheets. The following sections describe how to clear cell contents and how to delete cells, rows, and columns.

Clearing Cell Contents

Clearing cell contents is not the same as deleting a cell. Deleting a cell moves, for example, cell B4 to where cell B3 used to be. All affected cells must shift to accommodate the space left by the deletion. Clearing cell contents, on the other hand, just erases the data inside the selected cell.

If you select a cell and try to erase its contents and nothing happens, you probably are clicking a cell with data that is spilling over from the cell on the left. Just click the cell to the left of the one you are trying to clear and look in the formula bar to verify what is in the cell. Then try erasing again.

- To clear cell contents, select the cells you want to clear and right-click. Then choose Clear Contents from the shortcut menu. Any numbers or text that were inside the cell will be removed. You can also simply click the cell and then press the DELETE key.

For an advanced set of clearing options, choose Clear from the Edit menu. For example, select All to erase both the cell formatting and the cell contents (cell formatting includes, currency or fraction number formatting, as well cell borders and background color choices).

To delete entire rows and columns (and thus move the neighboring rows and columns in to fill the gap), just right-click the affected row or column headings and press DELETE.

Expert Selecting

If you want to delete only a portion of a row or column, choose only those cells you have in mind, right-click them, and press Delete. Excel will then ask how you want remaining cells to move when they fill in the newly emptied space.

Earlier in this chapter, you learned the basics of selecting cells. But quite often, you'll want to apply formatting (add borders, background colors, change justification) to an oddly shaped selection. For example, what if you want to create a thick line around only your labels and headers, but not the cells between them? This section also touches on how to expand a selection of cells and automatically add data as you do so.

Selecting New Cells and Adding Content Simultaneously

In Excel, you can add cells to a selected group and fill them simultaneously. You can add data to a whole row or column of cells by simply typing in one and then dragging the cell downward or to the right.

To create a column or row and add an automatic sequence, do the following:

1. Type the data you want to start with into a cell; then place the cursor over the lower-right corner. The cursor turns into a small cross.

2. Drag downward or to the right, and the number sequence will continue, as shown in Figure 3.7.

To create a more complex sequence, do the following:

1. Type two or more cells of data, enough to suggest the pattern you want to extend to a larger selection.

2. Select the cells you just created to lock your pattern in place.

3. Drag the right corner downward or to the right, and the sequencing pattern suggested by the cells you created will continue for as long as you drag (see Figure 3.8).

When determining how to fill a list, Excel provides many options. To see them, keeping the right mouse button pressed, drag downward on the right corner of the cells, selecting the ones you want to fill. You'll see options for filling the new cells with various types of data and formatting.

Using Excel's Add-and-Repeat Labels Feature

Excel predicts that you'll want to quickly add date and time columns to some of your worksheets, or perhaps drag to create columns for every day of the week or month of the year. To see this automatic filling in action, type any day of the week in a cell and drag

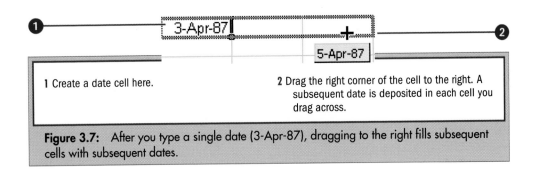

① 3-Apr-87
5-Apr-87 ②

1 Create a date cell here.

2 Drag the right corner of the cell to the right. A subsequent date is deposited in each cell you drag across.

Figure 3.7: After you type a single date (3-Apr-87), dragging to the right fills subsequent cells with subsequent dates.

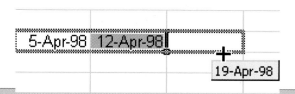

Figure 3.8: Two dates were typed, a week apart, suggesting a pattern sequence. Any new cells you select and drag will continue the sequence.

downward, and Excel adds subsequent days, repeating if you drag far enough; dates will also repeat.

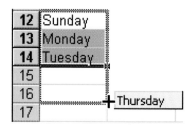

Creating Data and Label Patterns

Excel allows you to create your own data or label pattern and save it for later use. To do so:

1. From the Tools menu, click Options.

2. When the Options dialog box appears, select the Custom Lists tab (see Figure 3.9).

3. In the List Entries panel, type any list that would be of help to you, pressing ENTER after you type each line. To use a list that you've already typed in your spreadsheet, click the Import button and select the cells to use for this list.

4. After typing your list, you can click the Add button to continue to add more lists at this time, or you can click OK if you are finished. Your custom list appears with those Excel provides.

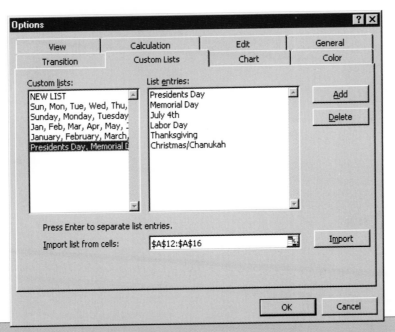

Figure 3.9: Create an automatic list by using the Custom Lists tab in the Options dialog box.

5. From now on, type any entry from the list you created and drag downward on the right corner of that cell, and Excel will add entries from your list, repeating if necessary.

Avoiding Data Growth in a List

Sometimes, you'll want numbers to repeat, rather than go up incrementally. The preceding examples demonstrated how to create lists that increment automatically when dragging; for example, dragging two cells that contain 5 and 10 will create new cells that contain 15 and 20. But what if you want cells to simply repeat 5 and 10 over and over? To avoid incremental growth, select the cells you want to repeat and press the CTRL key while dragging downward or to the right. (See Figure 3.10.)

5	10	15	20	25	30	35

5	10	5	10	5	10	5

Figure 3.10:   The top row was created by selecting both the 5 and 10 cell and then dragging. The bottom row was created the same way, while pressing the CTRL key.

Checkpoint

Now that you've learned how to select, move, and edit cells, you're ready for prime time: Chapter 4 gives you the lowdown on numbers and formulas, Chapter 5 shows nifty formatting tricks that will help add pizzazz to your worksheets, and Chapter 6 gives you pointers on organizing large projects.

CHAPTER 4

The Basics of Numbers and Formulas

INCLUDES

- Formatting number cells
- Creating custom number formats
- Creating formulas
- Using arrays and lookup tables in formulas
- Triggering actions with formulas
- Controlling recalculation in formulas
- Gathering data without formulas
- Understanding what happens when you move formulas

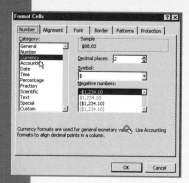

Format Number Cells ➡ pp. 78–79

1. Select the cell(s) you want to format.
2. Choose Cells from the Format menu.
3. Click the Number tab in the Format Cells dialog box to bring it to the front.
4. Scroll through the Category list and choose the number type.
5. Select other number options, such as number of decimal places and negative number display.
6. Click OK.

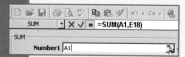

Treat Numbers as Text ➡ pp. 79–80

To get Excel to treat numbers as text, just precede the entry with an apostrophe (').

Create Formulas ➡ p. 81

1. Type an equal sign (=) in the formula bar.
2. Point to a cell and click.
3. Type the operator for your equation in the formula bar.
4. Point to another cell and click.
5. Press ENTER to finish the formula.

Use Excel's Formula Palette ➡ pp. 82–86

1. Click the target cell that will hold your formula.
2. Click the equal sign on the formula bar to display the Formula Palette
3. Click the down-facing arrow on the Formula Palette to choose a formula type.

   The Formula Palette will change to reveal fields to help build your formula.
4. Click the Range Selector button on the top line of the Formula Palette and locate the first cell reference for your formula.

   After displaying your first number choice, Excel adds the necessary operator for that portion of your formula. Notice that the Formula Palette disappears, leaving only the field needed.

5. Click the second Range Selector button and choose a cell for the next portion of your formula.

Excel will add the necessary operators.

6. Click OK to finalize your formula. The results will be displayed in the target formula cell.

Use Ranges ➡ p. 87

1. Start a formula in the formula bar.

2. Select all the cells you want to include in the range.

These cells appear referenced as a group in the formula.

3. Click OK.

The formula cell displays the *results*, while the formula bar displays the *range of cells* that are referenced in the formula. In this case, the results are the average number of students in school attendance, culled from cells E3 through E8.

=AVERAGE(E3:E8)	
D	E
	2443.8333
	Attendence
	1232
	1432
	4554
	4321
	1248
	1876

Trigger Actions with Formulas ➡ pp. 89–90

10	N/A

1. Create a cell in your worksheet that is watched by a formula. Here you will see the IF function, watching to see whether or not cell C1 displays the number 2.

2. Determine actions or results based on the presence of a certain condition in that cell. In this example, if cell C1 does display the numeral 3, then the number in cell D1 is multiplied by 2. That's why the formula cell (A1) displays the result 10.

3. Create a Formula that carries out an action when a condition is not present. If some other number besides 3 is present in cell C1, then the formula cell displays "NA."

Gather Data Without Formulas ➡ p. 95

1. Select cells and look at the middle of the status bar. The sum of the selected cells is displayed. Right-click the worksheet status bar to see perhaps an average or maximum calculation rather than a sum.

2. Project future data based on numbers currently in your worksheet.

3. Use Excel to fill in data incrementally between two known numbers. Right-click and drag downward on the bottom number of a series of cells. Click the Series option.

Attendance	Year		Attendance	Year
1123	1997		1123	1997
1276	1998		1276	1998
	1999			1999
	2000			2000
	2001			2001
	2002			2002
1888				

| D7 | $D7 | D$7 | $D$7 |

Change from Relative to Absolute to Mixed Cell References ➤ pp. 98–99

When you want to move cells around and not have the cells' related formulas move with them, make the cell references absolute, rather than relative.

1. Select the cell containing the formula to be changed.

2. In the formula bar, select (or just click anywhere in or adjacent to) the reference to be changed (B1, for example).

3. Press F4 repeatedly, watching the reference change until you see the desired effect ($B$1, for example).

4. Press ENTER or click the Enter (check mark) button on the formula bar to change the formula.

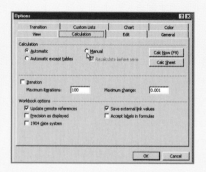

Overrule Automatic Recalculation ➤ p. 98

1. Choose Options from the Tools menu and select the Calculation tab.

2. Select the Manual option.

Numbers and formulas are the key to Excel. You'll enter numbers to represent money, dates, percents, quantities, time—anything numbers are used for in everyday life, and formulas manipulate them. They do the work.

Formulas start with the numbers you provide, apply a calculation, and return a result. In a few seconds, you can create a formula that multiplies two numbers, divides the results by yet another number, and then returns the result to you as a percentage (see Figure 4.1). Here are some examples of the alchemy of formulas:

1. First the formula multiplies the contents of cells D1 and E1.

2. Then it divides the product by the contents of cell F1.

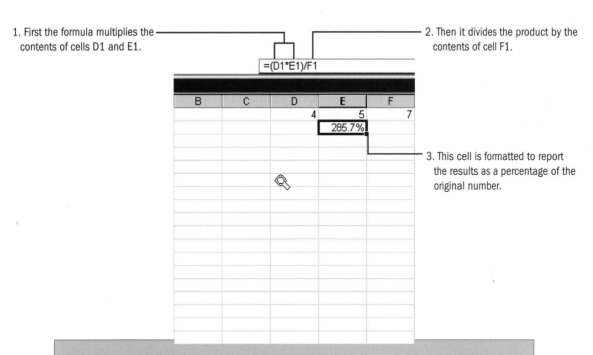

3. This cell is formatted to report the results as a percentage of the original number.

Figure 4.1: The selected cell contains the formula shown in the formula bar. The results are formatted to be displayed in a percentage

You can create a formula that calculates the numbers you choose, and then, if the result is larger than, say 35, the formula will automatically display another calculation (Figure 4.2). In this IF function example, you can see from the formula bar that if the number in cell D2 is larger than the number in cell D1 (which is the case here), then the contents of cells F2 and F1 will be multiplied (since the True condition is met, the formula completes the instructions). Since the number 35 is

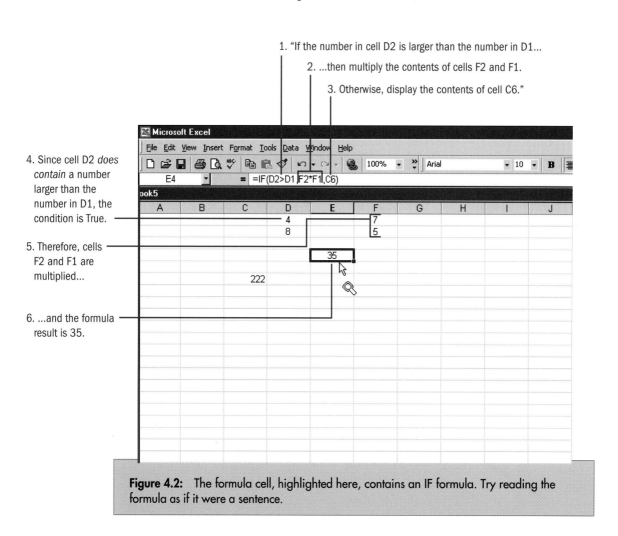

1. "If the number in cell D2 is larger than the number in D1...

2. ...then multiply the contents of cells F2 and F1.

3. Otherwise, display the contents of cell C6."

4. Since cell D2 *does contain* a number larger than the number in D1, the condition is True.

5. Therefore, cells F2 and F1 are multiplied...

6. ...and the formula result is 35.

Figure 4.2:   The formula cell, highlighted here, contains an IF formula. Try reading the formula as if it were a sentence.

displayed in the formula cell (F2 * F1), we know that the True condition has been met. As you can see from the formula bar, if the condition is not met (if D2 turns out to be smaller than D1), then the number found in cell C6 is displayed. Look again at Figure 4.2, and notice the formula in the Formula Bar. The two commas help clarify how to read the formula. The first comma signifies the word "then," and the second comma can be read as "otherwise."

> *"IF D2 is greater than D1, then multiply the contents of cell F1 those in cell F2. Otherwise, display the contents of cell C6."*

Working with Numbers

You can enter numbers in Excel two ways:

- You can use the number keys (above the letter keys) on your keyboard.
- You can use the numeric keypad (to the right of the letter keys) with NUM LOCK on.

In addition to the numerals 0 through 9, you can enter the following special symbols:

```
+ - ( ) , . $ % E e
```

When using these special symbols, keep the following in mind:

- Excel ignores the plus sign in numeric entries.
- Excel considers a number to be negative if you precede it with a minus sign (hyphen) or enclose it in parentheses.
- Excel treats commas and dollar signs correctly and accepts numbers entered in scientific notation (2.5E+2, for instance).
- When you enter dollar signs, percentages, or commas, Excel changes the number's format—that is, the way the number appears to you—without changing the number itself.

TIP

If you see
(####),
indicating that a number is
too large for the cell,
double-click the line
between the heading for
that column and the one to
its right, at the top of the
screen. This expands
the entire column width
to accommodate the
widest entry.

TIP

Create your own
type of number
formatting by selecting
Custom on the Numbers tab
of the Format Cells dialog
box and scrolling through
the options in the Type list.

Understanding Number Formats

When working with numbers, you will likely encounter numbers that are too long for a cell to contain. Excel handles this problem in one of three ways:

- It rounds off the numbers (displaying 990.32 rather than 990.32345).
- It displays the numbers in scientific notation (2.24E+02 rather than 223.5758).
- It displays the numbers as a series of pound signs (####), if the cell is too small to display the numbers in scientific notation.

Don't worry, though, Excel stores and calculates your numbers exactly as you enter them, not as they're displayed on the screen.

Formatting Number Cells

If you notice Excel using too many decimal places when presenting your data, limit the number by right-clicking the column in question, selecting Format Cells, and choosing Number (Figure 4.3). Notice the check box for specifying the number of decimal places to be displayed in a cell. Reduce this value to accommodate a narrower cell.

Understanding Dates and Times

Enter dates and times by typing them in the most commonly accepted American formats. Take a look at the Number tab in the Format Cells dialog box to see all the nifty date and time formats.

CELLS WITH DATES MAY SUDDENLY CHANGE THEIR APPEARANCE   Excel is often required to perform date-and-time math (to determine the number of days between two dates or the number of hours between two time entries, for instance), so it stores

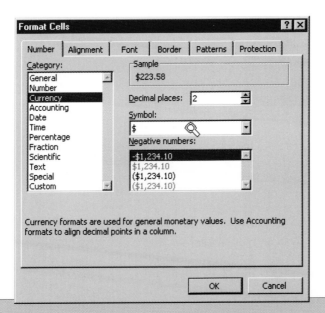

Figure 4.3: To change the appearance of numbers to reflect their use in your worksheet, click the Number tab of the Format Cells dialog box and make any changes you want.

dates and times as serial numbers, using January 1, 1900, as the starting date. Here's what you need to remember:

- The serial number 1 represents January 1, 1900; the serial number 2 stands for January 2, 1900.
- If you reformat a cell containing a date and display it as a number, you'll see the serial number instead of the date.
- Excel still treats the cell's contents as a date for computations, even though the cell may look strange to you.

Forcing Excel to Treat Numbers as Text

Suppose that your XYZ Widget company keeps inventory by listing part numbers using a ##/## format—like 12/63. Normally, Excel would try to treat this as a date, and instead of seeing your part number in the cell, you'd see something like Dec-63 after you finish the entry. However, if you precede the entry with an apostrophe, Excel will treat the number as a text entry rather than a date. Here's an example:

=	'12/63

C	D
	12/63

You would enter '12/63. The apostrophe will not be displayed on the screen or printed after you enter the number.

Working with Formulas

Formulas are used to add, subtract, multiply, or divide numbers in your worksheets. They are made up of two parts:

- The cells you want to include in the formula
- The operators, which tell Excel what calculation you want to perform

To accommodate Lotus 1-2-3 users, Excel also lets you introduce a formula with a (+) sign, changing it automatically to an equal (=) sign.

Excel formulas always start with an equal sign (=), which tells Excel that you want to create a formula. So a simple formula might look like this:

```
=B3-B2
```

EXPERT ADVICE

To see all of the formulas in your worksheet, choose Options from the Tools menu, select the View tab in the Options dialog box, and then place a check mark in the Formulas check box. You can also press CTRL-` (the backquote symbol found at the top left of the keyboard).

Creating Formulas

Creating formulas isn't nearly as hard as it may sound. Let's try a formula that will subtract the number in cell B3 from the number in B2 and then put the answer in cell B4. This formula is shown in Figure 4.4.

1. Put numbers in cells B2 and B3. Make the number in cell B2 larger than the number in B3.

2. Move your cursor to cell B4 and type the equal sign (=).

3. Click inside the formula bar.

4. Click cell B2. Cell B2 is surrounded by what look like marching ants, indicating that it is selected. The cell's address appears in the formula bar.

5. Making sure your cursor is still in the formula bar, to the right of the B2 reference, type the minus sign (hyphen) for your equation.

6. Point to cell B3 and click. Again, the cell's address appears in the formula bar.

7. Press ENTER to finish the formula. If you have entered values in cells B2 and B3, the value in B3 is subtracted from the value in B2, and the difference appears in cell B4.

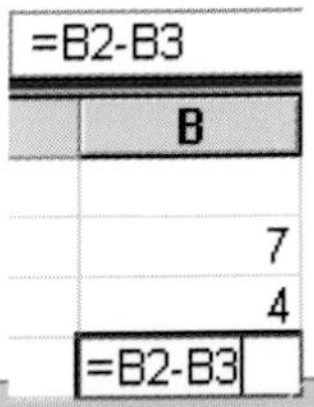

Figure 4.4: This formula instructs Excel to subtract the number in B3 from the number in B2. The formula cell is B4. We've not pressed ENTER yet, so B4 still shows the formula, not the result.

Formulas Refer to Cells, Not Numbers

When working with formulas, remember that:

- A formula with cell references (such as B6*B7) will perform the calculation indicated in the formula regardless of the numbers in those cells. You can change the cell numbers, and the formula will still perform the task you assigned it.

- You can also create a formula that contains numbers, not cell references. However, formulas with lots of numbers in them will require you to go back to the formula to make any needed adjustments; you will not have the convenience of simply updating the numbers in the cells.

- Many formulas are a mixture of cell references and fixed numbers. Data that is likely to change belongs in cells, while a fixed value can be inserted directly into a formula as a number. For example, when creating a tax formula equation that considers the number of children you have, if this condition is not likely to change, then feel free to type the number of children directly into the formula instead of creating a cell reference.

The Order of Operations in Formulas, or Operation Precedence

Whenever you add more than one operator to a formula, Excel must decide which operation to perform first. The results depend on rules governing which operators are calculated first. Here's an example of two formulas that use the same numbers but yield different results:

=5+2*10 yields 25
=10*5+2 yields 52

Why is this? Because in each instance, *Excel performs multiplication first.*

- In the first formula, Excel arrives at 20 (2 times 10) before adding the 5.
- In the second example, Excel arrives at 50 (10 times 5) before adding the 2.

Here is a list showing the order of operations:

1. Parentheses containing operations

2. Exponents

3. Multiplication and division

4. Addition and subtraction

Applying Formulas to New Cells

Sometimes you will want to copy formulas from cell to cell. For instance, if you create an equation to add all numbers in column D, you may want a similar formula for columns E and F.

Washington	23400	25600	26500
Utah	79681	100220	124110
	=SUM(D3:D7)	=SUM(E3:E7)	=SUM(F3:F7)

Each of the following formula-copying techniques produce different results:

- To apply a formula you created in one column and move it to others, simply select the bottom-right corner of the formula cell and drag it horizontally, over all the other target columns (see Figure 4.5). This process copies the formula to each column, and in each instance, *the formula changes to refer to the cells in its own new column.* This is called a *relative cell reference* (versus an absolute reference).

- To move a formula to a new cell, taking its references with it, click the formula cell with the arrow mouse pointer (click the edge of the cell) and drag it to a new location. Unless the

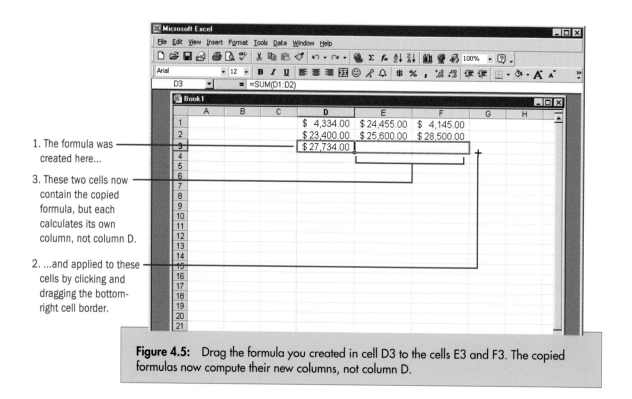

1. The formula was created here...

3. These two cells now contain the copied formula, but each calculates its own column, not column D.

2. ...and applied to these cells by clicking and dragging the bottom-right cell border.

Figure 4.5: Drag the formula you created in cell D3 to the cells E3 and F3. The copied formulas now compute their new columns, not column D.

mouse pointer is right at the edge of the cell, it won't look like a pointer.

- If you want to move your formula to a new cell (not copy it) and have the formula refer to cells in the column where you moved it, press the CTRL key while dragging the formula.

Moving Formulas Simultaneously

To move or copy a group of formulas together, hold the SHIFT key while selecting the formulas, release the SHIFT key, and then move them. When you drag grouped formulas to a new location, the formulas will still refer to the original set of cells.

If instead you hold down the CTRL key, the formulas will be copied and will refer to the cells in the new column.

Moving a formula up and down a column does not affect the cells it refers to.

Excel's Formula Operators

For purposes of explanation, Excel operators can be divided into four general categories: arithmetic, comparison, text, and reference. Most of the time, you will use arithmetic operators. The others are useful for more complex projects.

The following sections provide an overview of these four types of formula operators.

Arithmetic Operators

You've already seen *arithmetic operators* at work: the plus sign (+), for example, and the minus sign (−). Here's the standard collection of arithmetic operators:

Operator	Meaning
+	Addition
−	Subtraction
*	Multiplication
/	Division
%	Percentage
^	Exponentiation

Simply include these symbols at the appropriate places in your formulas to perform the desired calculations. Here are two examples:

- =B5*10% computes 10 percent of the contents of cell B5.
- =B5^2 computes the square of cell B5's contents.

EXPERT ADVICE

Formulas will add all the numbers in a column, even if you specified only the first few. This feature can be important for totaling lists. For example, if you write the formula =Sum (C2:C4), which tells Excel to add the numbers in cells C2, C3, and C4, you can keep typing numbers in column C—in cells C5, C6, and so on—and they will be added as well. Excels assumes that you want to add all the numbers in column C, even if your formula specifies only a few of the top cells. That's why, when using Excel to create invoices, for instance, you should leave room for additional itemized purchases: that is, place your formula cell pretty far down in the column.

Comparison Operators

Comparison operators let you inspect two values and come to a conclusion about their relative values. They are usually coupled with Excel's logical functions (discussed in Chapter 7).

Here are the comparison operators:

Operator	Meaning
=	Equal to
>	Greater than
>=	Greater than or equal to
<	Less than
<=	Less than or equal to
<>	Not equal to

Text Operator

Excel's only *text operator* is the ampersand (&). It is used to combine text. For instance, if you have the word "cow" in cell C7 and the word "boy" in C8, the formula =C7&C8 will create the text string "cowboy."

Reference Operators

Excel also offers *reference operators*. The most common reference is to a range of cells. For instance, the expression B1:C3 refers to cells B1, C3, and all the cells between them. The reference operator is the colon: that is, you use a colon to separate the first and last cell addresses in a cell range.

Referencing Cells in Your Formulas

When you type the name of a cell into a formula, you've created a *cell reference*. It gives the formula a map to that cell. Let's look at the difference between formulas that refer to one single cell, and formulas that work their magic on a range of cells all at once.

Some formulas perform a calculation to one particular cell. This is called a *single-cell reference.* If you want your formula to refer to a cell, just click the cell or type the cell address in the formula bar. Here's an example of a single-cell reference:

=(8/B3)*115%

This formula divides the contents of cell B3 by 8 and then multiplies the result by 115%.

Some formulas calculate an entire range of cells. In the following example, cells B3 through B5 represent the *range reference* upon which the formula act.

=(8*SUM(B3:B5)*115%)

In this example, the formula multiplies the sum of cells B3 through B5 and then multiplies the product by 115%. As you can see, to specify a cell range, you insert a colon between two cell addresses. The formula will then know to examine all the cells between, and including, the two named cells.

Using Lookup Tables

Lookup tables are special arrays (cell ranges) that you create to help you look up and provide different cell contents as conditions warrant. Here is an example:

> **TIP**
>
> Rather than type a cell range in a formula, click and drag your mouse over all the cells you want to include, and Excel will insert the range into your formula.

B10		= =LOOKUP(A10,$A$3:$B$5)		
A	B	C	D	E
1				
2 Guests	Rate			
3	10	$ 14.95		
4	25	$ 10.95		
5	50	$ 7.75		
6				
7				
8	10			
9	100			
10	25	$ 10.95		

The lookup table consists of the range of cells A3:B5. Cells A3 through A5 contain quantities for each of three price breaks. Cells B3 through B5 contain the prices.

In the above example, the quantity you type in column A (as shown, 10, 25 or 50) causes a certain ticket price to appear in Column B. The Lookup Table was set to offer lower prices ($7.75, Column B) for purchasing a higher volume of tickets (50 and above, Column A). Purchasing a lower volume of tickets (say, 10 and under), triggers the adjacent cell in Column B to display a higher price-per-ticket. The purpose of a Lookup Table, then, is to let you specify what range of numbers typed in a certain column will trigger a particular result in another column. As you can see from the example, cell B:10 contains a Lookup Table formula, and it displays the results of the applicable formula.

Incidentally, you can use lookup tables with text as well as numbers. In the following example, Excel inserts different words based on order quantities. All that was done to create this table was to replace the cell contents in B3, B4, and B5 with text.

B9		=	=LOOKUP(A9,$A$3:$B$5)	
	A	B	C	D
1				
2	Guests	Rate		
3	10	Small group		
4	25	Medium group		
5	50	Large group		
6				
7				
8	10	Small group		
9	100	Large group		
10	25	Medium group		

EXPERT ADVICE

Lookup tables need not be on the same page or even the same sheet as the cells containing the lookups. Consider putting your lookup tables out of sight.

Advanced Formula Techniques

Here are a few other examples of how formulas can make your life easier. These formulas trigger actions based on certain criteria, such as the presence of a certain text phrase, number, or date.

Triggering an Action with a Text Entry

If you sell (and sometimes ship) merchandise, you can create a formula that adds sales tax for customers in your state, but which doesn't add it for customers in other states. The same spreadsheet can also add a shipping and handling charge to only those accounts you specify. How would this work? The formula would watch the cell in which you regularly type your customer's state (see Figure 4.6). If you type your home state, the spreadsheet would automatically add the sales tax.

This formula says, "If cell G7 contains 'CA,' then multiply cell B19 by 1.08. Otherwise, just repeat cell B19."

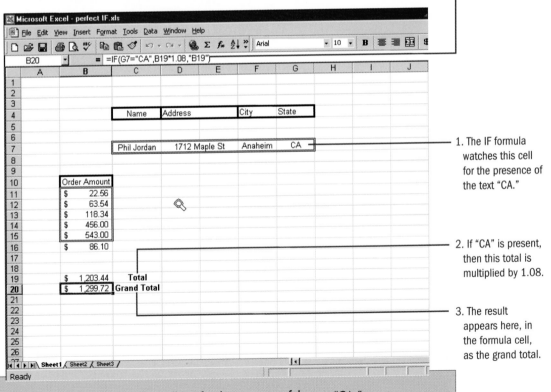

1. The IF formula watches this cell for the presence of the text "CA."

2. If "CA" is present, then this total is multiplied by 1.08.

3. The result appears here, in the formula cell, as the grand total.

Figure 4.6: The formula watches cell G7 for the presence of the text "CA."

Putting a Formula to Work

The formula we will now examine involves a *function*. Functions simply combine formulas, performing several calculations at once. They are discussed in Chapter 7, but since the following example is very practical, we'll get a little ahead of ourselves and begin our exploration of functions.

A Worksheet with a Text Trigger

Figure 4.7 shows a portion of the invoice shown in Figure 4.6. Cell B19 shows the sum of all the purchases (the order amounts) that are listed in column B. To create a formula that adds the numbers in column B and displays the results in B:19, you would type: **=Sum(B11:B15)**.

To create the purchase sum, do the following:

1. Select where you want the sum of the purchases to appear (in this example, the sum appears in cell B19).

2. Click the equal sign on the formula bar.

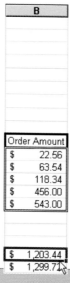

Figure 4.7:　Column B contains the sums to be added, and the formula for calculating sales tax when appropriate.

3. Type the formula **Sum(B11:B15)** (Excel automatically adds the equal sign). To finalize the formula, press Enter or click the equal sign again.

Your sum will not appear in the cell you clicked until you click the equal sign on the formula bar or press ENTER. Clicking the equal sign finalizes the formula and places the results of the formula in the cell. (In reality, the results of the formula and the formula itself both live in the same cell.)

As you'll soon see, you can now tell your spreadsheet to add sales tax to a sum only if the customer on this invoice is from a state where sales tax applies (you determine whether sales tax applies—not Excel). To make a spreadsheet choose between two actions, you have to tell it to watch for a certain condition.

Building the Formula

The spreadsheet in Figure 4.6 has a state field, in which the person preparing the invoice always types the state where the customer lives. Think of the formula as a sentence that reads: "Any time the State field contains 'CA,' add sales tax to the purchase total."

What components does this formula need? First, we need the cell locations.

- The State field is cell G7.
- The purchase sum is in cell B19.
- This formula will appear in a field labeled Grand Total, which will contain the sum of the purchase total plus the tax. Cell B20 will be the formula cell that both contains the formula and displays the grand total.

Here's the formula close up:

```
=IF(G7="CA",B19*1.08,"N/A")
```

Think of it as a sentence that reads: "If cell G7 contains 'CA,' then multiply cell B19 by 108 percent. Otherwise, display N/A."

Now let's build a formula like the one in the illustration. If you'd like, follow along and create a spreadsheet containing an "Order Amount" column like the one shown in Figure 4.7. The formula we create will appear below the Order Amount subtotal, since it will be the grand total, including sales tax.

SETTING UP A CONDITION USING THE IF FUNCTION   To create the grand total, we need the IF formula. IF looks at the cell we specify to see whether a certain condition is met. In this case, if the condition we specify is present (is True), then we want the formula to calculate the appropriate sales tax.

1. Click the cell where you want the formula to appear and then click the equal sign on the formula bar.

2. Click the down-facing arrow on the left and scroll down. Select the IF function. A dialog box that steps you through the IF formula appears (see Figure 4.8).

    The dialog box has three data lines for you to enter different parts of your formula.

    Logical_test   Specify the condition the formula should look for. In this example, we'd direct the formula to look for "CA" in the cell we designate as the State cell. That cell is G7.

    Value_if_true   Specify what should happen if the condition is True. In the example, if "CA" appears in the State cell, then sales tax should be added to the purchase sum.

    Value_if_false   Specify what should happen if "CA" does not appear in the State cell. In this case, a simple N/A (not applicable) would appear in the sales tax column.

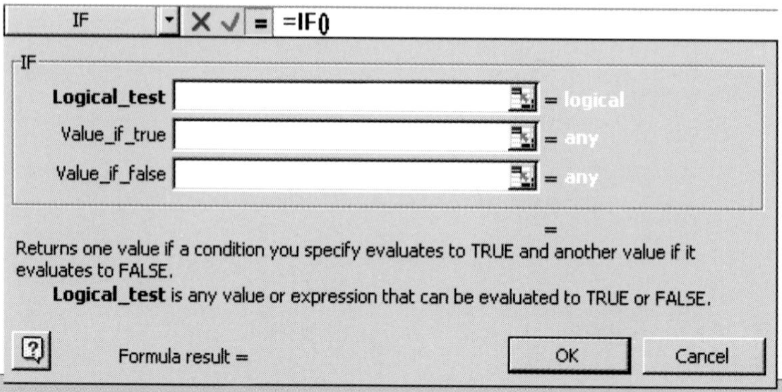

Figure 4.8:   The IF formula dialog box as it appears when first opened

SETTING UP THE LOGICAL_TEST LINE   You need to set up the condition you want the formula to look for.

1. Click the Range Selector button on the right side of the first line, and the main formula dialog box is replaced by a single data strip at the top of the screen.

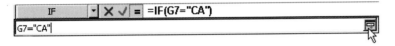

2. This part of the formula begins with a cell reference. Rather than typing the cell address, just click the cell (in this case, G7), and the cell reference will appear in the formula.

3. Type **="CA"** (include the quotation marks) to set the condition that the formula will look for, which is the presence of the abbreviation for California. You can specify Calif. or California, if you like, but whatever text you specify will have to be typed in the state cell (G7) for the formula to work.

    You've just provided all the data you need for the Logical Test line. Now bring back the IF formula dialog box.

4. Click the Range Selector button again (in the figure, it is near the label "G"), and the IF formula dialog box will expand, allowing you to make the rest of the formula entries.

Verifying Your Results
To verify your formula, do the following:

1. Type **CA** in cell G7, and the Grand Total cell will add sales tax to the value in the Total cell (see Figure 4.9).

2. Type any other state abbreviation in cell G7, and the Grand Total cell will simply repeat what appears in the Total cell.

3. To test more functionality, type new purchases in any of the upper cells in column B and watch the Total amount change, causing the Grand Total cell to be updated as well.

TIP

When building a formula as described, do not click the OK button until you've completed your entire formula. If you accidentally click OK, click the equal sign on the formula bar again, and your formula will reappear right where you left off.

While creating a function like we've done here, you don't really have to minimize the function's dialog box to click a cell and have it appear in a function's data line. If the cell is visible on the screen, just click inside the formula dialog box where you want the cell to appear and then click the cell itself—or just move the dialog box out of the way.

	=	CA				
B	**C**	**D**	**E**	**F**	**G**	

	Name	Address		City	State

	Phil Jordan	1712 Maple St		Anaheim	CA

Order Amount
$ 22.56
$ 63.54
$ 118.34
$ 456.00
$ 543.00

$ 1,203.44	**Total**
$ 1,299.72	**Grand Total**

Figure 4.9: Test your IF formula by typing **CA** in the State cell and then replace it with a different state in this cell.

Instant Calculations

Some important calculations can be performed without directly invoking a formula.

Quickly Adding Numbers

To add a row or column of figures, just use the AutoSum feature. Simply select the whole row or column of numbers you want to add and then click the AutoSum button.

The line immediately below or to the right of the group of numbers you selected will display the sum of all of them.

AutoSum actually generates a formula that resides in the cell that contains the sum. You can move the formula cell, and it will continue to refer to that same group of cells. This freedom of movement can be important if your list of added numbers grows and you need to make room for more.

Performing Common Calculations to Get Information on Selected Cells

When you need information from particular cells, you can quickly perform common calculations without using formulas. Simply select the cells, right-click anywhere along the status bar in Excel, and select the appropriate function (see Figure 4.10). You can use this approach for a fast column or row total, or even to total cells that are not contiguous. You can also find the average of a group of numbers, locate the minimum or maximum value, or count the number of filled cells in a selection. However, you cannot copy the results to the clipboard or move the results to a different cell. This feature is for your information only.

Projecting Data without a Formula

Not all data collection requires a formula, either. With just a couple of mouse clicks, you can make projections based on a series of numbers, predicting what values will follow. Excel uses the relationships among the numbers in the group of cells you select and provides the next logical sequence of numbers in the neighboring cells.

This feature is helpful, for example, if you have a monthly sales chart and want to determine how sales will grow in the coming months based on previous months' growth (see Figure 4.11).

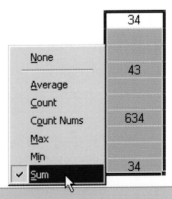

Figure 4.10:   Select cells, and their sum appears at the bottom of the Excel screen. Right-click the bottom of the screen to see the results of other calculations.

Region	January	February	March	April	May	June
North	10111	13400				
South	22100	24050				
East	13270	15670				
West	10800	21500	32200			
				42900		

Figure 4.11: By selecting figures for January and February and then dragging rightward, you can create sales projections for subsequent months.

PROJECTING FUTURE DATA ON THE FLY To have Excel look at the relationship between a set of numbers and then determine what numbers would logically follow, do this:

1. Select the numbers to start your projection *from*. For example, sales totals for the last four months. Select them by clicking the top number in your series, pressing the SHIFT key, and then clicking the bottom number in the series, or by clicking and dragging from the first to the last numbers.

2. Place your mouse over the right-bottom corner of the bottom cell of your selection (you'll notice a small black square), and your mouse will turn into a small cross. Click the mouse button and drag downward, selecting as many new cells as you like. If you are measuring months, for example, determine how many months you want to predict for and then drag to select a corresponding number of cells.

The new cells continue on in the pattern established by the previously selected cells. The new cells are filled with text or number data, not formulas.

PROJECTING VALUES BETWEEN GIVEN NUMBERS If your spreadsheet has beginning and ending values (for example, odometer readings before and after a long trip), Excel can fill in the cells in between your two values with incremental steps. Use this feature when you need to know what may have gone on in between two results. For example, if you weigh a certain amount, have a new target weight in mind, and have a specific number of weeks in which you want to reach this new ideal weight, use this feature to fill in the amount you will want to weigh at the end of each week along the way (see Figure 4.12).

To project the values between two numbers, do the following:

1. Select the original and the target numbers, pressing the SHIFT key while you click each number (or select the range from the original to the target number by clicking and dragging).

2. With the range selected, select Fill from the Edit menu and choose Series. The Series dialog box appears.

3. On the Series In panel, click Columns. Make sure Linear is selected and click OK.

Excel will fill in the cells between your starting and target cells.

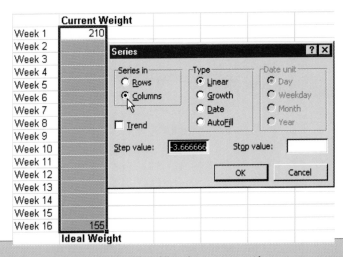

Figure 4.12: Use the Series command to fill in the increments between two existing numbers at either end of a column or row.

Excel's Automatic Recalculation Feature

Normally, Excel recalculates each time you change any number in a worksheet. Unless you instruct it otherwise, Excel always recalculates before saving. If you want to turn off automatic recalculation, choose Options from the Tools menu and click the Calculation tab. Under the Calculation settings, check the Manual option. From then on, to recalculate a worksheet manually, press F9.

Using Relative, Absolute, and Mixed Cell References

Relative, absolute, and mixed cell references are particularly handy when you plan to copy and paste or otherwise move cells around in your worksheets. A relative reference will vary depending on where the formula is copied. For example, suppose a formula in cell A15 references cell A1. If you copy the formula from A15 and paste it into cell B15, the relative reference will then point to cell B1. All references are relative unless you specify them to be absolute.

An absolute reference, on the other hand, always refers to the same cell, no matter where the formula is copied and pasted in the worksheet. For example, if a formula in cell A15 references cell A1, then the formula will always reference cell A1, even if you copy and paste the formula to other cells.

A mixed reference, as the name indicates, is part relative and part absolute.

You can create three types of mixed references:

- Mixed references that point to a specific column and a relative row (like $A1)

- Mixed references that point to a specific row and a relative column (like A$1)

- Mixed references that point to a specific worksheet and relative row and column (like Sheet2:$A$1)

To ensure that formulas always refer to a specific cell (like the one containing the markup percentage in the example earlier in this

An absolute reference has a dollar sign preceding it. To quickly change a cell reference to a particular type, click inside the formula bar and select the reference. Select a cell reference type by pressing the F4 key until the reference type you want appears.

chapter), you should specify an absolute reference. To change the type of reference, just follow these steps:

1. Place the insertion point inside or adjacent to the cell address.

2. Press F4.

Look at the address. An absolute reference looks like this: $G$1. A relative reference looks like this: G1. A mixed reference can look like $G1 (with the column absolute) or G$1 (with the row absolute).

Keeping Formulas in Place

Sometimes we need an absolute reference in a formula. The spreadsheet shown in Figure 4.13 proposes an increase of 2% per month. This added 2% is expressed in cell D1. The formula used to apply the 2% increase is =(D5*D1)+D5.

D1 is the data cell that will be increased each month by 2%. D5 represents February spending. The formula multiplies that number by 2% by creating a reference to cell D1.

APPLYING THE FORMULA TO OTHER MONTHS   Of course, we are interested in more months than just February. We'd like to quickly apply that 2% multiplier progressively to future months. The best way to do so is to drag the formula across to include the new

			= =(D5*D1)+D5				
B	C	D	E	F	G	H
		0.2				
Region	January	February	March	April	May	June
North	10111	13400	16080	16080	16080	
South	22100	24050				
East	13270	15670				
West	10800	21500				

Figure 4.13:   The budget amount does not grow incrementally because the reference is entirely relative. When the formula is dragged to a new cell, it looks for the incremental percentage amount in cell E1, then F1, and so on. If the formula were made absolute, it would know to look only for the calculation in D1.

months. The formulas will dutifully change references to compute the new columns they find themselves in.

Region	January	February	March	April	May	June
North	10111	13400	16080	19296		
South	22100	24050				
East	13270	15670				
West	10800	21500				

The percentage we are using to affect these budget increases is set in D1. We do not want the reference to D1 to move, even though we want the other references in the formula to change to compute each new month we drag our formula to. So how do we get the one formula component to refer to the same cell no matter what (to always call up D1) and leave the other formula component free to roll along (to change to a new month's column each time it is moved)?

We have to create a formula with an absolute reference for cell D1 (by placing dollar signs in front of the D and 1) and a relative reference for the remainder of the formula. That way, we can drag the formula to compute any month's column, and the reference to the cell with the percentage calculation (D1) will remain fixed. The mixed reference allows the formula to be applied to many months (a relative reference), yet continue to draw its budget increase amount from the same cell (an absolute reference).

Pasted formulas always create relative references unless a formula specifies absolute references. That means that a formula you cut and paste will change to reflect its new location.

D7	$D7	D$7	$D$7

Formula References and Moving Cells

When moving cells, rows, or columns, keep an eye on the formulas that refer to them. Some formulas will follow your movement of cells and update their references automatically. However, if you move a referenced cell to a new worksheet or workbook, error messages may appear. If you move worksheet items and receive unwanted results, use the Undo arrow to return your worksheet to the way it was before you moved things. Then change the cell references that are creating errors into absolute references. This reduces the confusion caused when a formula looks for a cell that has been moved.

If you've moved worksheet items and cannot use the Undo key to retrace your steps, use the Audit feature to help locate the formula a cell is looking for.

Checkpoint

In this chapter you've learned the true essentials of what Excel can do for you—take the numbers you've entered as formulas and calculate them. Specifically, you've learned about entering numbers and creating formulas, and you've even learned a bit about rearranging formulas in your worksheet. Armed with this information, you're prepared to start using Excel for your worksheet needs.

Up next in Chapter 5 is information about formatting your worksheets. There you'll learn about changing fonts, sizes, and colors as well as adding some cool effects to your worksheets. In Chapter 6, you'll learn some organization techniques that will help you work more efficiently on large projects. Then, in Chapter 7, you'll get a brief introduction to functions, which are pre-made formulas that are ready for you to use.

CHAPTER 5

Formatting Tricks

INCLUDES

- Saving time with AutoFormat, Styles, and Format Painter
- Resizing rows and columns or hiding them altogether
- Changing the appearance of text
- Formatting numbers
- Adding order with borders
- Highlighting key points with color and shading
- Inserting page breaks

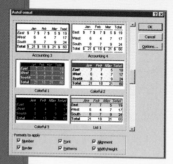

Apply Formatting Quickly
with AutoFormat → pp. 112–114

1. Select the cells you want to format.
2. Choose AutoFormat from the Format menu.
3. Scroll through the previews of available format options. Consider how your data would appear displayed in the same manner.
4. Use the Options button to include or exclude formatting options.
5. Select a format option and click OK.

Create a New Style → pp. 114–116

1. After formatting a cell, choose Style from the Format menu.
2. Type a new style name.
3. Clear the check boxes of any items you don't want included in the style; then click Add.
4. Click OK.

Use Format Painter → p. 116

1. Select a cell that has the formatting you want to copy
2. Click the Format Painter button on the standard toolbar.
3. Drag to select the area to receive the formatting.
4. Release the mouse button.

Change Row Height ➥ p. 117

Rows automatically adjust to fit their tallest entry.

- To make manual adjustments, drag the bottom edge of a row label to a new height.
- To specify a row height in points, select the row and choose Format | Row | Height, or select the row, right-click, and choose Row Height from the shortcut menu.

Row Height	? X
Row height:	14.25
OK	Cancel

Change Column Width ➥ p. 118

- To automatically adjust a column to fit its widest entry, double-click one of the lines separating the column labels.
- To make manual adjustments, drag the right edge of a column label to a new width.
- To specify a column width in number of characters, select the column and choose Format | Column | Width, or select the column, right-click, and choose Column Width from the shortcut menu.

Width: 14.14 (104 pixels)

Hide and Reveal Rows or Columns ➥ p. 118

- To hide, select the row(s) or column(s) to be hidden. Then right-click the selection and choose Hide from the shortcut menu.
- To unhide, select the rows above and below the hidden rows or the columns to the right and left of hidden columns. Then right-click and choose Unhide from the shortcut menu.

-

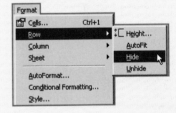

Change Fonts and Their Attributes ➡ pp. 120–121

1. Select cells or other objects containing text.
2. Click the format buttons on the formatting toolbar or right-click the selected cells and choose Format Cells on the shortcut menu.
3. In the Format Cells dialog box, make font and formatting selections on the Font tab.

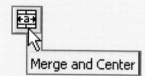

Center Text Across Columns ➡ p. 123

1. Select the text to be centered and the cells across which the text will be centered.
2. Click the Merge and Center button on the formatting toolbar.

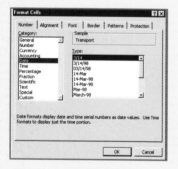

Alter the Appearance of Numbers ➡ pp. 123–124

1. Select the cell(s) containing the number(s) to be reformatted.
2. Click the format buttons on the formatting toolbar or right-click the selected cells and choose Format Cells from the shortcut menu.
3. In the Format Cells dialog box, make your selections on the Number tab.

Add Lines and Borders ➡ pp. 125–126

1. Select the cells to be formatted.
2. Click the down arrow next to the Borders button on the formatting toolbar to reveal a list of line and border choices.
3. Click the desired choice.
4. Click the Borders button again to add borders or to change the appearance of borders.

Change Colors and Shading ➡ pp. 126–127

1. Select the cells containing the text to be colored or shaded.

2. To change font colors (or gray shading on noncolor systems), click the down arrow next to the Font Color button on the formatting toolbar. To fill or shade cells with a different color or gray shade, click the down arrow next to the Fill Color button on the formatting toolbar.

3. Click the desired color or shade from the palette that appears.

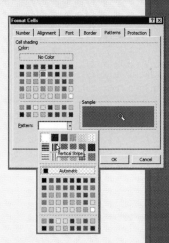

Add or Remove Page Breaks ➡ p. 127

• To insert a page break, select the row beneath the desired page break point or the column to the right of the desired break point and choose Page Break from the Insert menu.

• To remove a page break, select the row beneath the existing page break point or the column to the right of the break and choose Remove Page Break from the Insert menu.

Remove Formatting ➡ p. 128

Select the cell(s) and choose Edit | Clear | Formats. Then do one of the following:

• Select the cell(s), choose Style from the Format menu, and then select Normal from the drop-down Style name list.

• Right-click the cell(s), select Format Cells, select the Number tab, and click General.

Formatting sets the "look" of your spreadsheet. It lets you choose what your readers will focus on. What do you want them to see first? Formatting rescues your data from the labyrinth of rectangles that make a generic spreadsheet such an object of fear and loathing. Excel offers a number of formatting features that affect fonts, cells, backgrounds, rows, and columns. We'll get acquainted with all of them.

What Formatting Accomplishes

The purpose of formatting is not merely to make your spreadsheets more attractive. Data needs clarity, and formatting helps do the following:

- Draw attention to row and column labels. This helps people understand what your data represents.
- Create a sense of urgency so that your work will be read.
- Separate essential from nonessential information.
- Lead the reader's eye directly to the totals or results.

Examples of Formatting

What do we mean by formatting? Well, do you want people to see this...

Painter's last name	First name	Painting
Cézanne	Paul	Mont Saint Victoire
Delacroix	Eugène	Paganini
Monet	Claude	Gare Saint-Lazare
Picasso	Pablo	Les Demoiselles d'Avignon
Renoir	Auguste	Le Moulin de la Galette

...or this?

Painter's last name	First name	Painting
Cézanne	Paul	*Mont Saint Victoire*
Delacroix	Eugène	*Paganini*
Monet	Claude	*Gare Saint-Lazare*
Picasso	Pablo	*Les Demoiselles d'Avignon*
Renoir	Auguste	*Le Moulin de la Galette*

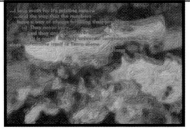

This...

Month	Classical	Rock	Jazz	Folk	Total Sales
Jan	900	1025	1000	500	2525
Feb	700	950	850	450	2250
Mar	950	1100	1000	400	2500
Totals	2550	3075	2850	1350	7275

...or this.

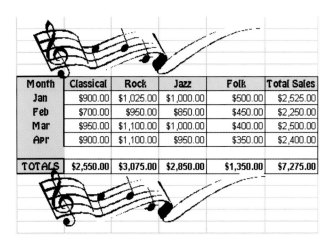

Month	Classical	Rock	Jazz	Folk	Total Sales
Jan	$900.00	$1,025.00	$1,000.00	$500.00	$2,525.00
Feb	$700.00	$950.00	$850.00	$450.00	$2,250.00
Mar	$950.00	$1,100.00	$1,000.00	$400.00	$2,500.00
Apr	$900.00	$1,100.00	$950.00	$350.00	$2,400.00
TOTALS	$2,550.00	$3,075.00	$2,850.00	$1,350.00	$7,275.00

Here's how to apply formatting where it counts:

Make your headers and labels stand out. To draw attention to row and column headers and labels, do this:

- Use a bolder font than that used for the data.
- Apply a different background to the row and column labels.
- Apply a unique border to set off the labels and headers from the data.

Figure 5.1 shows an example of these three techniques in action.

Announce your spreadsheet's intentions. Provide a title, using a larger font that is just slightly different than that used in the rest of the spreadsheet. Center it above the entire data area. Glance at Figure 5.2 to learn how.

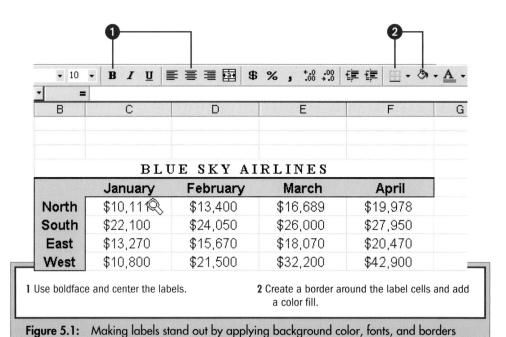

BLUE SKY AIRLINES

	January	February	March	April
North	$10,11⊘	$13,400	$16,689	$19,978
South	$22,100	$24,050	$26,000	$27,950
East	$13,270	$15,670	$18,070	$20,470
West	$10,800	$21,500	$32,200	$42,900

1 Use boldface and center the labels.   **2** Create a border around the label cells and add a color fill.

Figure 5.1:   Making labels stand out by applying background color, fonts, and borders

BLUE SKY AIRLINES			
January	February	March	April
North	10111	13400	16689	19978
South	22100	24050	26000	27950
East	13270	15670	18070	20470
West	10800	21500	32200	42900

Before formatting

After formatting

BLUE SKY AIRLINES			
January	February	March	April
North	10111	13400	16689	19978
South	22100	24050	26000	27950
East	13270	15670	18070	20470
West	10800	21500	32200	42900

Figure 5.2:   Create an eye-catching title with a larger font, centered, with a simple border.

To lead the reader's eye to the totals, employ a thicker border above the Total cells and apply a slightly different background color to the entire row that displays totals.

Mar	$950.00	$1,100.00	$1,000.00	$400.00	$2,500.00
Apr	$900.00	$1,000.00	$950.00	$350.00	$2,400.00
TOTALS	$2,550.00	$3,075.00	$2,850.00	$1,350.00	$7,275.00

EXPERT ADVICE

Make sure your row and column headers clarify the units of measurement for both the rows and the columns. For example, include the label "Number of people (in thousands)" or "Wholesale purchasers per state."

"Automagically" Formatting Your Worksheets

Excel comes with three tools that change the worksheet background color, font, and borders, all with a couple of mouse clicks:

- **AutoFormat**   Browse through previews of completed worksheets, click the mouse, and your worksheet automatically takes on the formatting of the previewed example.
- **Styles**   Create a "look" for your cells that you like, save it as a style, and apply it any time, even to other projects.
- **Format Painter**   Change the appearance of some cells and then sweep across other cells with the Format Painter. The format of the first cells will be applied to the ones you sweep across.

Let's explore each automatic formatting tool in more detail.

Using Excel's AutoFormat Feature

AutoFormat lets you pick an example and automatically apply the formatting from the example to your own spreadsheet. Here's what can be changed with AutoFormat:

Item	Changes
Fonts	Type, color, size, style, and justification
Backgrounds	Color, pattern, or image
Cells	Border, color, and pattern
Rows and columns	Height, width, and shading

AutoFormat can change colors, typestyles, borders, shading, row heights, and column widths—with hardly any work on your part. Excel comes with a variety of predefined formats, each designed to make your work easier to read and more professional in appearance. You can apply them to an entire worksheet or just to selected areas.

Here's how to use AutoFormat:

1. Select the cells you want to format.

2. Choose AutoFormat from the Format menu.

3. In the AutoFormat dialog box, click Options to reveal a panel of check boxes. Use these check boxes to limit the types of changes that are made to your sheet. For example, perhaps you don't want to change font size, but you do want the data automatically centered.

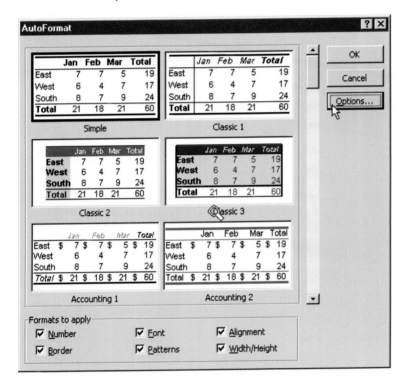

4. Scroll through the list of available formats. Each will apply a unique border, color, and font style scheme to your spreadsheet. Number formatting will be transferred as well (currency symbols will be applied, for example).

5. Try to imagine the effect each suggested format would have on your presentation. Would it be complimentary? Figure 5.3 shows a "before and after" formatting example.

6. When you find a format you like, click OK. Excel reformats your worksheet. If you selected only a portion of your worksheet with the selection tool, then only that segment will be formatted.

If you are displeased with the results of formatting, click the Undo button.

Using Styles

Styles are named collections of preformatted cells that you create. You can choose a font, cell alignment, borders, patterns, or coloring and save it for later use. Once you create and name a style, it is available at any time. For example, if you want every row name to appear in Arial 10-point bold, you can create a style with these

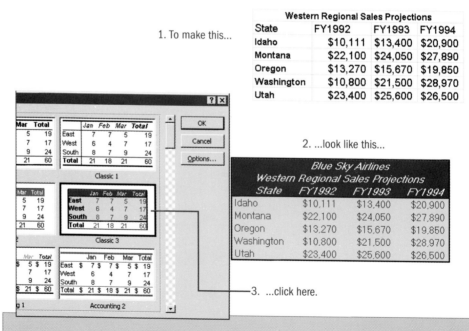

Figure 5.3: A "before and after" example of AutoFormatting

attributes and apply it wherever row names appear. Here's how to create a style and apply it later:

1. Create a cell or group of cells that contain formatting you want to use later.

2. With those cells selected, choose Style from the Format menu. The Style dialog box appears, ready to save all the stylistic choices you applied to the selected cells (see Figure 5.4).

3. Name the style. The name you choose will appear in the drop-down menu you are typing in right now. Even in other workbooks and worksheets, this created style you are naming will be available to you.

If you've never used Style before, the option will not appear until you click the down-facing arrow at the bottom of the dialog box. This is true for many toolbars and menus.

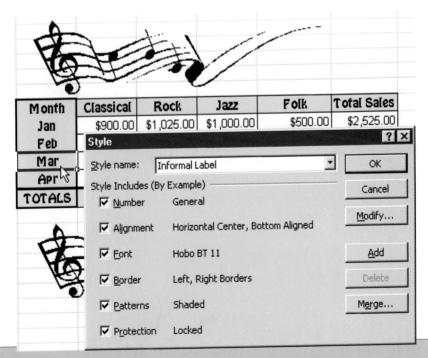

Figure 5.4: The Style dialog box saves your formatting choices for later use.

4. Remove the check mark next to any style option you do not want saved for later use. For example, if you think the border choices you created here are really not going to apply to other spreadsheets, remove the check mark next to Border.

5. Click Add, and from now on your style will be listed with the others.

Notice the Modify, Delete and Merge buttons, available for making changes to your styles, combining two styles into one, or getting rid of a style forever.

Using Format Painter

Format Painter lets you apply formatting options on a row-by-row or cell-by-cell basis. You simply create a cell or two that looks the way you want, select the Format Painter on the toolbar, and sweep it across the area you want to format. The formatting of the first set of cells is applied to the new area. Here's how to use Format Painter:

1. Select the cell you want to copy the format from.

2. Click the Format Painter on the standard toolbar (see Figure 5.5). The mouse cursor changes to a paintbrush. If you want to apply this format choice to several areas of your document, double-click it.

3. Drag to select the area that should receive the formatting.

4. Release the mouse button. The selected cells are formatted.

If you're not happy with the formatting results, choose Edit | Undo.

Format Painter does not save styles for later. Format Painter is for on-the-fly use only.

TIP

Double-clicking the Format Painter locks the formats so you can paint several areas. Click the tool again to release the formatting.

	A	B	C
1	Painter's last name	First name	Painting
2	Cézanne	Paul	*Mont Saint Victoire*
3	Delacroix	Eugène	*Paganini*
4	Monet	Claude	*Gare Saint-Lazare*
5	Picasso	Pablo	*Les Demoiselles d'Avignon*
6	Renoir	Auguste	*Le Moulin de la Galette*

Figure 5.5: The Format Painter picks up formatting from one cell and applies it to another.

Creating Formats

We've discussed how to quickly apply formatting you've created to other cells. We'll now discuss how to create formatting, so you'll have something to copy and save.

Modifying Rows and Columns

Modifying rows helps you accommodate extra-long (or short) strings of text or numbers. Columns and rows are very flexible. They can stretch or shrink the way you want them to.

Changing Row Height

Row height automatically increases or decreases to match the largest font in the row. You can also manually change heights (to give a label some extra head room, for example).

1. To change a row's height, click the bottom edge of the row label, drag your mouse, and release the mouse button when the height suits you.

2. To specify a row height in points, select the row and choose Format | Row | Height, or select the row, right-click, and choose Row Height from the shortcut menu.

Changing Column Width

Columns all start out at a default width, but the default width won't always meet your needs. For example, the information you type in a column may be too long, which results in one of three outcomes:

- Text spills over into the adjacent cell if the cell to the right is empty.

- Text is truncated (the text is still there—you just can't see it all) if the cell to the right is not empty.

- Numbers are replaced with pound signs (####) if cells containing numbers are too narrow.

If you want to be able to see all the information in your columns (which you probably do), here are three methods you can use to resize worksheet columns:

- Click the right edge of the column's label (when the cursor is a double-headed arrow), drag the mouse to the right or left, and when the column width suits you, release the mouse button.

- Double-click the line at the right of any column label that separates it from its neighbor, and Excel automatically resizes the column to accommodate the text width.

- To specify exact column widths, select the column, right-click, and choose Column Width from the shortcut menu, or choose Format Column Width from the menu bar.

EXPERT ADVICE

To see only the data that's important to you at the moment, you may want to temporarily hide rows or columns from view. To do so, select the rows or columns to be hidden, right-click, and choose Hide from the shortcut menu. The hidden items will return when you right-click the row or column border and choose Unhide.

Fitting Text into Cells

Excel makes it easy to fit a long title into a small number of cells. For example, suppose you have a title that stretches across three cells, like this:

To squeeze the title into just two cells, select the number of cells you want the title to fill (in this case, two), right-click, and choose Format Cells. On the Alignment tab, click Shrink to Fit and Merge cells, as shown here.

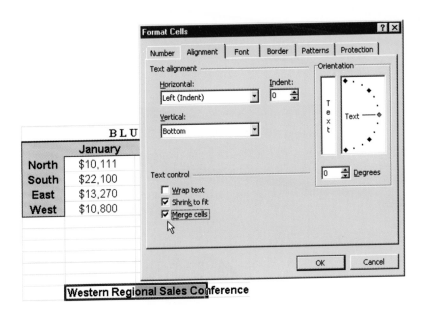

Formatting Your Text

After you're done wrestling with columns, you might want to add some life to the text. Excel lets you change fonts, sizes, and colors, which all add some excitement to your worksheets. It's easy—just use the formatting toolbar.

Customizing Font Sizes and Text Attributes

You can quickly change font attributes in Excel by selecting text in any cell that is formatted the way you like, then clicking the Format Painter on the toolbar. Next, click once in the cell containing the text you want to change. The text will now contain the formatting of the first cell you selected. However, you cannot apply the formatting to a second set of cells just by clicking on it. If you are going to apply formatting to more than one cell of text, double-click on the Format Painter before you begin applying the format.

Just as with other Office applications, you can use the drop-down Font and Font Size menus, justification tools, and type style tools to make your text format changes. Figure 5.6 shows some of the text-formatting options.

Click this arrow to select a font type. —

Click this arrow to choose a font size.

Boldface, underlining, italics, and justification settings can be applied to all text and numbers.

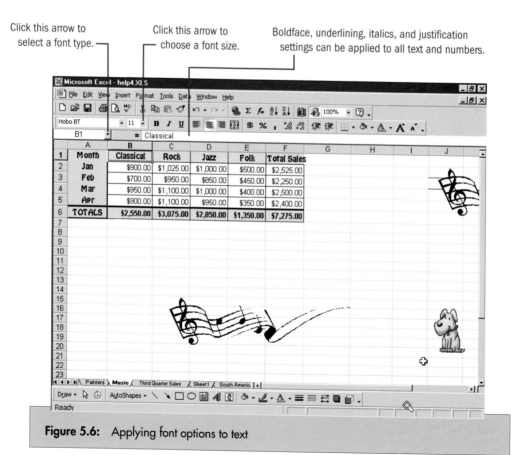

Figure 5.6: Applying font options to text

To change font size or type, do the following:

1. Select the cells that contain the text you want to modify.

2. Select the drop-down Font or Font Size menu on the formatting toolbar.

3. Choose the font or font size you want.

After you select the font or size from the list, you are done. To change font attributes, use the Format Cells dialog box.

You don't have to apply the same formatting to all the words in a cell. For example, a cell can contain bold and normal text or even two different types of fonts.

Changing Text Alignment

Text alignment, or justification, determines whether your text is positioned starting at the left or right edge of the cell, or centered. By default, numbers are right-aligned and text is left-aligned. Alignment options on the standard toolbar look like this:

The Alignment options can be applied to both text and digits with a single mouse-click.

Rotating, Wrapping, and Force-fitting Text

The Alignment tab in the Format Cells dialog box provides options for rotating, shrinking, and merging text to fit selected cells (see Figure 5.7).

To rotate text, click the cell with the text you want to rotate, right-click, and then select Format Cells from the shortcut menu. Choose the Alignment tab, and in the Orientation panel, drag the red marker near the horizontal line to suggest a rotated text position. You can also enter a rotation angle using the Degrees menu.

To make text fit, select the cells that contain overflowing text and, from the Format Cells dialog box, select the Alignment tab. Under Text Control, choose Shrink to Fit. The text that once overflowed into other cells will now shrink to fit in the cell.

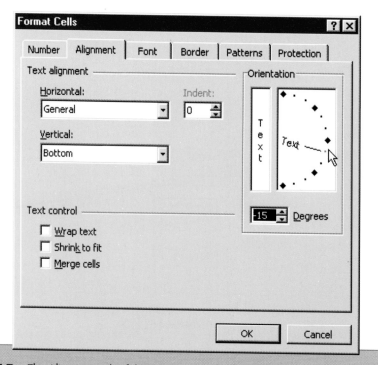

Figure 5.7:   The Alignment tab of the Format Cells dialog box

Centering Text Across Columns

Sometimes it's nice to have a label float over more than one column. This format lets you place general headings over more specific column headings. Here's an example:

CD, Cassette and LP Sales				
Month	Classical		Jazz	
	Chamber	Orchestra	Solo	Band
Jan	$900.00	$1,025.00	$1,000.00	$500.00
Feb	$700.00	$950.00	$850.00	$450.00
Mar	$950.00	$1,100.00	$1,000.00	$400.00
Apr	$900.00	$1,100.00	$950.00	$350.00
TOTALS	$2,550.00	$3,075.00	$2,850.00	$1,350.00

Here's how to create this format:

1. Select the cell containing the word(s) and the cells over which you want the text centered.

2. Click the Merge and Center button on the formatting toolbar. You'll see your data appear centered across your entire selection, no matter how many cells were originally included.

Formatting Numbers

The same formatting tricks you apply to text (changing font size, type, style, and alignment) can be applied to numbers as well. However, numbers come with extra baggage, such as commas, currency symbols, and decimal points. In this section, you'll learn how to format numeric data to appear just as it should. You'll learn that all the numeric settings can be applied uniformly across an entire worksheet section.

EXPERT ADVICE

Select only the cells you want included. When you select an entire worksheet row, Excel selects cells moving to the right into infinity. Data that is merged and centered in an entirely selected row will appear well to the right of your screen. Your title will end up about 3 feet to the right of the monitor!

To apply Excel's number formatting to a selection of numbers, do the following:

1. Select the cell(s) to be formatted.

2. Select Cells from the Format menu. The Format Cells dialog box appears:

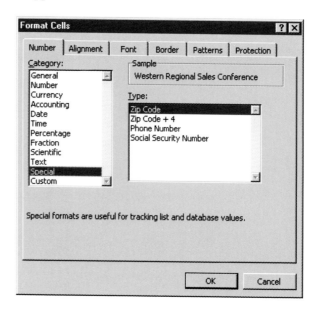

3. Click the Number tab if necessary to bring it to the front; then select a format type from the Category list.

   Unless the active cell is empty, you'll see a sample of the formatting applied to the first of your selected cells in the Sample area of the dialog box.

4. Click OK when you're done.

I f your formatting calls for zip codes, phone numbers, or social security numbers, click Special to reveal a list of formats for those types of numbers.

Borders, Colors, Images, and Page Breaks

So far in this chapter, you've learned about formatting text and numbers. Now you'll explore how to add borders to cells and spreadsheets, provide background colors and images, and format page breaks.

At times, just thickening a border and "adding" a dash of color will be enough to make your data stand out. If you want more, you can always add images and use multiple border types and sizes.

Defining Your Data with Borders

Borders can surround a cell or a group of cells, or a border can simply be a straight line that separates a group (for instance, to separate sums and totals from the rest of your data).

You can create borders in one of two ways:

- Select the cells and click the Borders button on the formatting toolbar. Click the down-facing arrow to reveal various border options. You can create a box around your data, or add a single separation line. Notice that some border options provide thicker lines than others. Click a border option, and the selected cells will reflect your border choice.

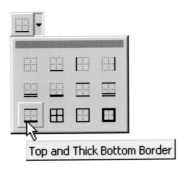

Top and Thick Bottom Border

- Choose Cells from the Format menu and click the Border tab in the Format Cells dialog box (see Figure 5.8). This dialog box has an interactive border builder, where you can click a border option and see it applied in the center of the dialog box. Note that you must select the line style option first, on the right side of the dialog box, and then click the Border options. You can actually click right inside the interactive border box itself, adding and removing lines as you prefer.

Borders are not necessarily complete rectangles. Use a single line to separate any data segment from another, according to your taste.

If you want to explore various border colors and line types (such as dashed or diagonal border lines), then you must use the Format Cells dialog box rather than the border tool found on the formatting toolbar.

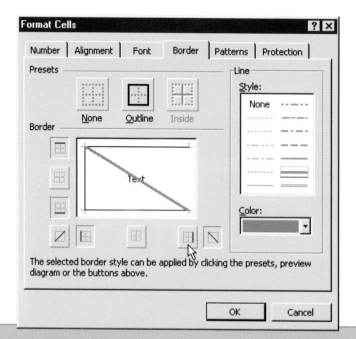

Figure 5.8:   The Border tab of the Format Cells dialog box has many more features than the border tool on the toolbar.

Adding Colors and Shading for Emphasis

If your computer and printer are color capable, you can add interest and emphasis to your masterpiece with the Fill Color and Font Color buttons, both located on the formatting toolbar.

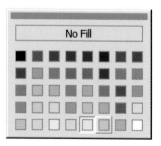

As with the Borders button, you can click the down arrows next to the Fill Color and Font Color buttons to choose colors from a palette. If you don't specify a color from these palettes, the default colors for fill (yellow) and font (red) are used. Remember to select your cells first and then click the appropriate button to make your selection.

Inserting and Removing Page Breaks

Another way you can format your worksheets is to add page breaks. Normally, Excel decides where to break pages when printing, based on the Page Setup specifications you've made. Use manual page breaks to override Excel's choices. If, for example, you think that a particular page is becoming too cluttered with data, you can force the page to end sooner, providing a roomier look. Manual page breaks cause a page to end and another to begin, regardless of how full the first page is.

- To insert a page break, select the row that follows the desired page break point or the column to the right of the desired page break point. Choose Page Break from the Insert menu.

- To remove a break, select the row that follows the existing page break point or the column to the right of the break; then choose Remove Page Break from the Insert menu. (This choice is available only when an appropriate row or column is properly selected.)

You can also interactively move page break lines by selecting Page Break Preview and dragging the blue lines with your mouse, as shown in Figure 5.9.

EXPERT ADVICE

If you want to see where your page breaks are, select Page Break Preview from the View menu. Remember that if you've not used this option before, you may have to click the arrow at the bottom of the View menu to display the Page Break Preview option.

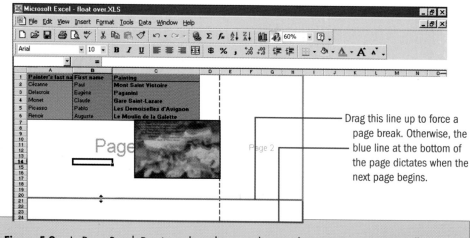

Figure 5.9: In Page Break Preview, drag the page lines with your mouse to manually adjust page breaks.

Removing Formatting

You can remove formatting in two ways:

- Select the cells and then choose Edit | Clear | Formats.
- Select the cells, choose Style from the Format menu, and then select Normal from the drop-down Style list. You can also right-click the cells, select Format Cells, and on the Number tab, click General.

Checkpoint

You've learned a lot in this chapter! You've learned how to let Excel do some of your formatting for you, as well as how to do it yourself. Now you know how to make rows, columns, and cells look their best.

Up next is Chapter 6, where you'll learn some organizing techniques that will help you with your more complex Excel projects. In Chapter 7, you'll lean how to insert built-in formulas into cells that will perform complex computations for you. And in Chapter 8, you'll learn all about including cool charts in your Excel worksheets.

CHAPTER 6

Managing Large Projects

INCLUDES

- Naming cell ranges
- Referring to named ranges in your formulas
- Freezing columns and rows to keep them in view
- Naming your worksheets
- Moving and copying worksheets
- Collaborating on large projects

FAST FORWARD

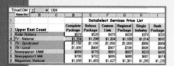

Name Ranges ➡ pp. 133–136

1. Select the cells of interest.
2. Choose Name from the Insert menu and choose Define from the submenu.
3. Look at the Refers To box and change the reference, if necessary.
4. Examine the range name Excel proposes and change it if you want (remember not to include any spaces).
5. Click OK. Range names are saved when you save the worksheet.

Go to a Named Range ➡ p. 136

1. Click the Name box arrow at the left end of the formula bar.
2. Select the named range to which you want to go. The range is highlighted.

Refer to Named Ranges in Formulas ➡ pp. 137–139

1. Begin the formula as usual.
2. At the point where you want to insert a name, press F3.
3. Pick the name from the resulting list.

Generate a List of Named Ranges ➡ p. 140

1. Select the cell where you want your list to start.
2. Choose Name from the Insert menu and choose Paste from the submenu.
3. Click the Paste List button.

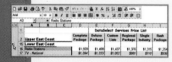

Create Collapsible Spreadsheet Segments ➡ pp. 141–143

1. Select the rows or columns you want to collapse or expand with the click of a mouse.
2. Choose Group and Outline from the Data menu and select Group.
3. Collapse cells or rows by clicking the plus sign above or to the right of them. They will disappear for a moment. Expand them again by clicking the plus sign.

Filter Worksheets to Quickly Locate Data ➡ pp. 143–145

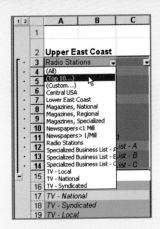

1. Select Filter from the Data menu and choose AutoFilter. Drop-down menus appear at the top of each column of your worksheet.

2. Click any drop-down menu, specifying filtering criteria for that row. Some drop-down menus will affect more than one row or column. Filtering criteria choices you make with these drop-down menus will determine how many cells appear on the screen at that moment.

3. Remove AutoFilter by again selecting Filter from the Data menu and clicking AutoFilter.

Freeze Columns or Rows ➡ pp. 147–149

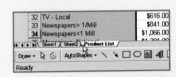

1. Select the row below the one you want to freeze on the screen or the column to the right of the column you want to freeze.

2. To freeze both rows and columns, select the intersecting cell below and to the right of the row and column to freeze.

3. Choose Freeze Panes from the Window menu. When you scroll, the frozen items will not scroll off of the screen.

Name Worksheets ➡ pp. 149–150

To name a worksheet, double-click its tab and type a new name

Move Worksheets ➡ pp. 150–151

1. To move a sheet within the same workbook, point to the worksheet tab at the bottom of the window and drag it to a new position. (As you drag, the mouse pointer changes to include a page icon.)

2. To move sheets from one open workbook to another, either tile both workbooks on your screen (choose Window | Arrange) and drag worksheets from one book to the other, or use the Edit menu's Move or Copy Sheet command.

Copy Worksheets ➥ p. 151

1. Hold down CTRL and point to the tab for the sheet you want to copy.

2. Drag your mouse to the tab position in the workbook where you want to place the copy. (The mouse pointer changes to include a page icon with a plus sign.)

3. Release the mouse button. The copy is created and inserted. Rename the new sheet if you want.

4. To copy sheets from one open workbook to another, either tile both workbooks on your screen (choose Window | Arrange) and drag worksheets from one book to the other while holding down the CTRL key, or use the Edit menu's Move or Copy Sheet command. (When using the Move or Copy dialog box, make sure you check the Make a Copy check box if copying is your intention.)

Some spreadsheet tools will not seem essential to you until your project grows beyond a page or so. It's fairly easy to manage data that you can see on your screen. Scrolling up or down an inch to locate a missing row or column is not really an inconvenience. But what about spreadsheets that are 40 or more rows (or columns) deep?

Creating a new worksheet to accommodate new rows or columns may not be the best answer. You will generally want to create a new sheet when you add new aspects or data types to your project, but there's no reason to create a new sheet just because you have too many rows or columns.

So to immediately locate a row or column of cells without having to scroll and hunt aimlessly, what should you do?

Understanding Named Cell Ranges

CAUTION

Named ranges are always absolute references. Since the name is visible, and not the values, you cannot inspect or easily copy formulas included in the range.

You select the row or column you want immediate access to and then type a name for that cell range in the Name box (at the upper left of the screen). Later, no matter where you are in your project, you can type the name you chose, and that same cell range will appear centered on your screen. Figure 6.1 illustrates this process.

In this chapter, you'll learn all the ins and outs of how to work with named ranges, create collapsible worksheet segments, keep column and row titles visible, and work with multiple views and worksheets.

Creating and Applying Range Names

Figure 6.2 shows a spreadsheet that's easy to get lost in. The distinction between the headings is slight; each type of service is repeated as you move down the list, separated only by the region in which the service is offered. It may be hard, for example, to locate the

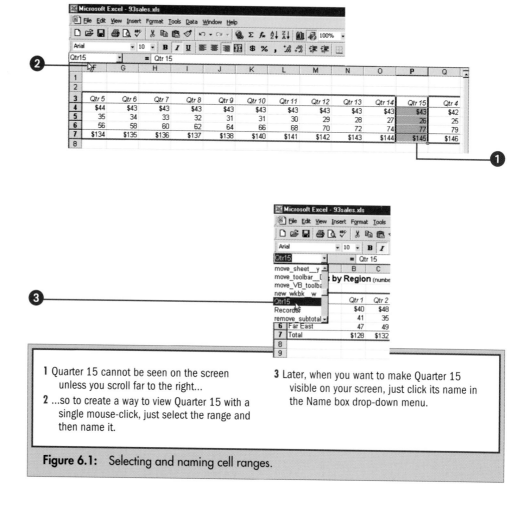

Figure 6.1: Selecting and naming cell ranges.

1 Quarter 15 cannot be seen on the screen unless you scroll far to the right...

2 ...so to create a way to view Quarter 15 with a single mouse-click, just select the range and then name it.

3 Later, when you want to make Quarter 15 visible on your screen, just click its name in the Name box drop-down menu.

cost of a list of national TV stations in the Western United States. How could the spreadsheet user find this information quickly, or change items on the price list, without spending an hour doing so? Figure 6.2 shows how all the newspaper listing services for the Lower East Coast area can be selected and then named. The spreadsheet user will then be able to locate prices for that entire range of services with a couple of mouse clicks.

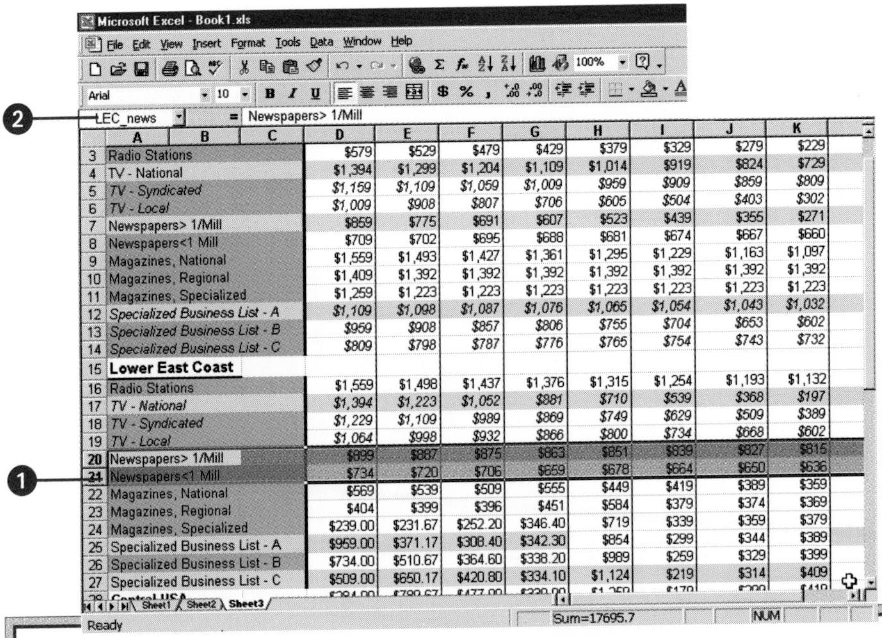

1 These cells represent all newspaper listings for the Lower East Coast region. Select them and then create a named range.

2 To create a named range, just make up a name and type it here.

Figure 6.2: Naming similar cells to quickly access them later as a group

To create and name a range, just do the following:

1. Select the range of cells you want quick access to. Use any selection tools discussed in earlier chapters; for example, press SHIFT or CTRL while clicking individual cells.

2. Place the mouse cursor in the Name box in the upper-left corner of the screen and type a name for your cell range. Pick a name that will be easy for you to later identify. This is important especially if you are going to be naming many cell ranges. Easy identification is the key here. In this example, we named the cell range LECnews, for Lower East Coast Newspaper services.

Type this name instead of a list of cells.

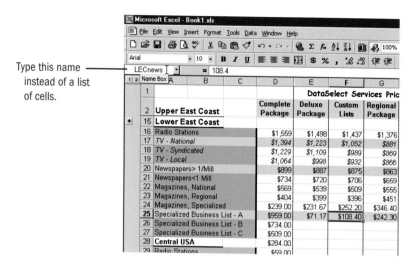

3. When you are done typing a name, press ENTER.

4. The name you entered will now appear in the drop-down menu, available by clicking the DOWN ARROW right next to it. Select the name from the list; the range of cells will appear on the screen, no matter what you were previously doing with your spreadsheet.

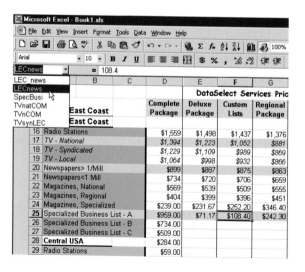

Think of situations in which you'd have to quickly access certain cell groupings. Create and then name as many groups as you like. This process automatically saves them in the Name box drop-down menu. Remember to assign memorable names to your cell groups so, as your list grows, you'll be able to remember which is which.

Creating Formulas with Your Named Groups

Cell ranges can become arguments in your formulas. For example, select a group of cells and call the group Advertising. Then, instead of creating a formula that reads =SUM(F16:F24)*5, just use the name of the selected cells and create a formula that reads =SUM(Advertising)*5.

The Font drop-down menu is right above the Name box. To differentiate between the two, hold your mouse momentarily over either feature. A tooltip appears, identifying the item.

To name cells for quick access later, you need not select a cell range. Select a single cell, name it, and later move to that cell simply by clicking its name in the Name box drop-down menu.

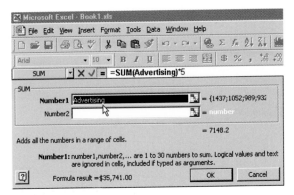

Here's how to apply such a formula using our example. Let's create a discount for those customers who purchase two types of TV services. To show how much this service will cost after we apply the discount, we can simply create a formula cell that adds two named cell groups and then multiplies the sum by 90%. Follow these steps (see Figure 6.3):

1. Create a cell group called **TVnatCOM** to represent the price for complete services for national TV listings.

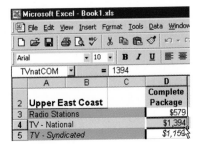

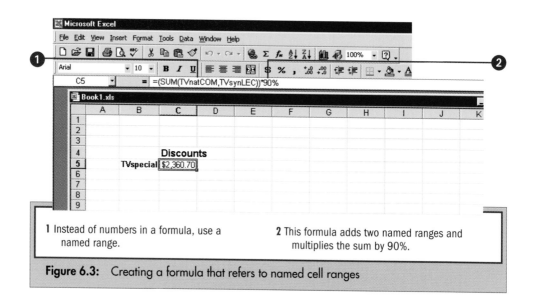

Figure 6.3: Creating a formula that refers to named cell ranges

1 Instead of numbers in a formula, use a named range.

2 This formula adds two named ranges and multiplies the sum by 90%.

2. Create another named cell group called **TVsynLEC** to represent the cost for syndicated TV listings in the Lower Eastern United States area.

You could now create a formula that refers to these two ranges. The example here creates a discount formula, adds the sums of these two groups together, and then applies a 10% discount (multiply the sum by 90%).

You can change the numbers in your named range, and any formulas that refer to that name will calculate the new numbers associated with that named range.

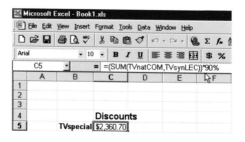

However, you want to create a formula based on cell range names.

1. Create a formula, and instead of using a range of cells as an argument, type the name of your cell range, placing it in

parentheses. This name becomes your argument: for example,
=SUM(TVnatCOM)*90%

> This formula says to multiply the range of cells called
> TVnatCOM by 90 percent.

> The formula cell itself will display the results of the formula,
> as always, and will treat your named range no differently
> than the numbers it represents.

The formula shown in Figure 6.4 creates a sum of two named
ranges and multiplies them by 90%. To create many automatic
discount cells like this, just create named ranges and apply them in as
many formulas as you like. Don't forget that even if you change the
numbers in the cell ranges (such as individual prices), your named
ranges will still be valid and need not be changed.

Working with Named Ranges

Once you have your ranges named, you can use them to help you
manage your worksheet. You can view a list of your named ranges,
refer to named ranges in formulas, and update or delete them.

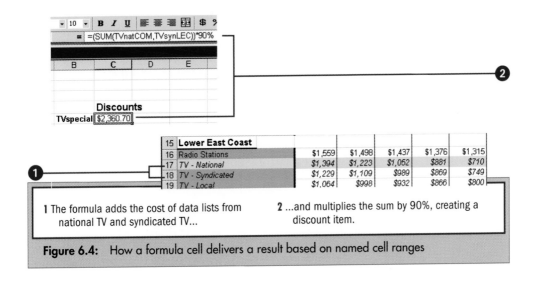

1 The formula adds the cost of data lists from national TV and syndicated TV...

2 ...and multiplies the sum by 90%, creating a discount item.

Figure 6.4: How a formula cell delivers a result based on named cell ranges

Listing All Your Named Ranges

Sometimes you'll want to list all your named ranges—for example, if you forget a range name or want to inventory the information in the worksheet. If you're looking for a quick listing of the ranges, just use the Name box drop-down list by clicking its down arrow. You'll see a list of all the named ranges.

However, if you want to print the list of named ranges, you have to use a slightly different process:

1. Make sure you are finished naming everything in your workbook.

2. Select the cell where you want the top-left entry of your list to appear. (Remember that the paste operation will overwrite several cells below and to the right of the selected cell, so you might want to put the list in a new worksheet.)

3. Choose Name from the Insert menu.

4. Choose Paste from the submenu.

5. In the Paste Name dialog box, click the Paste List button.

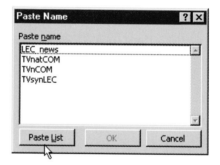

Updating and Deleting Ranges

As your worksheets change with new or discarded information, you might need to update or delete ranges as well. Use extreme caution, though, because updating and deleting ranges can affect any formulas that refer to them.

Here's how to update or delete named ranges:

1. Choose Name from the Insert menu.

2. Choose Define from the submenu.

3. Type the name for the new range (remember: no spaces).

4. Use the "get-out-of-the-way" button at the right edge of the text box and select the range of cells to which the name will apply. Click the "come-back-now" button to restore the dialog box.

5. Click Add to add the range.

6. Either repeat steps 3 through 5 to define an additional range or click OK to finish.

Expanding and Collapsing Worksheet Segments

Excel lets you select any group of rows or columns and make them into a collapsible unit. Click a marker, and those cells you selected will temporarily disappear, or collapse. Click again, and the hidden segments reappear. You can choose any size of segment you wish. In this way, you can turn your spreadsheet into a cabinet of sorts, opening and closing "drawers" filled with your columns and rows. Close a group, and you'll see only the rows and columns next to the group you closed (see Figure 6.5).

Creating expanding and collapsing spreadsheet segments allows you to "reel in" sections that are below the bottom of your screen or too far to the right. Here's how it's done:

1. Select the rows or columns you want to make collapsible. You need to select entire rows or columns.

2. From the Data menu, choose Group and Outline and then select Group. The rows or columns you chose will now appear bracketed with a line, and a minus sign will appear at the top of the group.

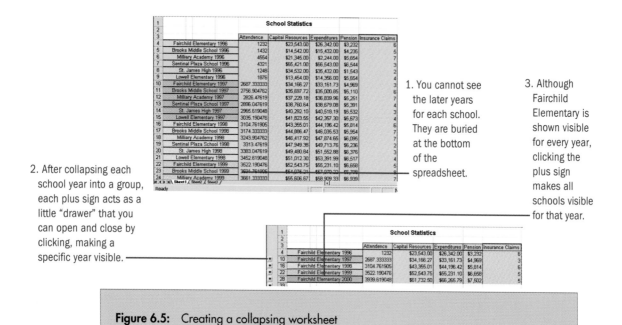

1. You cannot see the later years for each school. They are buried at the bottom of the spreadsheet.

3. Although Fairchild Elementary is shown visible for every year, clicking the plus sign makes all schools visible for that year.

2. After collapsing each school year into a group, each plus sign acts as a little "drawer" that you can open and close by clicking, making a specific year visible.

Figure 6.5: Creating a collapsing worksheet

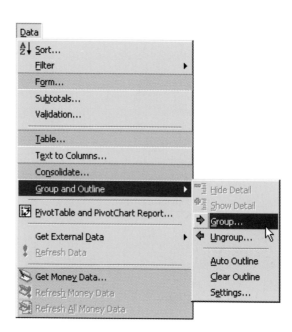

3. Click the minus sign to collapse your group. It now disappears, and in its place a plus sign appears.

4. Click the plus sign, and your group reappears.

Using the Collapse/Expand Feature

You've seen how to apply a single collapsible segment. Now you will apply what you know using this chapter's common example; you will see how to divide each segment of the U.S. within this company's sales reach into collapsible segments.

The examples so far show only collapsed rows. Notice in Figure 6.6 that columns are also collapsible, allowing you to view segments that are far to the right of your immediate viewing area.

Each time you group a segment and make it collapsible, a new minus and plus sign bracket appears. Each segment operates independent of the others, allowing you to open only the spreadsheet portion you want to view at any given moment.

This collapsible spreadsheet feature allows you to create projects that are hundreds of cells deep (or wide) and facilitates quick viewing of, perhaps only 10 or 15 columns at a time. Spreadsheets of any size can be made manageable and navigable.

To remove your collapse settings and restore your worksheet to the way it was before you used this feature, select Group and Outline from the Data menu and choose Clear Outline.

Using Filters to View Specific Data

Excel lets you instantly filter your data through various criteria, zeroing in on cells you find the most significant. When you use

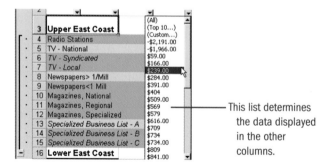

Figure 6.5: How a "busy" spreadsheet is made more convenient by expanding and collapsing it.

Excel's AutoFilter feature, drop-down menus are placed at the top of your columns. You make choices from these menus, working from top to bottom and left to right. By clicking drop-down menu selections, you apply criteria that determines which cells appear on your screen.

Each time you add a condition from a drop-down menu, you've applied a stricter criteria for determining which cells appear. Thus, the more menu choices you make, the fewer the number of cells that are displayed on the screen.

Use AutoFilter, for example, to view your very own Top 10 selection. This view could contain the ten highest numbers in your spreadsheet, or it could be based on some other criteria you choose (see Figure 6.7). You can also use AutoFilter to view only certain columns or rows according to their labels.

To use AutoFilter, select Filter from the Data menu; then from the submenu that appears, choose AutoFilter. Drop-down arrows appear at the top of each column in your sheet.

To see the most dramatic, instantaneous results, use the drop-down menu at the far left and choose to view data for only one row, as shown in Figure 6.8. To restore the normal, nonfiltered view, open the drop-down menu you just manipulated and this time select All. You may have to scroll up to locate it.

Using the AutoFilter Top Ten

To view the highest or lowest number of any criteria, select a drop-down menu near the middle top of your worksheet and choose Top 10. A

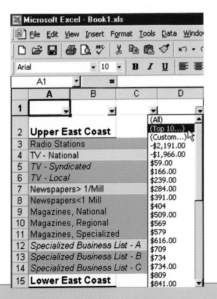

Figure 6.6:   Using AutoFilter to locate far-flung data on a busy spreadsheet

Figure 6.7: Using AutoFilter to narrow the spreadsheet view to a single row

dialog box appears, allowing you to choose to view the 10 items with either the top or bottom values or the top or bottom 10 percent. This dialog box simply reads the number values in your sheet. (You can change the numeric or percentage values used in this dialog box. For example, you can report the top 50 items or the bottom 6%.)

Creating a Custom Filter

Creating custom filtering criteria can give you instant access to information that you'd normally have to spend a good deal of time searching for and scrolling to locate. Here's an example:

1. After applying AutoFilter, select the column or row you want to search or filter for a certain criteria.

2. Click the drop-down menu and choose Custom. The Custom AutoFilter dialog box appears.

3. In the top-right field, specify what to search for—perhaps a particular number or data value or a label.

4. In the top left field, specify how to use the search criteria; for example, should the filter include numbers that are greater than, less than, or equal to sum you selected, or should it include all numbers that begin or end with your chosen digit or text string?

5. In the bottom left and right fields of the Custom AutoFilter dialog box, set up any additional criteria for your custom filter, to narrow your search even more. You can, for example, type a date or the name of a company and thus filter out all data that does not include this second criteria, as shown in Figure 6.9.

In the fields here, you can type entries or use a criteria from the drop-down menu. For example, you can specify a number range, such as >100 and <300.

To remove AutoFilter and the drop-down menus that accompany it, select Filter from the Data menu and click AutoFilter. This toggles the feature off and restores full view of the data.

Freezing Rows and Columns

Keeping all your columns and rows in sight is a real chore. As soon as you scroll to the left, you find yourself wanting access to the column just a little to the right. Scroll down, and suddenly you forget what was in the rows at the very top of the sheet.

Excel provides a tool for keeping selected rows and columns always on the screen. Imagine scrolling in any direction and having certain columns and rows stay right where they are. The rest of the sheet

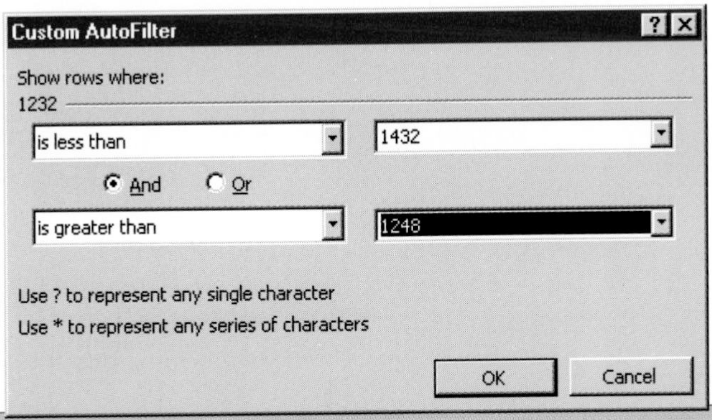

Figure 6.8: Using the Custom AutoFilter dialog box

moves as you scroll, but the rows and columns that you designate will be frozen in place.

In this section, you'll learn how to freeze rows and columns. This technique makes it much easier to work on big sheets because you always have the specified rows or columns right in front of you. Take a look at Figure 6.10.

To freeze rows or columns, do the following:

1. Select the column to the right of (or the row below) the section that you want to remain stationary. In other words, if you want the row titles to not move, select the column immediately to the right of the row titles.

2. Choose Freeze Panes from the Window menu.

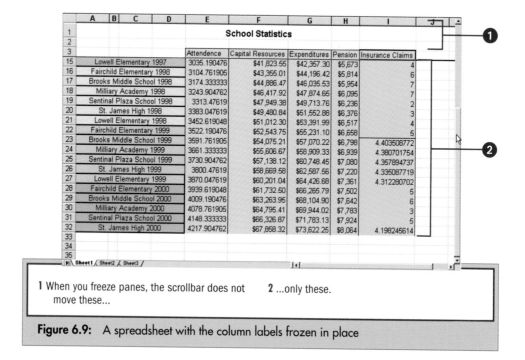

1 When you freeze panes, the scrollbar does not move these...   2 ...only these.

Figure 6.9: A spreadsheet with the column labels frozen in place

In this illustration, rows are frozen so that the labels to the side never move as you scroll from side to side. The data moves as the scroll button moves, while the row labels do not.

Working with Multiple Worksheets

As you have no doubt noticed, when you start a new project, Excel opens a workbook containing three worksheets. You can add additional worksheets if you like, and obviously there is no requirement that you use all three sheets for a given project. You can name individual worksheets, change their locations in the workbook, and move or copy them to other workbooks. Let's take a look.

Naming Your Worksheets

Each worksheet has a name. When you open a new workbook, Excel names them Sheet1 through Sheet3. Their names appear on the tabs used to bring the sheets to the front of the screen.

Here's how to rename a worksheet:

1. Double-click the worksheet's tab.
2. Type the new worksheet name.

3. Press ENTER. Then click one of the other tabs or click anywhere in the sheet to accept the changed worksheet name.

Moving and Copying Worksheets

You can move or copy worksheets within the same workbook or between workbooks. These features are particularly handy when your projects get large and you start having to move big chunks of information to new worksheets or workbooks.

Moving Worksheets Within a Workbook

Moving worksheets within a workbook is as easy as clicking and dragging. Find the worksheet tabs at the bottom of your screen; then follow this procedure:

1. Click (and hold) the tab you want to move. The mouse pointer changes to include a page icon, and a small triangle appears to help you see where the tab will land when you release the mouse button.

2. Drag the tab to the new location.

3. Release the mouse button.

Copying Worksheets Within a Workbook

Copying worksheets is particularly handy when you want to use the basic structure of an existing worksheet. Copying worksheets is very similar to moving worksheets—the only difference is that you also use the CTRL key. Here's how:

1. Click the sheet's tab.

2. Hold down the CTRL key and drag. Your mouse pointer changes to include a page and plus sign.

3. When you reach the desired location for the copy, release the mouse button. Make sure to release the mouse before you release CTRL or the sheet will be moved instead of copied.

4. Rename the copied sheet by double-clicking the tab and typing the new name—unless you like names like Sheet1 (2) for the second copy of Sheet1.

Moving and Copying Worksheets to a Different Workbook

Just as you can move or copy worksheets within a single workbook, you can also move and copy worksheets to a different workbook. Here's how to move or copy a sheet from one workbook to another:

1. Open both workbooks and place the workbook that has the original worksheet on the top with the sheets selected.

2. From the Edit menu, choose Move or Copy Sheet. The Move or Copy dialog box appears.

3. If you want to make a copy of the worksheet, click to put a check mark in the Create a Copy check box. If you don't check the box, the worksheet will be moved.

4. In the To Book box, choose the name of the workbook that will receive the copy. The names of all open workbooks will appear in the drop-down list. You can also choose to start a new workbook.

5. Click OK.

DRAGGING WORKSHEETS TO A DIFFERENT WORKBOOK   If you are comfortable with tiling multiple windows, and if you have a big enough display area, you can display both workbooks on your screen at once and drag the desired worksheet from one workbook to the other. Just follow these steps:

1. Open both workbooks and choose Arrange from the Window menu; then choose Tiled. You should be able to see portions of both windows on your screen.

2. To move the worksheet, click the worksheet's tab and drag it to the other workbook. To copy the worksheet, click the worksheet's tab while pressing CTRL and drag it to the other workbook.

Checkpoint

You should now be pretty well prepared to take on large projects and use Excel to help you organize them. However, you can let Excel do even more of the work for you by using the information in the next few chapters. For example, up next, in Chapter 7, you'll learn how to add functions to your worksheets. Functions are built-in formulas that you can insert into cells that perform complex computations. In Chapter 8, you'll learn how to create charts, which are graphs that can help explain the relationship among data items. And, if you want to include some really nifty effects, check out Chapter 9, which tells you all about including graphics in your Excel worksheets.

CHAPTER 7

An Introduction to Functions

INCLUDES

- Understanding the parts of a function
- Inserting functions in formulas
- Reading error messages in functions
- Installing the Analysis ToolPak add-in for even more functions
- Seeing Excel's functions in action

Insert a Function ➥ pp. 161–162

1. Click the cell where you want to put the function.
2. Click the Paste Function button.
3. Select the function category.
4. Select the name of the function.
5. Click OK. Then enter your arguments or select them from the Formula Palette.

Apply Functions Manually ➥ pp. 162–163

1. In the formula bar, type = and then the function's name and an opening parenthesis, or pick the function's name from the list reached by choosing the Insert menu's Function command. The Function dialog box appears.
2. Type any necessary arguments, or point to cells containing the arguments and click to include them.
3. Be sure to include any necessary closing parenthesis and any required commas, as prescribed in online help for the particular function you are using.
4. Press ENTER to complete the function entry.

Get Help with Functions ➥ p. 163

- For help with a specific function, click on the Office Assistant, then type the function's name in the text box.
- For an overview of functions by category, click on the Office Assistant and enter the name of a category. Then click an entry in the topic index of functions.
- For help while in the Formula Palette, click the Office Assistant button. A special help screen will appear.

Include Function Add-Ins ➡ pp. 165–166

1. Place your Office 2000 CD in your CD-ROM drive.
2. Open Excel and, on the Tools menu, click Add-Ins. You may have to click the double arrow at the bottom of the menu to reveal the lower part of the menu.
3. When the Add-Ins dialog box appears, scroll through the Add-Ins Available list and place a check by Analysis ToolPak (while you're there, select any other add-ins that appeal to you, such as the Conditional Lookup Wizard, which we'll be examining in this chapter).
4. Click OK, and Excel will search the CD for the add-in you requested.
5. Be patient while the program installs the add-in. After this installation, you'll notice that additional functions will be available from the Paste Function menu.
6. Follow any additional on-screen instructions for completing the installation of the Analysis ToolPak. You won't need your CD to access these additional functions in the future.

Back in Chapter 4, you learned a bit about numbers and formulas. These are the heart of worksheet programs like Excel because they are what the program uses to perform your calculations. In this chapter, you're going to go one step further and delve into the world of worksheet functions.

Worksheet functions are built-in formulas that you can insert into cells and use to perform complex computations. When you use functions, there's no muss or fuss in creating formulas. Excel has hundreds of functions that facilitate engineering computations, manipulate text, and do much, much more.

In the first part of this chapter, you'll learn about functions, what they are, and how to use them. Later in this chapter, you'll learn about the broad categories of functions Excel provides and get an idea of how to apply them to your projects.

Using Worksheet Functions

Back in eighth grade, my math teacher, Mr. Rand, told me about a very useful concept called "plug-n-chug," which basically means that you plug a number into a formula and chug out the answer. The same principle applies to worksheet functions because basically all you do is plug numbers into a function and let Excel chug out the answer.

Different functions do different things. Some functions inspect items and take actions based on what they find. For example, the function ISNONTEXT( ) can check a cell and tell you whether the cell contains text. Other functions perform conversions: for example, the text function LOWER( ) converts text to all lowercase; the engineering function CONVERT( ) transforms values from one unit of measure to another (Fahrenheit to Celsius, feet to meters, and so on). The following sections provide an overview of functions, how to use them, and how to get help if you need it.

Most functions are already installed with Excel. Others (like CONVERT) may need to be installed as add-ins. You'll see how to install add-ins later in this chapter in the section "Using Functions That Require Excel Add-Ins."

Understanding the Parts of a Function

Worksheet functions consist of two parts:

- The operator, which tells Excel what to do with the numbers
- The argument, which provides the numbers you plug into the function

Let's take a look at the SQRT( ) function as an example. The SQRT portion of the function is the operator. The ( ) portion will contain the number you want to find the square root of. For example, if you enter SQRT(9), Excel finds the square root of 9.

Function arguments often refer to places in your worksheet. For instance, =SQRT(A2) computes the square root of the contents of cell A2. If you use named items in your worksheets, functions can sometimes refer to them as well. For example, =SQRT(VOLTAGE) might be a legitimate formula if your worksheet contains a positive number named VOLTAGE or a formula named VOLTAGE that computes voltage.

Arguments can also be text, logical values (TRUE and FALSE), or arrays. For example, you might see functions and their arguments expressed as follows:

SQRT(number)

or

SUM(number1,**number2**...)

or

FV(rate,nper,pmnt,pv,type)

Notice that in the FV example, some of the arguments are bold and others are not. Often, if you don't provide an argument, Excel supplies a default value. Arguments with default values appear in bold.

For instance, look at the following function:

DOLLAR(**number**,decimals)

This function converts numbers into text with dollar signs and, optionally, decimal places for cents. Let's look at three examples of this function:

Function	Result
=DOLLAR (200)	$200.00
=DOLLAR (200,1)	$200.0
=DOLLAR (200,)	$200

CAUTION

Commas are important in functions and sometimes there is a big difference in the results if you delete a comma instead of leaving it and not entering an argument after it.

In the first case, leaving out the optional second argument and the comma that separates it causes Excel to use the default argument (a decimal point and two places, in this function). In the second case, the comma separates the second argument, which specifies the number of decimal places (1). In the third case, where there is a comma and no second argument; the comma suggests to Excel that there is a second argument (an argument specifying neither decimal point nor decimal places).

You can frequently use other functions as arguments, too. For instance, you can combine the ROUND and SQRT functions to compute the square root of a number and then round the results:

=ROUND(**SQRT(A1)**,2)

This formula computes the square root of the contents of cell A1 and then rounds the answer to two decimal places.

Now that you've seen some of what functions can do, you're probably wondering just how to get these into your worksheet so you can try them. No problem—read on!

Pasting Functions

The Paste Function button greatly simplifies the use of functions. It leads you through the necessary steps, displaying the results as you work, and even provides examples of the functions in use.

1. Activate the cell where you want to paste the function.

2. If you need to begin your own formula before inserting the function, type it first, stopping when the insertion point reaches the place where you want to insert the function.

3. Click the Paste Function button on the standard toolbar, or choose Insert | Function.

The Paste Function dialog box appears. This dialog box lists functions in 11 categories (Financial, Date & Time, and so on). In addition, it offers the categories Most Recently Used and All.

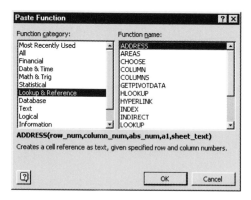

4. Click a category in the Function Category list on the left. Scroll through the Function Name list on the right and click the desired function. Its name and arguments appear near the bottom-left corner of the dialog box. Read the description of the function to be sure it's the one you want.

5. Click OK to open the Formula Palette. Here, you'll see a list of arguments that are required, and possibly, some that are optional (and labeled as such). The arguments are explained on the screen, and the Office Assistant button, as always, summons help on the particular function or on the use of the Formula Palette. If you don't know what to enter, click to select the entry box in question and then click the Office Assistant button.

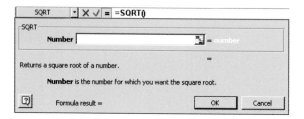

6. You can type directly in the Formula Palette's entry boxes or just click the cells in the sheet to select the data you want to use

as arguments. Click the button in the Formula Palette to compress it and move it out of the way so you can select the cells you're interested in.

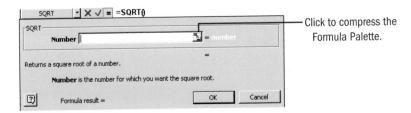

Click to compress the Formula Palette.

7. After you've selected the cells, click the button at the right of the compressed Formula Palette to restore the full palette.

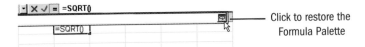

Click to restore the Formula Palette

As you work, Excel displays the results of its calculations in the Formula Result area at the bottom of the Formula Palette.

8. Click OK when you are finished using the Formula Palette. As you can see in Figure 7.1, when you click OK, Excel pastes the function into the active cell and displays the results of the current arguments in the cell. You see the formula in the formula bar. Add to or edit the rest of the formula if necessary. Then press ENTER to finish the formula.

Each Formula Palette dialog box is different and depends upon the function for its appearance and content. For instance, SQRT has only one argument, while PV has many.

As you're learning to use functions, remember that you can click on the Office Assistant, and then type the function's name in the text box. For an overview of functions by category, click on the Office Assistant and enter the name of a category. Then click a function name in the topic index of functions. For more information about using help, see Chapter 2.

Dealing with Error Messages

When you leave out or misuse arguments in functions, cryptic error messages like "Error in formula" may appear, or a message like #NAME? or #NUM! may appear in the cell containing the flawed argument.

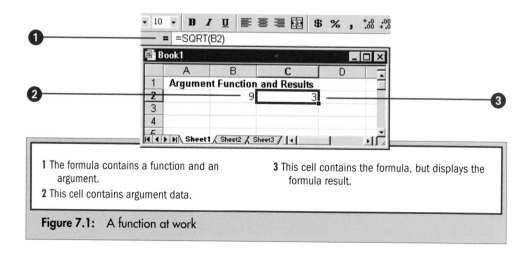

1 The formula contains a function and an argument.

2 This cell contains argument data.

3 This cell contains the formula, but displays the formula result.

Figure 7.1:   A function at work

It is common to get messages like these when you work with names or text strings as arguments. Text strings must be enclosed in quotation marks, while names (references to areas, for instance) must not be in quotation marks.

For instance, suppose you are using a math function such as SQRT. If you enter the formula argument =SQRT(VELOCITY), Excel expects to be able to find a named numeric value or range of cells in your worksheet called VELOCITY. If it can't, it displays the message #NAME? in the cell containing the formula. If you do have a positive numeric value named VELOCITY, the formula uses its contents as the function's argument. If the value of VELOCITY is negative, you'll see the error message #NUM!. Suppose you accidentally enclose the name VELOCITY in quotation marks and then try to use it as an arithmetic argument? The expression =SQRT("VELOCITY") produces the error message #VALUE!, since SQRT needs a numeric value to do its thing, and Excel treats any data in quotation marks as text. Refer to Chapter 14 for more information about error messages.

EXPERT ADVICE

Formula entries can be the actual data (like the number 90), cell addresses (like A1), range names (like SALES), or even other functions. Be consistent when entering arguments. For example, if you name a cell range A1:D12 SALES, don't use A1:D12 sometimes and SALES other times.

Using Functions That Require Excel Add-Ins

Some functions require add-ins—additional software (such as a utility program) that is provided with Excel but is not automatically loaded when you run Excel. When you attempt to use functions that require add-ins, Excel loads the add-ins automatically for you. For example, the BESSELI and DELTA engineering functions need the Analysis ToolPak. If Excel can't load the required add-in, it may be because you chose not to install add-ins when you initially installed Excel on your hard disk. Try rerunning the installer program to add these features.

Here are the general steps for adding the Analysis ToolPak:

1. Place your Office 2000 CD in your CD-ROM drive.

2. Open Excel and, on the Tools menu, click Add-Ins. You may have to click the double arrow at the bottom of the menu to reveal the lower part of the menu.

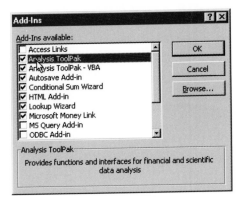

3. When the Add-Ins dialog box appears, scroll through the Add-Ins Available list and place a check by Analysis ToolPak (while you're there, select any other add-ins that appeal to you, such as the Conditional Lookup Wizard, which we'll be examining in this chapter).

4. Click OK, and Excel will search the CD for the add-in you requested.

5. Be patient while the program installs the add-in. After this installation, you'll notice that additional functions will be available from the Paste Function menu.

6. Follow any additional on-screen instructions for completing installation of the Analysis ToolPak. You won't need your CD to access these additional functions in the future.

Types of Functions

So far in this chapter, you've learned quite a bit about the basics of functions, but the best way to really learn about functions is to experiment with them. This section presents a few examples to get you started, organized in the same categories that Excel uses to group the functions (except for user-defined functions, because I don't know what you'll define).

Date and Time Functions

Excel has two types of date and time functions; some simply report the current date and/or time, and others handle date-and-time math.

Date and time functions in Excel can be very useful for many busy people. Forget your wristwatch? No problem! Excel has a reporting function that finds and displays the current time: the NOW( ) function. When you use it, NOW( ) inserts (returns) a new number corresponding to the current date and time whenever the worksheet is recalculated. For example, if you simply paste the formula =NOW( ) into a cell, Excel displays the current date followed by the current time and then updates the cell's contents every time the worksheet is recalculated (and only when it is recalculated).

Other date and time functions calculate dates, days, and times. For instance, the DAYS360( ) function computes the number of days between two dates, assuming a 360-day year (used by many accounting folks).

You can change the appearance of cells containing date and time functions by using the different date and time types found on the Number tab of the Format Cells dialog box. Excel's default date format displays the date and time in the format *m/dd/yy hh:mm*, for example, 7/25/98 3:21.

You can choose from a number of other variations with or without including the time. To change the format, use the following procedure:

1. Select the date and time cells you want to reformat.

2. Choose Format | Cells.

3. Scroll through the listed types until you find the format you need.

4. Select the format of your choice and then click OK.

When you do any kind of date math, check your work very, very carefully. It is quite easy to produce technically correct answers that are not the ones you need. For instance, when computing working days, Excel does not automatically know that December 25 is a holiday for many people. Your formulas will need to take things like this into consideration.

Database Functions

You can take advantage of Excel's database functions to look up values based on specific criteria. Need to find out how many of your customers owe between $1,000 and $5,000? Try DCOUNT( ). What if you need the average number of items in inventory from your master Excel file? DAVERAGE( ) gets you there. Each of the database functions require three arguments: the database, the field to be checked, and the criteria or conditions to select.

Engineering Functions

Engineering functions are available, but they require the Analysis ToolPak add-in macro, which you will probably need to install manually (that is, you'll need to get out your installation CD or disks) if you didn't opt to install it when you first installed Office. (Add the ToolPak using the steps described earlier in the section "Using Functions That Require Excel Add-Ins.")

EXPERT ADVICE

Note that you can move the Formula Palette around. Just click and hold somewhere in the dialog box (except in boxes or on buttons, of course) and drag.

The CONVERT( ) engineering function, for example, is a worthwhile addition to your collection. Create the Convert Formula with the Formula Palette, specifying which cells should contain the original number, the From unit, and the To unit.

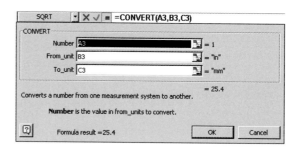

In Figure 7.2, CONVERT( ) converts inches to millimeters.

Financial Functions

Excel's many financial functions are pretty well documented in online help. Many of them can be used together or can be included as arguments, one function within another.

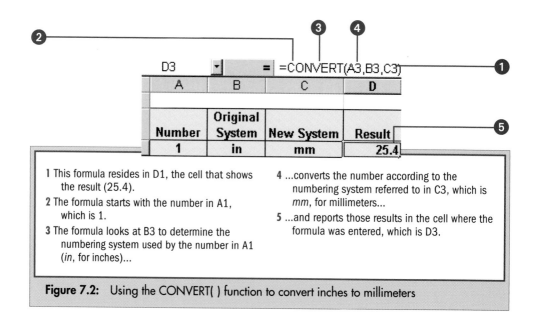

1 This formula resides in D1, the cell that shows the result (25.4).

2 The formula starts with the number in A1, which is 1.

3 The formula looks at B3 to determine the numbering system used by the number in A1 (*in*, for inches)...

4 ...converts the number according to the numbering system referred to in C3, which is *mm*, for millimeters...

5 ...and reports those results in the cell where the formula was entered, which is D3.

Figure 7.2: Using the CONVERT( ) function to convert inches to millimeters

Look at PMT( ), Excel's payment function. Officially, according to the online help, this function "returns the periodic payment of an annuity based on constant payments and a constant interest rate." In other words, it tells you what your payments will be, given the loan amount, number of payments, and a fixed rate of interest. Here, you can see PMT( ) at work:

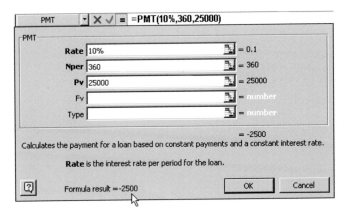

Here is the syntax of the function:

PMT(rate,nper,pv,fv,type)

The rate argument indicates the interest rate per period. For instance, if you borrow at an annual fixed interest rate of 10 percent and then make monthly payments, the interest rate is 10 percent divided by 12. This explains the division portion of the formula in the formula bar.

The Nper argument needs the total number of payments. Thus, if you borrow for 30 years and make monthly payments, you'll make 30*12, or 360 payments.

The Pv argument indicates the present value, or total the amount that the series of payments is worth now—the loan amount, in this case. Notice in our example that the optional Fv (future value) and type arguments were omitted; Fv (future value) is a desired cash balance after the last payment is made, and type is either a 0 (zero) or 1. Omitting the type argument or entering 0 indicates that you will make payments at the end of each period. Entering 1 tells Excel that the payments will be made at the beginning of the period.

Related financial tools include FV( ), IPMT( ), NPER( ), PPMT( ), PV( ), and RATE( ) as separate functions.

Information Functions

Some functions perform inspections and report what they found. For example, ISEVEN( ) lets your formulas know whether a cell contains an even number. Other information functions can check things external to Excel, such as the amount of RAM in your computer or which DOS version you are using. The function's syntax is as follows:

INFO(type)

Remember that if you use the actual name of the type (instead of a cell reference), you need to include quotation marks around the word, as in this example:

INFO("directory")

Here you can see INFO( ) at work:

	A	B
	Argument	**Result**
1		
2	directory	C:\My Documents\
3	memavail	1048576
4	totmem	2047836
5	release	9.0
6	numfile	16
7	origin	$A:$A$1
8	system	pcdos
9	osversion	Windows (32-bit) 4.10

Cells B2 through B9 each have the same formula that refers to corresponding cells in column A, which contain the arguments that produce the results you see.

Logical Functions

You use logic all the time. Chances are, you say things like, "If I finish writing this chapter in time, I can go out to lunch; otherwise, I'll nuke some frozen pizza." You can use logic in Excel, too. Take the IF function, for example. Its syntax is as follows:

IF(logical_test,value_if_true,value_if_false)

Let's look at a real-life example, as shown in Figure 7.3. The IF( ) function here checks to see if the ending odometer reading is greater than the starting reading (B3>B2). If the readings look okay, the IF function causes Excel to subtract the beginning reading from the ending reading (B3-B2). If B3 isn't greater than B2, chances are the user has made a typing error when entering the readings, or perhaps the odometer has reached its limit and rolled over, and started again at zero. If there seems to be an error, the function displays a text message in the cell ("Check OD").

Lookup and Reference Functions

Lookup and reference functions go to cells you specify and return with answers. These functions can inspect ranges, names, or specific cell addresses. They can be used to create invoices that look up and insert different unit prices based on quantities purchased.

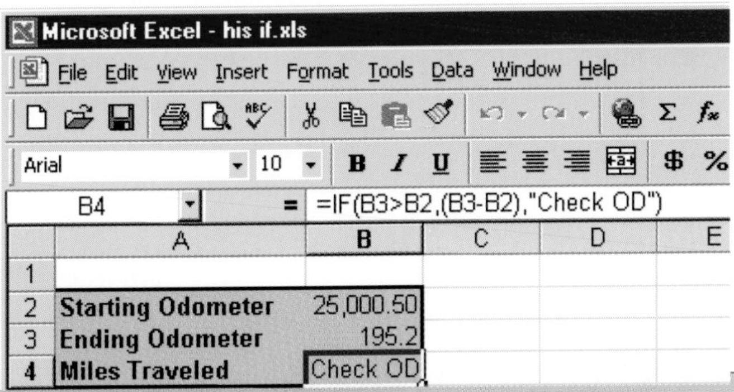

Figure 7.3: Excel's IF function tests for conditions and responds with different actions, based on what it finds.

For instance, you can use a lookup function such as VLOOKUP( ) to find the appropriate price for a specific quantity of sales:

B10	▼	=	=VLOOKUP(A10,Reference,2)

	A	B	C	D	E
1		**Reference Table**			
2		Quality	Unit Price		
3					
4		1	$5.75		
5	Over	10	$5.50		
6	Over	50	$5.05		
7	Over	100	$4.86		
8					
9	**Quantity**	**Unit Price**	**Total**		
10	13	$5.50	$71.50		

In this example, the formula compares the value in cell A10 to the range named Reference and finds the corresponding unit price from the reference range. In this example, 13 is lower than 50 yet higher than 10, so the unit price is $5.50.

Math and Trigonometry Functions

You've already seen several of the mathematical functions in action—SQRT( ) and SUM( ), for example. There are many others, enough to make an eighth grade math teacher weep with joy. Most are quite straightforward and are well documented in online help. Math and trig functions can refer to cell references, names, or plain old numbers.

Two of the math and trig functions simply produce numbers whenever a worksheet is recalculated. RAND( ) produces evenly distributed random numbers greater than or equal to zero and less than one, each time you recalculate—handy if you play the lottery or need to check probabilities. The PI( ) function inserts 3.141592654.

Statistical Functions

Pollsters and statisticians will want to check out the many statistical functions, from AVEDEV( ) to ZTEST( ). (AVEDEV returns the average of absolute deviations; ZTEST returns the two-tailed P-value of a Z-test, don't you know.)

Text Functions

To manipulate or analyze strings of text in cells, use text functions. For example, CLEAN( ) strips away any nonprinting characters stored in a cell. UPPER( ) converts text to all uppercase. DOLLAR( ) converts numbers to their spelled-out dollar equivalents and formats them in currency format.

Checkpoint

Wow. That's some creative calculating, if I do say so myself. And just think: You can have Excel do it all for you—from figuring dates to statistics to small business expenses. What you have learned in this chapter is how to identify parts of a function and how to insert a function in your Excel worksheet, and you have seen a sampling of the various Excel functions. There's a lot more to learn about functions—much more than I can include in this book. You'll be able to learn a lot by experimenting and exploring Excel's online help, although if you get really intensively into formulas and functions, you may also benefit from a reference book designed specifically for Excel functions.

Coming up are chapters that will help you add dimension to your Excel worksheets. Specifically, in Chapter 8, you'll learn how to include charts—which illustrate the relationship among sets of information. In Chapter 9, you'll learn about Excel's graphics capabilities (bet you didn't know Excel was creative, did you?). In Chapter 10, you'll get a brief introduction to command macros, which can help you create solutions to common problems.

CHAPTER 8

Charts

INCLUDES

- Understanding chart terminology
- Creating charts using the Chart Wizard
- Modifying charts
- Resetting chart defaults
- Using Microsoft Map
- Printing charts
- Deleting charts
- Publishing charts on the Internet

Create a Chart Using the Chart Wizard ➡ pp.182 – 184

1. Select the cells to be charted.
2. Click the Chart Wizard button.
3. Answer the Wizard's questions, clicking Next to move forward or Back to change your mind.
4. Click Finish when you're done.

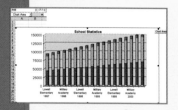

Resize a Chart ➡ pp. 186 – 187

1. Click the chart to select it.
2. Drag with the size handles to resize the chart. You'll notice that more data becomes visible.
3. If parts of your chart data are missing, reduce the font size to show more data.

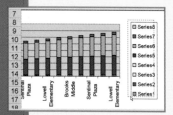

Move a Chart ➡ pp.186 – 187

1. Click the chart to select it.
2. Drag the chart with your mouse; release the mouse button when you've moved the chart to your satisfaction.
3. Drag and reposition the data area or legend to suit your needs.

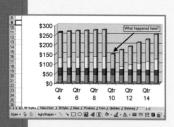

Add Notes and Arrows ➡ pp. 187 – 190

1. Use the Text Box button on the drawing toolbar to add text. (Click the Drawing button on the standard toolbar, if necessary, to bring up the drawing toolbar.)
2. Use the Arrow button on the drawing toolbar to add arrows.
3. Double-click text boxes and arrows to change their appearance.

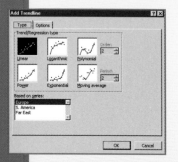

Add Trendlines ➡ p. 191

1. Click a chart to select it.
2. Select the data series for the trendline by clicking one of its markers.
3. Right-click and choose Add Trendline from the shortcut menu.
4. In the Add Trendline dialog box, pick a trend/regression type. Click the Options tab to change options, if necessary.
5. Click OK.

Add Overlay Charts ➡ pp. 192 – 193

1. Select the data series you want to change and choose Chart | Chart Type.
2. Choose the new type for the series.
3. Click OK.

Change the Axis Default ➡ pp.193 – 194

1. Select the chart.
2. Using the chart toolbar, click either the By Row or By Column button to readjust the data.

Change the Chart Type Default ➡ p. 194

1. Click the chart to select it.
2. Right-click the chart and choose Chart Type from the shortcut menu.
3. Click the chart type you want as the default.
4. Click the Set as Default Chart button at the bottom of the dialog box.
5. When Excel asks whether you're sure you want to reset the default, click Yes if you do or click No if you've changed your mind.

Use Microsoft Map or MapPoint 2000 ➡ p. 195

1. Select a range of cells (one column in the cell range must contain geographic data).
2. Click the Map button on the standard toolbar or select Map from the Insert menu.
3. Click and drag your mouse to specify where the map should go. If the data you select is ambiguous or if there are misspellings in your data, a dialog box asks you how to proceed. Otherwise, the map appears on your screen.

Print Charts ➡ pp. 197 – 198

Charts print automatically when you print your worksheets.

- To inhibit automatic printing, remove the check mark from the Print Object option on the Properties tab of the Format Chart Area dialog box. (Reach this box by selecting Chart Area from the Chart Objects drop-down list on the chart toolbar and then clicking the Format Chart Area button on the same toolbar.)
- To tailor options for printing a single chart by selecting the chart, choosing File | Page Setup, and clicking the Chart tab.

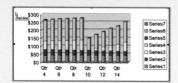

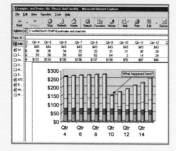

Delete Charts ➥ p. 198

1. Click the chart to select it.
2. Press DEL.

Publish Charts on the Internet ➥ p. 198

1. Create the chart.
2. Choose File | Save as Web Page. The chart appears in your Web pages just as it does on your worksheet.
3. Get a preview of how your chart will look online by selecting Web Page Preview.

Remember the old adage about how numbers can lie? Well, charts can seduce. Excel charts (which are often called graphs) make it easy for people to understand the relationships among data. It's one thing to write that a small percentage of our tax dollars go toward education; it's another thing to see a graphic representation of the relationship between education and defense expenditures. By the same token, a 3D bar representation of the same government budget that has been rotated just right will portray the little education bar bigger than it really is; the defense bar will look smaller.

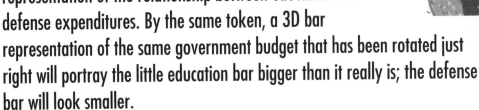

This chapter introduces you to charts. You'll learn some basic terminology. Then you'll learn how to create and modify charts, how to change chart defaults, and how to print and delete charts. When you finish this chapter, you'll be an expert chart creator!

Understanding Chart Terminology

Two immediate tasks await: First, learning terminology to understand the chart creation process. Second, learning key chart terminology in case you need to look up something in Excel Help. The following sections will introduce you to some basic chart terms and help you understand how to read and put together your own charts. Refer to Figure 8.1 as you learn about these new terms.

Axes

An axis is a reference line denoting one of the dimensions of a chart. Excel can plot using up to three axes: category (X), value (Y), and series (Z). The category axis runs horizontally (left to right), and the value axis runs vertically (bottom to top). For instance, on the

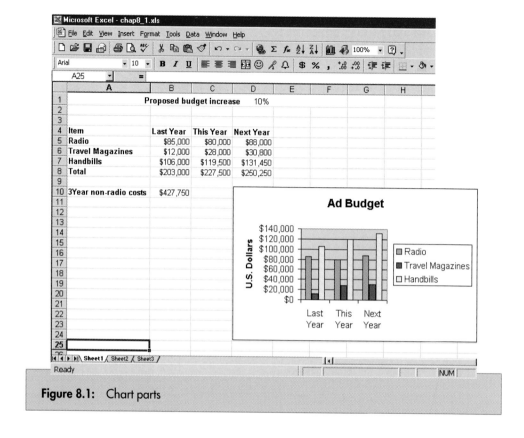

Figure 8.1: Chart parts

two-dimensional (2D) chart shown in Figure 8.1, the years run along the category axis, and the dollars runs along the value axis.

In three-dimensional (3D) charts, the series axis runs vertically, and the category and value axes are at angles to display perspective.

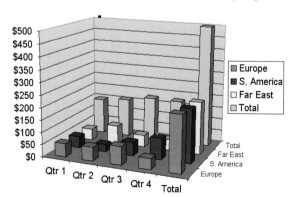

Tick Marks and Grid Lines

Tick marks are short lines that intersect an axis to separate parts of a series scale or category. Horizontal grid lines are similar, except they not only intersect the axis but also run across the chart. Figure 8.1 shows horizontal grid lines.

Chart Text

Chart text is the text used to identify the title and data labels. In Figure 8.1, "Ad Budget" and "U.S. Dollars" are chart text.

Chart Data Series

A chart data series is a collection of related values that are plotted on the chart. For instance, the chart in Figure 8.1 shows three data series: the numbers in row 5 ($85,000, $80,000, and $88,000) make up the first data series; the numbers in row 6 ($12,000, $28,000, and $30,800) make up the second data series; and the numbers in row 7 ($106,000, $119,500, and $131,450) make up the third data series.

Chart Data Series Ranges

Chart data series ranges are the cell addresses that contain all of the data series. For example, in Figure 8.1, the data series range is B5:D7. The cells between (and including) B5 and D7 are all the cells that are used to plot the graph.

Chart Data Series Names

Chart data series names usually correspond to worksheet labels for the data being plotted on the Y (vertical) axis. For instance, in Figure 8.1 the chart has three data series names, one for each series. Data series names are usually displayed in a box (and called a legend) alongside a sample of the color, shade, or pattern used for each data series. The Chart Wizard automatically identifies data series names and creates legends.

Category Names

Category names usually correspond to worksheet labels for the data being plotted along the X (horizontal) axis. For instance, in Figure 8.1 the category names are Last Year, This Year, and Next Year.

Chart Data Series Markers

Chart data series markers are the bars, pie wedges, dots, pictures, and other elements used to represent a particular data point (a single value in a series). For instance, the nine shaded columns in Figure 8.1 are each separate data markers.

When charts have more than one data series, the markers for each series usually look different. This is also illustrated in Figure 8.1, where the Radio columns are blue (or a shade of gray or a pattern when viewed on monochrome screens), the Travel Magazines columns are red, and the Handbills columns are yellow.

You can also use different types of markers for a different series on the same chart. You can, for instance, use columns for one series and lines for another.

Creating Charts

Creating a chart is a cinch. All you have to do is use the Chart Wizard, which allows you to choose the way you want the chart to look—then it creates the chart for you, even faster than you can say "humuhumu" (the nickname of the Hawaiian state fish). Following are instructions for using the Chart Wizard.

Start by creating a worksheet containing the data you want to chart. Then follow these steps:

1. Select the data to be included in your chart (probably most easily done by dragging to highlight the relevant cells). You should include labels for data in your charts, but don't include empty rows, columns, or totals.

2. Click the Chart Wizard button. The first Chart Wizard dialog box appears on your screen.

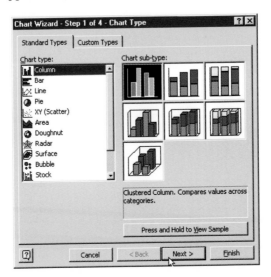

3. Select the chart type on the left, select a subtype on the right, and click Next. Note that you have different subtype choices based on the type you select. You can preview the way a chart type will look before you decide to use it. In the first Chart Wizard dialog box, use the Press and Hold to View Sample button (which, of course, you press and hold to use) to display a sample chart with the data you selected above the button. Think about the general presentation of the data at this point. Does the chart help you understand the data? Does it use the correct axis? Do you like the chart type? If not, release the button and keep trying chart types.

4. If you create a chart and decide that you've included too much or too little information, you can always change the data series ranges. In the second dialog box (Chart Source Data) of the Chart Wizard, you can redefine the data range by typing cell references or by dragging over the data range in the worksheet with your mouse.

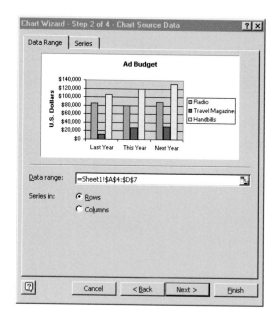

5. Work through the next three Wizard dialog boxes. Answer the questions, clicking Next to move forward or clicking Back if you change your mind. Click Finish when you're done. Your chart appears on your worksheet, illustrating the data you selected. Additionally, the chart toolbar appears so you can more easily modify the new chart.

Modifying Charts

Excel lets you change chart types and formats, embellish text, choose patterns and colors, add grid lines, and much more.

The next several sections give an overview of how to modify your charts. You'll learn the basics of resizing and moving charts, adding text boxes and arrows, and adding trendlines and overlays.

Before you start these sections, be sure that you have the chart toolbar displayed (choose View | Toolbars | Chart). This nifty toolbar can take care of all your chart editing needs. Table 8.1 give details for each button on the toolbar.

Button	Function
Value Axis ▾	Selects the various parts of the chart you want to work with
	Lets you format the part of the chart you've selected
	Lets you select a chart type
	Lets you show or not show a chart legend
	Lets you view the specific numbers used to create the chart
	Shows the chart data by row
	Shows the chart data by column
	Lets you rotate selected text

Table 8.1: Chart Toolbar Buttons

Editing Chart Elements

The first step to modifying your charts is learning how to edit individual chart elements. Even though charts look like one object, they're really made up of individually selectable parts. You can select and edit most specific parts of a chart, such as text, grid lines, the shading used for markers, and so on, by simply double-clicking them. For example, referring back to Figure 8.1, you can double-click the legend text and edit the font, size, and style; or double-click a legend color to edit the color in the legend box as well as the color used on the chart. Additionally, you can select parts of the chart and use the regular fill, text color, and other drawing commands to customize them to your heart's content.

Here are some more starting points for editing charts:

- To select the entire chart, click anywhere outside of the plot area but not on other items such as titles or legends (or choose Chart Area from the Chart Objects drop-down list at the left end of the chart toolbar).
- To edit the title, select it and then double-click a word, or double-click and then drag to select a larger amount of text with the I-beam pointer.
- To edit a data series, double-click any marker in the series. For instance, to select the Radio spending series in your sample chart, you could click any of the Radio columns for any year. A description of the data series in your formula bar appears, where you can edit the series definition. Also, you can point to a data marker, and Excel's ScreenTips feature will appear, telling you what the series, data point, and exact value are.
- To select a single data marker (like the Last Year column marker in your sample chart), click any marker in the series to select the series and then click one of the markers in the series to select it.
- To select a grid line, click exactly on it, or click an axis to select it instead.
- To select just the plot area (the columns without their category names, for instance), click any part of the plot area not occupied by other things like grid lines or markers (or choose Plot Area from the Chart Objects drop-down list at the left end of the chart toolbar).
- When creating a chart, you're given a choice of where to display it. As shown in Figure 8.2, a chart can be displayed in a new sheet or as an object in an existing worksheet. If your current worksheet is already a bit cluttered, consider allowing Excel to create a new worksheet for this chart.

Resizing and Moving Charts

Once you finish a chart, you can resize it or move it to suit your needs. For example, you may find that the finished chart is too big to

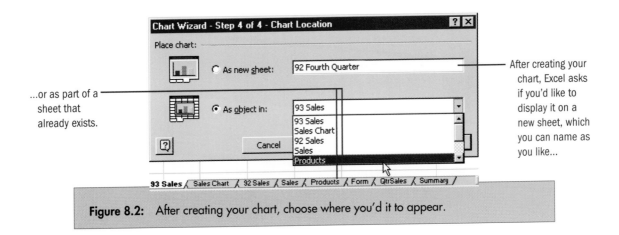

...or as part of a
sheet that
already exists.

After creating your
chart, Excel asks
if you'd like to
display it on a
new sheet, which
you can name as
you like...

Figure 8.2: After creating your chart, choose where you'd it to appear.

fit on a full worksheet. Or you may want to make a chart bigger to fill space on a worksheet. Either way, you can change the size (and shape!) of charts by using these quick steps:

1. Click the chart to select it. You'll see a box with little black handles (squares) surrounding the chart, as shown in Figure 8.3.

2. Click (and hold) one of the black handles.

3. Drag the handle until the chart is resized to your liking.

To move a chart, click and hold. (After clicking the chart, make sure the bounding boxes surround the chart itself, not the outer chart box area.) Drag the chart wherever you want to place it and then release the mouse button. While you have the chart selected, you can also cut or copy it using the buttons on the toolbar and then paste it into another worksheet, another workbook, or a different document.

Adding Text Boxes

You'll often want to draw attention to, or explain, certain items on your chart. You can do this by adding text boxes that contain additional information about the cell contents. Here's how:

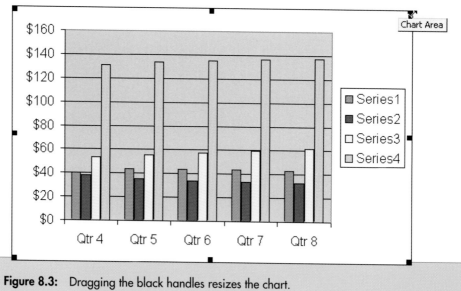

Figure 8.3:   Dragging the black handles resizes the chart.

1. Display the drawing toolbar if it's not already on the screen. (Click the Drawing button on the standard toolbar, or right-click a toolbar and choose Drawing from the shortcut menu.)

2. Click the Text Box button and click where you want the text box to appear.

3. Type and edit your note using the text-editing techniques that should be familiar to you by now.

4. Drag the handles of the text box to resize it if necessary.

5. Click outside the text box when you're done.

Text boxes are similar to regular text in a worksheet. You can change the way they look to improve appearance or to better fit with other text on the worksheet.

Resizing Text Boxes

To resize or move a text box, use these steps:

1. Click any edge of the text box. The outline thickens, and you'll see six size handles.

2. Drag and resize using the handles.

Restyling Text Boxes

To change text appearance, use these steps:

1. Select the text.

2. Use formatting toolbar buttons (such as bold and italic). (Or right-click your selection and then choose Format Text Box from the shortcut menu.)

To change the outline or fill pattern used for a text box or to add a shadow effect, double-click the edge of the text box. You'll see the Format Text Box dialog box, shown here:

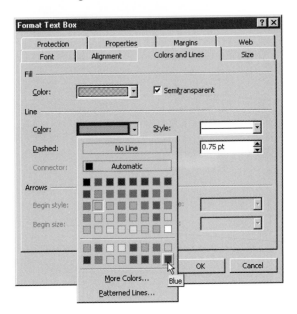

Drawing Arrows

Arrows are another great way to draw attention to information on a chart. Here's how to draw them:

1. On the standard toolbar, click the Drawing button to display the drawing toolbar.

2. On the drawing toolbar, click the Arrow button.

3. Point your mouse where you want the arrow to start; then click and drag to the ending point. (Notice that the pointer tool turns into a crosshair.) When you release the mouse button, an arrow appears.

Formatting Arrows

Changing the appearance of arrows after you've drawn them is fairly straightforward:

1. Click the arrow to select it (or SHIFT-click to select multiple arrows).

2. Right-click and choose Format AutoShape from the shortcut menu to bring up the Format AutoShape dialog box.

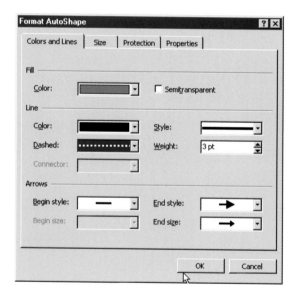

3. Choose from arrow format options, such as arrow styles, line thickness, and colors.

Creating Trendlines

Trendlines are used to plot the direction of data in a series. It's easy to add trendlines to Excel bar, column, area, and scatter charts. To create trendlines on charts, follow these general steps:

1. Click a chart to select it.

2. Select the data series for the trendline by clicking one of its markers.

3. Right-click and choose Add Trendline from the shortcut menu.

4. In the Add Trendline dialog box, pick a trend/regression type, as shown here:

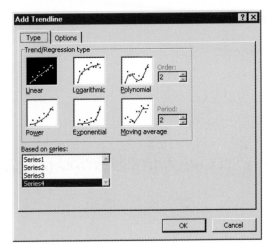

5. If necessary, click the Options tab of the Add Trendline dialog box and change options.

6. Below, we are extending the trendline for two periods to create a forecast.

7. Click OK. The trendline appears.

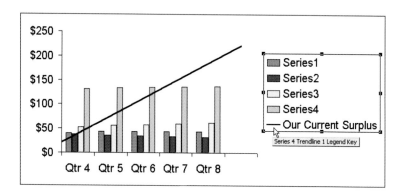

Adding Overlay Charts

Sometimes you'll want to overlay one kind of chart data on top of another. For instance, you might want to display projected ad expenditures as a line over the prior and current year bars.

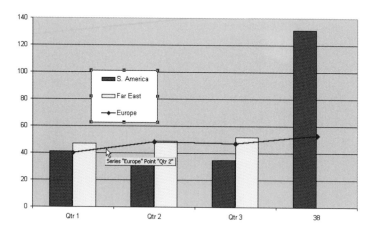

The easy way to do this is to set up your chart as usual and then follow these steps:

1. Select the data series you want to change.
2. Choose Chart | Chart Type.
3. Choose the new type for the series.
4. Click OK.

In the example, the line data series (Europe) was originally in bar form, like the other two series entries. Only the Europe bar was selected and changed into a line chart display.

Changing Chart Defaults

The Chart Wizard can create some awesome charts using its default settings. Once you've created a couple of charts, though, you might decide to change some of the chart default settings to ones that better suit your needs. This section shows you how to change the axis default and the chart type default.

Changing the Axis Default

Excel considers the numbers of rows and columns you've selected when determining how to plot your data. Although space prohibits showing each chart type and examples of the results with different row and column combinations here, it's easy to watch the sample as you work with the Chart Wizard and change the outcome. For example, look at this:

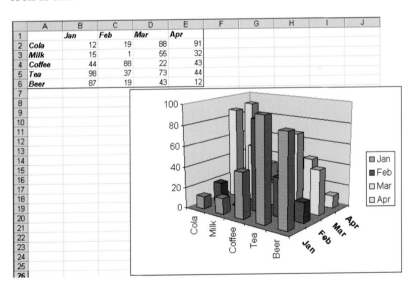

As you can see, Excel has plotted the months on the category axis and the departments on the value axis because of the number of rows and columns selected. To overrule this choice—and therefore change the axis default—use these steps:

1. Select the chart.

2. Using the chart toolbar, click either the By Row or By Column button to readjust the data.

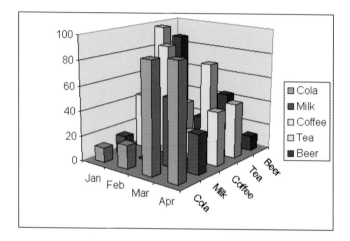

Changing the Chart Type Default

The Chart Wizard, by default, creates new charts using the Column chart type and first subtype. If you want to change this, use these steps:

1. Choose a chart from the current worksheet that you would like to use as the default.

2. Right-click the chart.

3. Select Chart Type from the shortcut menu.

4. Click the Set as Default Chart button at the bottom of the dialog box.

5. Excel asks whether you're sure you want to reset the default. Click Yes if you do; click No if you've changed your mind. By the way, you can always reset the default chart type later.

Using Microsoft Map

Excel has a terrific feature called Microsoft Map that allows you to insert actual maps into your spreadsheets. Figure 8.4 shows a map and the Map Control dialog box.

You can add titles, adjust shading, and even draw demographic data from files on disk. Follow along here to learn how to create a data map.

1. Select a range of cells. One column in the cell range must contain geographic data (such as country names).

2. Click the Map button on the standard toolbar (or select Map from the Insert menu).

3. Click and drag your mouse to specify where the map should go.

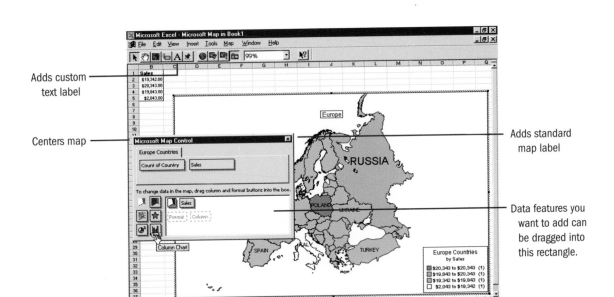

Figure 8.4: The Map Editor and Map Control dialog box

Editing Maps

Notice that when you're working with a map, the Excel screen changes to include the map toolbar, as shown in Figure 8.5.

To edit a map, use any of the following techniques:

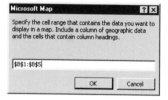

- Choose Insert | Data to bring up the Map dialog box. Here you can specify what data should be included on the data map.

- If you want a closer view of your map, click the Zoom Percentage of Map drop-down list and then choose a greater magnification.

- To refresh the map at any time, click the Map Refresh button.

- To change the shading or format of a column's data, drag the column into the Format box of the Map Control dialog box and click the appropriate button.

- To edit an existing map, double-click the map to get back to the map window.

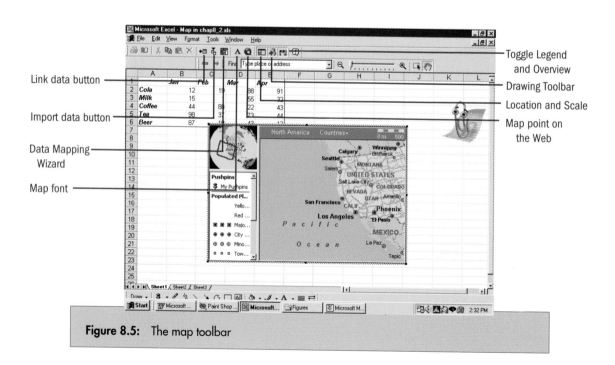

Figure 8.5: The map toolbar

Here's what a typical finished map looks like:

Using Demographic Information

You can link your maps to demographic data that comes with Excel in the file called Mapstats.xls found on your hard disk (probably in the \Program Files\Common Files\Microsoft Shared\Datamap\Data folder). You can then use this information along with your own sales results to monitor trends and predict demand. Consult a reference book on Excel for more details.

Printing Charts

Unless you tell Excel to do otherwise, it will print all the charts along with the worksheet they're in.

If a chart is in a separate worksheet, print it like any other Excel worksheet. Use the Page Setup and Print Preview features to format the documents, add headers or footers, and so on.

If you just want to print a chart without the accompanying worksheet, use these steps:

1. Click the chart to select it.
2. Choose File | Print.

3. In the Print dialog box, make sure that Print Selected Chart is selected.

4. Click OK.

After you select a chart, you can choose File | Page Setup to choose where on the page Excel will print your chart. Click the Chart tab to tailor the options.

Deleting Charts

To delete a chart, simply select it and press DEL. If you delete a chart by mistake, Edit | Undo will work.

Delete separate chart worksheets as you would any other unwanted Excel worksheet—that is, use the Delete Sheet command on the Edit menu.

Publishing Charts on the Internet

Excel even lets you publish your charts on the Internet! Charts on the Internet can often show information better and more efficiently than a worksheet—just as they do on paper. To publish a chart on the Internet, save it (or the worksheet it's created in) in HTML format (choose File | Save as HTML). Charts appear in your Web pages just as they do in your worksheets.

See Chapter 12 for the complete scoop on publishing your worksheets on the Internet.

Checkpoint

This chapter covered the basics of Excel charting and, as you've seen, the skills you learned in Windows and practiced in Word are often called for and applied in Excel. Many times, just reading the menu, dialog box, or the status bar will show you how to do new and useful things.

If you're looking for more information and nifty Excel chart tricks, you can always check out Excel's online help. Or you can check out

the hundred-plus pages on charts in your Excel manual, or pick up
Excel for Windows 95 Made Easy by Martin S. Matthews (Osborne/
McGraw-Hill, 1995).

Coming up in Chapter 9 is all you ever wanted to know about
graphics but were afraid to ask—well, okay—some really useful
information about Excel's graphics capabilities. In Chapter 10, you'll
learn about command macros. Then, in Chapter 11, you'll learn how
to let Excel answer those nagging "what-if" questions.

Graphics

INCLUDES

- Identifying graphic types
- Effectively choosing graphics
- Creating and importing graphics
- Editing graphics

Graphic Types Available to Excel ➥ pp. 206–209

- Simple line drawings
- Complex fills and shapes
- Text bubbles and callouts
- Word art
- Clipart and photos
- Imported and scanned images

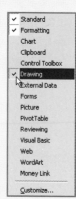

Adding Graphics to Your Spreadsheet ➥ pp. 209–217

1. Right-click any toolbar.
2. Choose Drawing. The drawing toolbar appears at the bottom of the screen.
   - Create a graphic by using the tools on the left half of the toolbar.
   - Modify a graphic by using the tools on the right.
   - Group, arrange, and select graphics by using the drop-down menu (on the far left) labeled Draw.

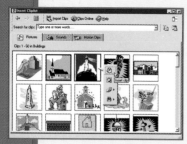

Inserting Clipart Graphics into Your Spreadsheet ➥ pp. 217–218

1. Click the face on the drawing toolbar.
2. Choose a graphic category from the picture catalogs shown.
3. Search a catalog to choose just the right graphic.
4. To insert a graphic, click it once; a fly-out menu appears with four options. Choose the top option, Insert Clip.

Inserting Imported Images
into Your Spreadsheet ➡ pp. 219–220

1. From the Insert menu, choose Picture; then choose From File.
2. Use the browse menu to locate the file you want to add.
3. Click the Look In drop-down menu to locate the drive and folder that contains the correct graphic.
4. To insert a picture into your spreadsheet, select the graphic and then press ENTER.

Editing Spreadsheet Images ➡ pp. 220–227

- To move an image, click it and drag it to a new location.
- To resize an image, drag inward or outward on one of the bounding boxes that surrounds it.
- To fill an image with color or a pattern or to create a border, select the image; then use one of the tools on the right side of the drawing toolbar.
- To add a text box to an image, click the Text Box icon on the drawing toolbar; then click the image and start typing your text message.
- To change a picture's color depth, right-click the image and choose Show Picture Toolbar; then click the Image Control icon and select one of the four color depth options that appears.

Aligning, Layering, and
Grouping Images ➡ pp. 220–227

- To layer one image over another, or to send an image to the front or back of a composition of several images, select the image you want to move to a new layer and click the Draw menu on the draw toolbar. Click Order and then choose a layering option.
- To group images, first create a layout or composition of images you want to preserve and select them all, using the SHIFT key to facilitate multiple selection. (Or click the arrow at the bottom-left of the Draw menu and drag a box around all the objects you want to select .) Then click the Draw drop-down menu on the draw toolbar and choose Group.
- To align images along an imaginary margin, perhaps centering them horizontally or vertically, first choose all the images you want aligned; then click the Draw drop-down menu on the draw toolbar and choose Align or Distribute. Click an Alignment option.

Choosing a Graphic Insertion Method ➡ pp. 227–228

- Choose cut and paste to insert an image if only a handful of images will be used.
- Avoiding cutting and pasting images that are particularly large.
- If an image is used repeatedly in your spreadsheet, choose the Linking option.

Graphics add character to your spreadsheets. They create a visual context for all those numbers on display. A reader will associate a positive image with the conclusions your data presents. Graphics also clarify: Create an explanatory label and then draw an arrow pointing to a section of your spreadsheet that needs a little elaboration. Graphics tidy up your spreadsheet, helping the reader quickly identify each topic on your sheet.

As you'll see, Excel provides many graphics tools. Some create simple lines and arrows; some create complex shapes that you can resize and fill with color. Often, you'll simply import a graphic, either from Office 2000's extensive collection of ready-made pictures, a scanned photo, or another image source found on your computer. With Word Art, you can create visually compelling pictures from simple text phrases.

Showing Restraint: How to Employ Spreadsheet Graphics

With so many tools, it's easy to go overboard and clutter your spreadsheet with unnecessary eye candy. So after you've developed your data and determined that your spreadsheet could use a little creative pizzazz, make sure that you include only images and artwork that help emphasize your spreadsheet's content rather than get in the way of your message.

Figure 9.1 shows examples of how to employ graphics in a spreadsheet.

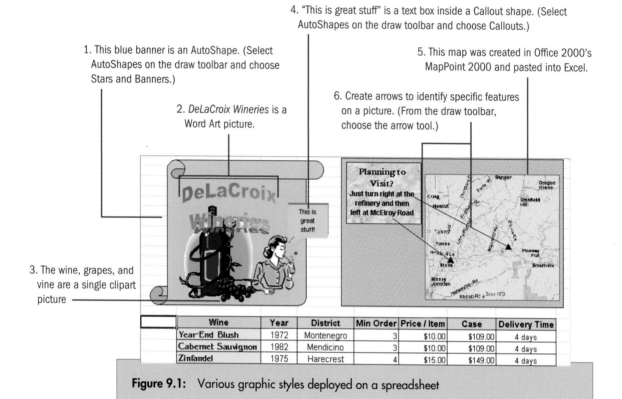

4. "This is great stuff" is a text box inside a Callout shape. (Select AutoShapes on the draw toolbar and choose Callouts.)

1. This blue banner is an AutoShape. (Select AutoShapes on the draw toolbar and choose Stars and Banners.)

2. *DeLaCroix Wineries* is a Word Art picture.

5. This map was created in Office 2000's MapPoint 2000 and pasted into Excel.

6. Create arrows to identify specific features on a picture. (From the draw toolbar, choose the arrow tool.)

3. The wine, grapes, and vine are a single clipart picture

Wine	Year	District	Min Order	Price / Item	Case	Delivery Time
Year-End Blush	1972	Montenegro	3	$10.00	$109.00	4 days
Cabernet Sauvignon	1982	Mendicino	3	$10.00	$109.00	4 days
Zinfandel	1975	Harecrest	4	$15.00	$149.00	4 days

Figure 9.1:   Various graphic styles deployed on a spreadsheet

Types of Graphics

There are several types of graphics you can create or import into Excel. The type you choose depends on your purpose.

Clipart

To employ a simple image in your spreadsheet, just drop in a clipart picture, which is a ready-made image that you can move and resize and otherwise adjust to fit your needs. Office 2000 comes with thousands of clipart images. These clipart images are arranged in catalogs, which helps you narrow your search for the right image. Office 2000's clipart catalogs include photographs as well as cartoons and drawings.

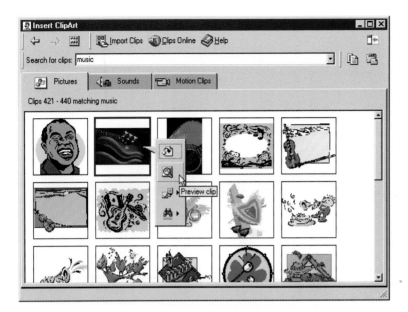

Simple Drawings

To highlight portions of your data and create explanatory or descriptive labels, use Excel's Draw tools. Create arrows, highlight data by circling it, and create text boxes that you can reposition near the data that you want to illuminate.

Word Art

To create artistic headlines, titles, and product names, use Word Art. Common to all Office 2000 applications, Word Art takes simple text phrases and reworks them into artistic images. You can reshape any text phrase, add a shadow, twist and rotate it, and add new background colors and fills. Be careful, though. It's easy to apply so many effects to a Word Art image that tinkering with all those interesting tools becomes an end in itself.

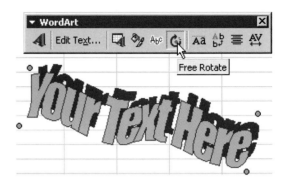

Flow Chart Tools

To show hierarchy, for example, the structure of an organization or the steps in a process, use the Flow Chart drawing tools (from the drawing toolbar, click AutoShapes and choose the Flow Chart drop-down menu). Create shapes that represent levels of your hierarchy and type text descriptions inside them. Then link them together to show their interdependence.

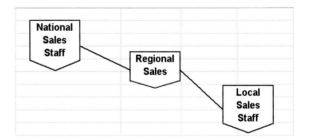

Imported Pictures

Images of all types can be inserted into your spreadsheet and resized and reoriented as needed. So if you've created or scanned a company logo or a photo using a graphic editing program, it can be easily employed in Excel.

Adding Graphics to Your Spreadsheet

First, we'll explore how to add graphics to your sheet, then edit, rearrange, and combine them to your liking. We'll see how to add simple lines and arrows and shapes and complex shapes with fills and borders, and then we'll discuss how to add clipart images and other files from your hard drive.

Adding Lines, Arrows, and Simple Shapes

Sometimes adding a line or two or an arrow, or circling key data, can be enough to give your spreadsheet the appearance you want. To create an arrow, line, or other simple shape, do the following:

1. First, look at the bottom of the spreadsheet to see if the drawing toolbar is visible (Figure 9.2). If it isn't, then right-click any toolbar and select Drawing.

2. Select the drawing tool you want. Right now, we're only discussing the line, arrow, rectangle, and oval tools. (To verify which tool you are about to use, momentarily hold your mouse over any tool icon. An identifying tooltip will appear.)

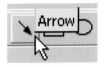

3. Once you've selected a tool, click and drag from the beginning of the line or shape to the end. If the image is a shape, click and drag from the top-left to the bottom-right. The mouse

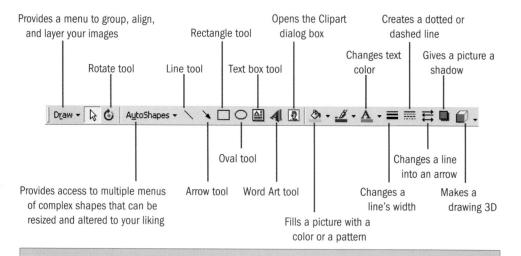

Provides a menu to group, align, and layer your images

Rotate tool

Rectangle tool

Line tool

Text box tool

Opens the Clipart dialog box

Changes text color

Creates a dotted or dashed line

Gives a picture a shadow

Oval tool

Arrow tool

Word Art tool

Provides access to multiple menus of complex shapes that can be resized and altered to your liking

Fills a picture with a color or a pattern

Changes a line's width

Changes a line into an arrow

Makes a drawing 3D

Figure 9.2: The drawing toolbar

cursor will appear as a crosshair. As you drag, the drawing appears in the spreadsheet.

3	$7.50	$67.50
5	$9.50	$98.00
7	$15.50	$152.00

A great deal for this time of year

Once you've created your shape, it will appear surrounded by bounding boxes. To resize or change the shape of your drawing, drag one of the bounding boxes. You'll see it change shape, expanding, or shrinking, depending on the direction you drag.

- Dragging a corner box changes the size of the image but keeps the basic shape the same (it retains the same aspect ratio).
- Dragging any other box changes the shape as well as the size. (Lines and arrows have only two bounding boxes).

Rotate an image to change the way an arrow points or the way a line is oriented. Click the Draw menu at the bottom-left of the drawing toolbar and select Free Rotate. Then drag any corner of the object to rotate it.

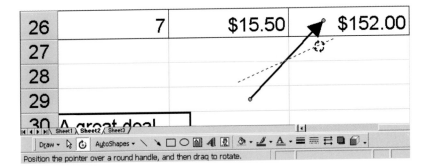

Creating Callouts, Starbursts, and Complex Shapes

You can create callouts, text bubbles, and other complex shapes, as shown in Figure 9.3. Follow these steps:

1. Click the AutoShapes icon on the drawing toolbar. A menu appears, revealing seven types of shapes you can draw (click the down-facing arrow at the bottom of the menu if fewer than seven categories appear).

2. Move your mouse to the right, over each category name, and a submenu appears, showing you all the different shapes that can be created just by clicking and dragging your mouse.

3. Use the same method for creating a shape as you did for creating a line: pressing and holding your mouse while you

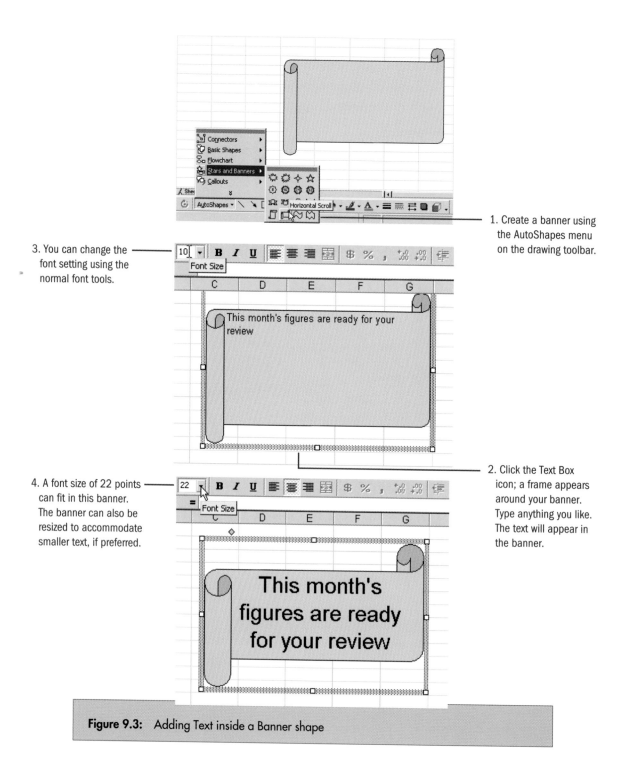

1. Create a banner using the AutoShapes menu on the drawing toolbar.

3. You can change the font setting using the normal font tools.

2. Click the Text Box icon; a frame appears around your banner. Type anything you like. The text will appear in the banner.

4. A font size of 22 points can fit in this banner. The banner can also be resized to accommodate smaller text, if preferred.

Figure 9.3: Adding Text inside a Banner shape

drag. Use the bounding boxes to resize and reshape
your creation.

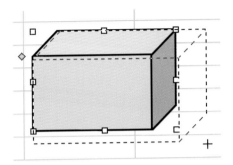

Changing Special Shape Features

Certain shapes have a special yellow box that you can use to change
some aspect of the shape's character. When creating a star, for example,
drag the yellow box to change the depth of the star's points. When
creating a scroll, drag the yellow box to make the page curl effect
narrower or wider.

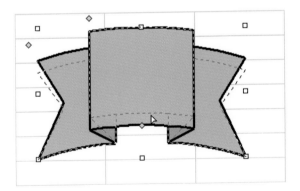

Using Fills and Outlines

When you first create a shape, it has a default thin black outline and
no fill. You can create a thicker outline, change the outline's color,
and fill the shape with the color of your choice by clicking the shape
and choosing the Fill Color (or Line Color) icon on the drawing
toolbar. This will fill the shape or line with the currently selected
color. To change the chosen color, click the down-facing arrow next
to the Fill Color (or Line Color) icon.

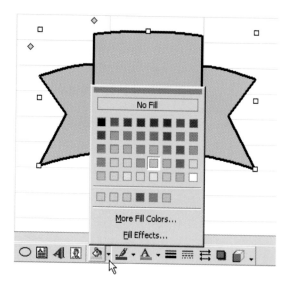

Rather than making changes via the toolbar, you can exert more control over fill and outline settings by right-clicking the object you want to transform and choosing Format AutoShape (or Format Line) from the menu that appears. You'll see a Format dialog box with five tabs. Click the Colors and Lines tab and do the following:

1. In the Fill panel, click the Color menu to choose a color for your shape. If you'd like the shape to not totally block out the objects you place beneath it, check the Semitransparent check box.

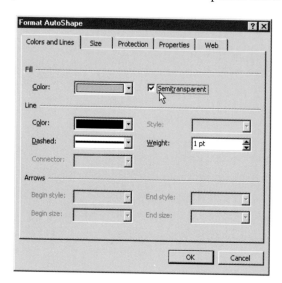

2. In the Line panel, specify the thickness (weight) of your arrow. You can also change your line into a dotted or dashed pattern. If the line you're creating has arrow qualities, use this dialog box to change the appearance of either end of your arrow.

Creating Text Boxes

To create a box that contains a text phrase, perhaps as much as a paragraph, do the following:

1. Click Text Box icon on the drawing toolbar (it looks like an "A" on a sheet of paper) and click in your spreadsheet. A blinking text cursor surrounded by a tiny box appears.

2. Just start typing, and the text box will expand to hold whatever you type.

3. Use any of the text tools (font, font size and style, color, and justification) to change the look of the text inside your box.

4. Once you've created your text box, add an outline or fill by right-clicking the text box border. Then select Format Text Box from the menu that appears. Click the Colors and Lines tab and add outline and fill features to your liking.

5. Move and resize your text box as you wish. You may have to change the font size to accommodate your new text box size and dimensions.

It's easy to place text boxes inside other objects, as in the example shown above, in which a text box was placed inside a sticky-note icon with a lifted lower-right corner to signify a reminder.

Creating Word Art

Word Art is appropriate for short phrases, perhaps four or five words at the most. Quite often, Word Art is used to create artistic titles or headings. The words you type can take on unusual shapes. The letters can be filled with brick patterns, crosshatches, and other 3D shapes and extrusions. However, Word Art creations can become toy-like very quickly and should be used sparingly.

To create a Word Art image, do the following:

1. Click the three-dimensional "A" on the drawing toolbar. The Word Art Style Gallery appears. You'll be given an opportunity to type text for your creation, but for now, just pick a design that appeals to you. You can make changes as you go along.

2. When the Edit Word Art Text screen appears, type your own text. Just start typing, and your own phrase will replace the Type Text Here placeholder text that appears on the screen. Click OK, and your text will appear in the spreadsheet, along with the Word Art toolbar.

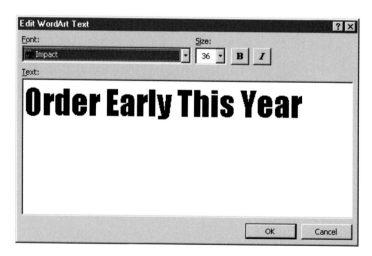

3. The Word Art toolbar lets you adjust how far apart your letters are, change the fill and letter outline qualities, and even change the entire shape and design of your Word Art creation. You can also make the Word Art text vertical rather than horizontal, rotate the text, and change the text justification.

4. Word Art creations also have a special yellow bounding box that allows you to interactively alter certain aspects of your text art shape: for example, to make the curve or slant of the text more acute or change the sharpness of a Word Art angle. Use the other bounding boxes to reshape and resize your Word Art image, just as you would any other clipart, drawing, or picture in Excel.

Adding Clipart to Your Spreadsheet

Clipart images are pre-drawn pictures that are included on your Office 2000 CD (see Figure 9.4). There are tens of thousands of them, arranged into catalogs. Some are rather cartoon-like, and some appear as hand-drawn artwork. The CD also contains photographs in the same clipart catalogs as the rest of the images. To insert a clipart image, first open a collection of catalogs and select one. Selecting a catalog helps narrow your search, so that you need not wade through more than 10,000 clipart images to find the one you want to use.

To place a clipart image in your spreadsheet, do the following:

1. On the drawing toolbar, click the Insert Clipart icon. The Insert Clipart dialog box appears, displaying icons that represent dozens of categories.

2. Either scroll through all the categories using the scroll bar on the right side of the dialog box and click the category that most relates to the topic you want for your image, or type keywords in the Search for Clips field at the top of the dialog box. For example, if you are looking for pictures of a business meeting, you might type keywords such as "business," and "people." The combination of these two keywords should narrow your search considerably. Then press ENTER, and the program will begin to search the clipart catalogs for images that match your

3. Click an image to reveal four options:

Insert Clip into Spreadsheet
Preview Clip
Add Clip to Favorites
Find Similar

1. After the Insert Clipart dialog box appears, type keywords to help narrow your search for the right image.

2. The images in the catalog change to reflect your search.

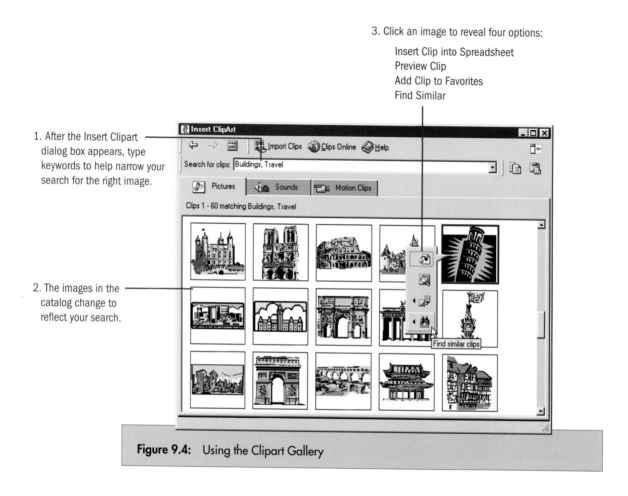

Figure 9.4: Using the Clipart Gallery

keywords. When Excel is finished, the Insert Clipart dialog box will display all the images that meet the criteria indicated by your keywords.

3. Whether you select your image by first opening a catalog or using keywords, the next step is the same. Once you see the image you want to use, just double-click it, and it will appear in your spreadsheet.

4. Use the bounding boxes to resize your clipart image and move it anywhere you like by dragging it with the mouse.

5. To add a border or fill to the clipart image, right-click it, select Format Picture, and choose the Colors and Lines tab.

Inserting Images from Other Sources

You are not limited to graphics from Microsoft's clipart collection. More than two dozen graphic file types are compatible with Excel. If you've scanned an image you'd like to use in your spreadsheet or created an image in a graphic editing program, it's easy to use such images in Excel. Here's how:

1. Click your spreadsheet where you'd initially like the graphic to appear. Remember that you can move and resize the graphic once you've inserted it.

2. From the Insert menu, select Picture and then From File. A browse menu appears.

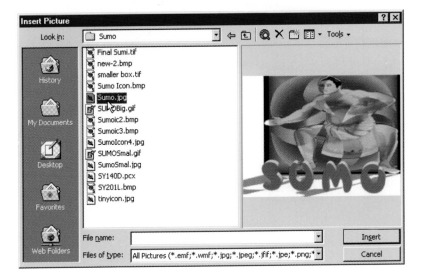

3. Use the browse menu to locate the image you want to include. In the drop-down Files of Type menu, make sure All Pictures appears in the field. This will ensure that your file type will be recognized during your search.

4. Click the drop-down Look In menu to locate the drive and folder that contains your image. When the Browse menu accesses an image, you'll see it appear in the Preview screen on the right.

5. To Insert the image, click it in the list of files and then click the Insert button. The image will appear in your spreadsheet.

6. The image will probably be too big, so use the bounding boxes on the corners to drag inward and resize it. You can move the image by placing your mouse anywhere inside the picture area. When your mouse cursor becomes a four-point arrow, you can click and drag the image to a new location on your spreadsheet.

7. To add an outline or otherwise edit the picture, right-click it and choose Format Picture. Select a tab and begin editing.

Editing Graphics

When you deploy a picture or any kind of graphic and you find yourself moving it around your page to maximize its appeal, remember this: you can do more than simply create a graphic and let it sit there. We'll now explore some tools for making graphics truly come alive on your page.

After initially creating or importing a graphic, you can:

- Resize it
- Move it
- Create a border around it
- Recolor it
- Place text inside it
- Draw on it
- Layer other graphics over or under it

Moving, Nudging, and Aligning Images

When you create a drawing or import a picture, you'll likely want to reposition it in relation to the other objects on your page. There are a number of tools for accomplishing this. You can simply move the image with your mouse or use the keyboard's arrow keys to gently nudge the image, little by little, to a new location, or you can use the Align tools to line up images along an exact center or margin. Here's how to move images around your spreadsheet once you've created them:

- After creating an image, place your mouse cursor somewhere near the center of it (not near a bounding box on the edge). When the mouse cursor becomes a four-point arrow, press and hold the mouse, dragging the image anywhere on your spreadsheet.

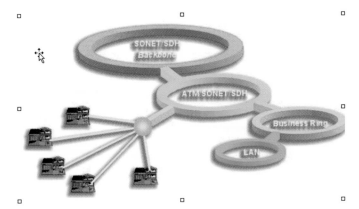

- To move your image only a centimeter or two in any direction, select the image and use the arrow keys. Pressing an arrow key nudges the picture in the direction indicated on the arrow.

- To evenly arrange a group of images so that they all line up along a particular margin, use the Align or Distribute command, as shown in Figure 9.5. The steps that follow show how.

  1. Select the images you want to align, using the mouse and the SHIFT key to select multiple images.

  2. Make sure the drawing toolbar is visible (if it isn't, right-click any toolbar and select Drawing) and then click the Draw menu at the left of the toolbar.

  3. Choose Align or Distribute and select one of the alignment options. (If you do not see Align or Distribute in the Draw menu, click the double-arrow at the bottom of the menu, and this option will appear. In Office 2000, some menu options do not appear until they are used a first time.)

1. These three images need to be aligned horizontally.

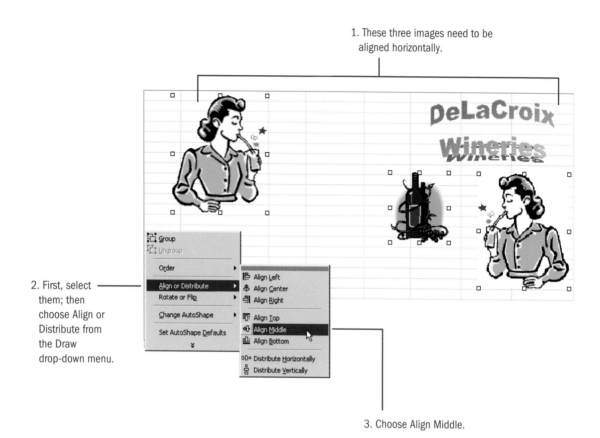

2. First, select them; then choose Align or Distribute from the Draw drop-down menu.

3. Choose Align Middle.

4. The three target objects will be aligned along their horizontal centers.

Figure 9.5: Use the Align or Distribute commands to center and evenly distribute pictures.

Grouping and Layering Images

Ideally, the images you use together on your spreadsheet should form some sort of composition. Even simple items like circles and arrows should be grouped to show that they belong together. Excel provides a few composition tools to facilitate this.

- Layer your images so they fit well together. For example, if you create a box filled with color, use that box as a background.

- To make sure the box you just created really sits behind the other images, right-click the image, choose Order from the shortcut menu that appears, and select Send to Back.

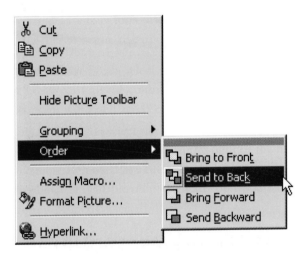

- To bring an image to the front (for example, if one picture has fallen behind something else and you'd rather it be near the front), right-click the image, choose Order, and select Bring to Front (see Figure 9.6).

Once you've organized and arranged your images to your liking, group them together so you can move them around as a unit instead of painstakingly moving them one at a time and then trying to get them back the way they were before. To group images, do the following:

1. Select each image you want to group together. To select multiple images, press SHIFT while clicking the images.

2. Right-click the images you want to group and select Grouping from the shortcut menu that appears; then choose Group.

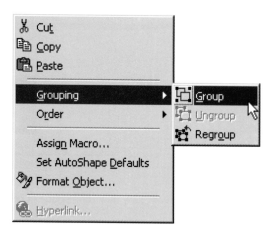

From here on, a single bounding box will surround all the images you've grouped. They can be moved and resized as a unit. To ungroup them, just select the group, right-click, choose Grouping, and then choose Ungroup.

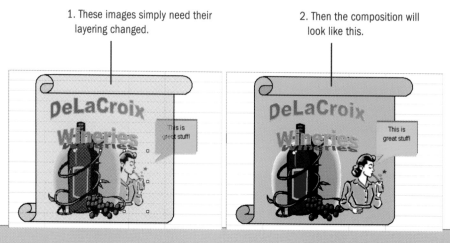

Figure 9.6: Layering images makes a big difference in how they appear together.

Cutting, Copying, and Pasting Images

Using just about any graphic editing program, you can create an image, copy it to the Windows clipboard, and paste it directly into Excel. However, this technique will increase your spreadsheet's file size greatly, so avoid pasting more than a handful of images into your spreadsheet.

Once you've pasted an image into your spreadsheet, all the resizing, reshaping, fill, and border tools are fair game. You can also change the image's color depth, insert text boxes, and otherwise treat this pasted image as you would any other object.

Paste Special

Sometimes Excel may not automatically recognize the type of image you are trying to paste into your spreadsheet. For example, if you paste an image from a graphic editing program that is not well known, you may have to identify this image as a bitmap to get Excel to display it correctly.

If you initially have trouble pasting an image into your spreadsheet, do the following:

1. Delete the image you've pasted.

2. Paste again, but this time try pasting with the Paste Special command (from the Edit menu, select Paste Special).

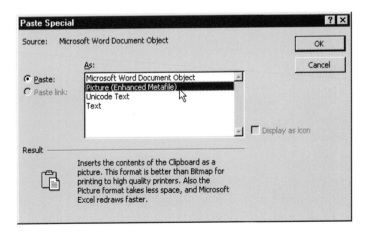

3. You'll see three or four options. These options force Excel to apply a certain file-type filter to your pasted image, allowing the image to appear as it should. It's sometimes hard to predict which option will work; simply try one option at a time until one of them works.

4. Each time Paste Special attempts unsuccessfully to paste your image, don't forget to delete whatever appears as a result of the unsuccessful attempt.

Changing a Picture's Color Depth

At times, you may want to use just a hint of a picture, faded into the background—something behind your spreadsheet. This is called a watermark. At other times, you may want to use a picture that uses no colors but, rather, is a mixture of shades of gray. Excel facilitates these techniques, allowing you to change a picture's color depth with a few mouse clicks.

To change a picture's color depth, do the following:

1. Click the image you want to change and make sure the picture toolbar is visible. If it isn't, right-click the picture and choose Show Picture Toolbar.

2. With the picture selected, click the Image Control icon on the toolbar (the second icon from the left). You'll see a menu with four color depth options:

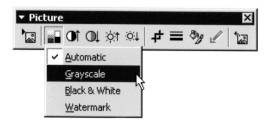

- **Automatic**   This setting retains the colors used by the original picture.

- **Grayscale**   Choose this option to remove all color information from the image. Rather than colors, the details of the picture will be redrawn in 256 shades of gray, ranging from black to white.

- **Black & White**   This setting is suitable only for simple line drawings. It removes all shading and colors from the image, using only black to draw the image details.
- **Watermark**   This option creates a very faded version of the image. Watermarks are suitable for backgrounds.

Graphic Insertion Methods

This section will be especially important to you if you have a slower computer, or if you plan to employ lots of graphics in your spreadsheets.

To place a graphic in your spreadsheet, you can:

- Insert an image from the Office 2000 Clipart Gallery or another picture source on your computer
- Copy an image from a graphic editing program to the Windows clipboard and then pasting it into your spreadsheet
- Link an image to your spreadsheet, so that the image appears in your spreadsheet but does not significantly increase the size of your spreadsheet file

Pay attention to the method you choose for adding graphics to your spreadsheet, especially if your computer is somewhat underpowered, or if you intend to use lots of graphics. When it comes time for inserting graphics, remember these tips:

- If you open a graphic editing program to view or edit a picture and then cut it to the Windows clipboard and paste the picture into Excel, the size of your spreadsheet file will increase significantly. Cutting and pasting images into spreadsheets causes your spreadsheet to move a little slower each time you edit it or make any kind of change. Therefore, if you intend to use more than one or two graphics in your spreadsheet, avoid cutting and pasting.

- Using images supplied by the Office 2000 Clipart Gallery will not diminish your spreadsheet's performance, so long as you don't use many more than five or six small- to medium-sized pictures. If you have a high-powered machine, you may not notice any performance difference at all.

- If you use a repeating image in a spreadsheet, for example, a company logo or diagram that appears several times, consider linking the image to your spreadsheet: From the Insert menu, select Object; then click the Create from File tab. Locate the image and then check the Link to Object check box. This method is superior to pasting or inserting the image for the following reasons:

  - When you change the image in a graphic editing program (for example, if you change the colors used in your company logo), then that new image will appear automatically in your spreadsheet.

  - When you link an image to your spreadsheet, then any change you make to that image is automatically reflected in any document it is linked to.

  - Linked images do not significantly increase your spreadsheet's file size. Even placing your company logo on every page of your spreadsheet will not make your computer run any slower or otherwise diminish performance. Note that if you link an image, Excel "remembers" the location of that image, so if you move the image, Excel cannot display it. If that happens, use the Edit | Links menu to reestablish the link.

- Employing arrows, lines, circles, and other drawn shapes will not interfere with your spreadsheet's performance.

Checkpoint

In this chapter, you learned all about using graphics in your spreadsheets. The next few chapters describe some more advanced techniques. You'll learn steps for reducing the tedium of some Excel tasks (by using macros, in Chapter 10) and leveraging Excel's power to predict trends based on your own criteria (by automating what-if projects, in Chapter 11), and you'll get acquainted with how your spreadsheets can be deployed on the Internet as well as on a company-wide intranet (in Chapter 12).

CHAPTER 10

Introduction to Macros

INCLUDES

- Recording your own macros
- Running macros—to save time!
- Using menu commands and toolbar buttons to run your macros
- Assigning macros to graphic objects
- Deleting macros
- Displaying your Personal Macro Workbook
- A brief introduction to ActiveX controls

Record a Macro ➡ pp. 235–236

1. Pull down the Tools menu, point to Macro, and then choose Record New Macro.
2. In the Record Macro dialog box, type a name for the macro, select a shortcut key for the macro if you want, and choose where to store the macro.
3. Click OK.
4. Perform the actions that you want to record.
5. Click the Stop Recording button.

Run a Macro ➡ pp. 237–238

1. Pull down the Tools menu, point to Macro, and then choose Macros.
2. Double-click the macro name in the list.

Assign a Macro to a Menu Command ➡ p. 238

1. Record the macro.
2. Choose Tools | Customize.
3. Click the Commands tab; then scroll down and select Macros from the Categories list.
4. Drag Custom Menu Item to a position on a menu (the menus drop down as you move Custom Menu Item toward them).
5. Right-click the new menu item. On the resulting shortcut menu, type a name for the item and then click Assign Macro.
6. Select the macro that the button should run and then click OK.
7. Click Close to close the Customize dialog box.

Assign a Macro to a Toolbar Button ➡ pp. 238–241

1. Record the macro.
2. If necessary, display the toolbar to which you want to add the macro with View | Toolbars.
3. Choose Tools | Customize.
4. Click the Commands tab; then scroll down and select Macros in the Categories list.
5. Drag Custom Button to a position on a toolbar.
6. Right-click Custom Button. In the resulting shortcut menu, type a name for the button, change the button image if you want, and then click Assign Macro.
7. Select the macro that the button should run and then click OK.
8. Click Close to close the Customize dialog box.

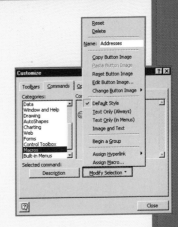

Assign a Macro to a Graphic Object ➡ pp. 241–242

1. Make sure you have an object in your worksheet that you want to use as a button.
2. Display the drawing toolbar and select the graphic object so it is surrounded by handles.
3. Right-click anywhere on the object and choose Assign Macro from the shortcut menu.
4. Double-click the macro that you want to assign to the object.

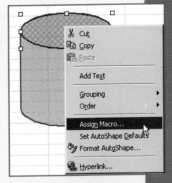

Delete a Macro ➡ p. 243

1. Pull down the Tools menu, point to Macro, and then choose Macros.
2. Click the macro name you want to delete.
3. Click Delete.

Display Your Personal Macro Workbook ➡ pp. 243–244

The Personal Macro Workbook is created automatically when you create a macro and opt to store your creation in the Personal Macro Workbook.

- To display your Personal Macro Workbook, pull down the Window menu, select Unhide, and select Personal.
- To hide the workbook again, select Hide from the Window menu.

We're creatures of habit. We develop patterns—ways of doing things—that we repeat, if not out of habit, then out of convenience. Perhaps you type the same heading on every worksheet or have a special format that you like to apply to cells. Maybe there's a formula that you use often or a certain template that's your favorite. Rather than repeat a series of actions each time you want to perform them, you can let Excel do it for you.

In this chapter, you'll learn about macros (in a macro, Excel remembers your actions and plays them back later); you'll learn how to record and run macros and how to delete them. In no time at all, you'll be sitting back and watching Excel do your work for you!

Understanding Macros

A macro is a collection of actions—keystrokes and menu and toolbar selections—stored together as one unit. So instead of having to perform two keystrokes, choose options from dialog boxes, and click a bunch of buttons. Later, select the macro from a list, press a key combination, or click a toolbar button. In a sense, a macro is just like a shortcut key, button, or menu item that's already built into Excel. The only difference is that a macro performs the functions that *you* tell it to perform.

Macros not only speed up your work with Excel but also help you to be consistent and to avoid mistakes. Suppose that you're creating a series of worksheets for the annual budget. You want all of the worksheets to have the same look and feel and to share some common elements. Rather than try to remember what formats to apply, just create one or more macros to apply them for you.

Recording Your Own Macros

Before you start recording macros, here are three points to keep in mind:

- When you play back your macro, the screen should look very similar to the screen you recorded the macro on. A macro remembers only your keystrokes. It does not take a snapshot of what the screen looked like before you started recording. For example, if you record a macro involving two spreadsheets that are open at the same time, you must open those two spreadsheets before you can play back your macro.

- Don't record a macro that involves clicking the mouse on an object that may not be there later. For example, a macro that includes selecting specific data in, say, cell A32, may not be useful to you, unless you plan to use it only on that spreadsheet with that exact data set.

- However, a macro can "memorize" chores that involve closed toolbars. If you record a macro that requires the presence of a particular toolbar—for example, creating a text box requires that the drawing toolbar be open—the macro can play back that task even if the toolbar is not visible. So even after you close the drawing toolbar (using this one example), the macro will create a text frame, even if that essential toolbar is not visible at the moment.

Here's how to record a macro (see Figure 10.1):

1. From the Tools menu, select Macro and choose Record New Macro from the flyout menu that appears (if Macro is not

visible on the Tools menu, click the double arrow at the bottom of the menu, and you'll see it).

2. In the Record Macro dialog box that appears, type a name and a description in the appropriate fields. Some characters are not allowed in macro names, so try to stick to letters. No spaces are allowed in macro names.

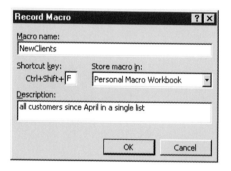

CAUTION

Some letters, when used in conjunction with the CTRL key, are already assigned by Excel to valuable shortcuts. For example, CTRL-C copies selected content to the clipboard. So try to pick a shortcut key that is not already spoken for. Assign a letter with SHIFT-CTRL rather than just CTRL.

3. Create a shortcut key combination if you like. The Record Macro dialog box provides the CTRL key. Type any other letter. Later, you can activate your macro by pressing CTRL plus the other letter you specified. For this macro, I pressed the SHIFT key and F at the same time. Therefore, pressing SHIFT-CTRL-F simultaneously will activate the macro I created.

4. When you're finished, click Close, and the Record Macro dialog box is replaced by a tiny "Stop" icon. The presence of this icon is the only indication that your keystrokes and mouse clicks will be recorded.

Creating a Sample Macro

Let's create a macro that types your return address in a single cell.

1. Click any Excel cell and type your first name.

2. Press ALT-ENTER and type your address.

3. Press ALT-ENTER again and type your city, state, and Zip code. Pressing ALT-ENTER prevents Excel from carrying over your address information into a new cell each time you press ENTER.

4. When you've finished entering your Zip code, click the green check on the formula bar.

5. Select the right border of the cell containing your address information and stretch it to the right, to accommodate the width of each line of data.

6. Click the address in the formula bar. This again makes the green formula check mark appear.

7. Click the check mark, which locks in the cell width adjustment you just made.

8. Click the Stop button (the black square) on the tiny Record Macro icon.

Although you'll see no indication on the screen, your macro is now saved and available to you. All that remains now is to determine the most convenient way to play it back and enjoy the time-saving benefit of this macro.

Running a Macro

When you want to use a macro, you just need to run it—that is, just tell Excel to do those tedious steps for you. To run a macro, pull down the Tools menu and point to Macro. Then choose Macros. You'll see the Macro dialog box, shown here. Double-click the name of the macro in the list, or select the macro name and click Run.

Rather than opening the Macro menu each time you want to run a macro, you can place a button on a toolbar or create a menu item in a regular Excel menu that you use every day—or, with the click of a mouse, you can turn any graphic into a clickable button that starts your macro (see Figure 10.1).

Using Menus and Toolbars to Run Your Macros

It's easy to run a macro by selecting it in the Macro dialog box, but it's even easier to just choose the macro from a menu or toolbar. When you assign a macro to a toolbar or menu, you don't have to open the workbook where the macro is stored—when you click the button, Excel opens the worksheet for you automatically. After you record the macro and assign it to a toolbar or menu, you're just a couple of clicks away from running the macro.

Assigning a Macro to a Toolbar Button

If you created a keyboard shortcut for your macro, you can always play back your macro with a couple of keystrokes. Otherwise, it's best to place the macro on a toolbar, so it will always be handy. To create a toolbar shortcut, do the following:

1. From the Tools menu, select Customize.

2. When the Customize dialog box appears, click the Commands tab.

3. In the Categories list, scroll down to Macros and click.

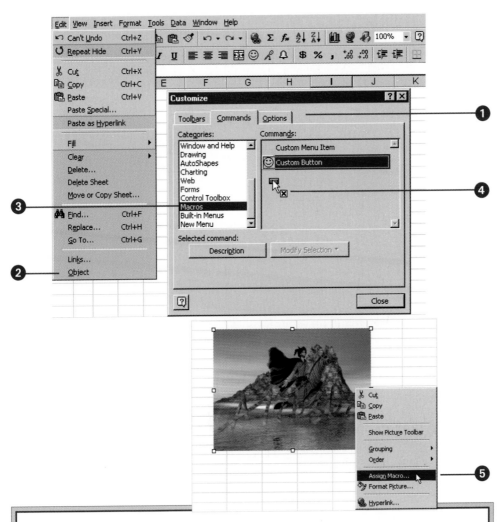

1 Select Customize from the Tools menu and click the Commands tab.

2 To turn your macro into a menu item and activate it from one of Excel's pull-down menus, click a menu now, to open it.

3 In the Categories menu, scroll down to Macros and click.

4 To create a toolbar button, drag Custom Button to an available toolbar. To create a menu item, drag Custom Menu Item to the menu you opened.

5 To use a graphic to activate your macro, right-click a graphic on your spreadsheet and select Assign Macro. In the Assign Macro dialog box, choose the macro you want to associate with this graphic.

Figure 10.1: Macro shortcuts can be saved on any Excel menu, as a button on a toolbar, or as a clickable graphic in your spreadsheet.

4. Click Custom Button and drag it to any toolbar you wish.

5. Back on the Customize tab, the Modify Selection drop-down button should now be available. Click it.

6. Scroll up to the Change Button Image option and click. A flyout menu appears, offering menu button selections for this macro tool button. Click your choice of button.

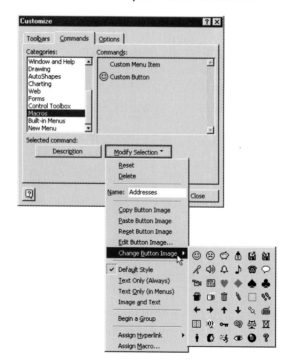

Clicking a new tool button on the Change Button Image menu automatically changes the tool button that you just edited on the toolbar above.

7. Click the Close button to close the Customize dialog box.

8. Click the tool button on the menu. The Assign Macro dialog box appears. You'll see the macro you created earlier in the list. (If your macro does not appear, click the Macros In drop-down menu, below the Macro Name menu, and locate the workbook where you earlier chose to save your macro.) Click the macro name.

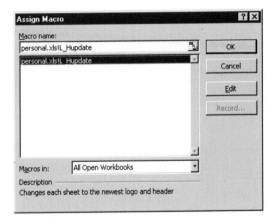

9. Click the OK button. This sets the tool button so that it always activates the macro whenever you click it.

From now on, every time you open Excel, the macro will be available to you when you click that tool button, as long as the toolbar you dragged it to is visible.

Assigning Macros to Graphic Objects

Assigning a macro to the toolbar is convenient, but a toolbar can hold only so many buttons. If you have a macro that you run only in a specific worksheet, why take up space in the toolbar? You can still run the macro with a click by assigning it to a graphic object on the worksheet itself.

In Chapter 9, you learned how to draw graphics. Well, you can convert a graphic into a button by assigning a macro to it. Because the graphic is saved as part of the worksheet, it is available whenever the worksheet is displayed on the screen.

To assign a macro to a graphic, use the following steps. Before you start, you need to make sure that you have an object in your worksheet that you want to use as a button. Using a text box is often a good choice, particularly if you want a text label on the button.

1. Display the drawing toolbar (choose View | Toolbars and select the drawing toolbar, if necessary). Select the graphic object so it is surrounded by handles.

2. Right-click anywhere on the object and choose Assign Macro from the shortcut menu.

3. In the dialog box that appears, double-click the macro that you want to assign to the object.

After you've assigned a macro to a graphic object, notice that your mouse cursor changes to a pointing hand whenever you move the mouse over the object. Just click the object to run the macro. Of course, if you click once to run the macro, that makes it a little tricky to select the object by clicking it. The easiest way to select a macro button or similar object is to right-click it, which both selects it and brings up the shortcut menu.

Deleting Macros

Before you delete a macro, stop and think a minute. Are you sure you want to undo all your hard work in creating the macro? (Just checking.)

Your first step in deleting a macro is to remove the corresponding menu item or toolbar button, if one was created. Follow these steps:

1. Choose Customize from the Tools menu.

2. Bring up the menu or toolbar with the macro item in it and right-click the item.

3. Choose Delete from the shortcut menu.

4. Click Close to close the Customize dialog box.

Here are some things to keep in mind about deleting macros:

- To delete a macro from another workbook, open the other workbook first before deleting.

- To delete a macro from your Personal Macro Workbook, you have to display the personal workbook first (this procedure is covered in the next section, "Displaying Your Personal Macro Workbook").

- To delete all of the macros from your Personal Macro Workbook, just delete the file Personal.xls stored in the Xlstart folder in your Excel folder (or Office folder, if you're an Office user). Don't worry, Excel will create a new Personal Macro Workbook the next time you choose to save a macro there.

Displaying Your Personal Macro Workbook

Before you can delete or modify a macro that you've assigned to your Personal Macro Workbook, you have to unhide the personal workbook—that is, make sure it is displayed in the window. The workbook is open when you start Excel, but it does not automatically appear in a window. To display your Personal Macro Workbook, use these steps.

1. Pull down the Window menu and click Unhide. You see a dialog box listing all of your hidden windows (there is usually only one).

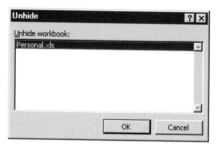

2. Click Personal; then click OK.

You can leave your Personal Macro Workbook displayed and switch to your other workbook using the Window menu. If you then exit Excel with your Personal Macro Workbook displayed, it appears on the screen the next time you start Excel. If you close the Personal Macro Workbook, however, you won't be able to use its macros until you open it again. So rather than close it, just hide it again. To hide the workbook, display the workbook (make it active) and then choose Hide from the Window menu.

Checkpoint

If it sounds like macros can help make your life easier, you're right. As you have learned in this chapter, macros can take the most tedious and time-consuming task and turn it into a simple keystroke or click of a toolbar button. Rather than typing the same information over and over and over again, you can just have Excel do it for you. Now that's using your noggin!

Up next is Chapter 11, where you'll learn a bit more about letting Excel do the work for you. Specifically, you'll learn about automating what-if projects. Then in Chapter 12, you'll learn to use Excel to publish information on the Internet or on an intranet (yes, Excel can even help you onto the information superhighway).

Automating What-If Projects

INCLUDES

- Organizing what-if projects
- Using scenarios
- Finding the right number with Solver

Create Scenarios ➡ pp. 250–253

1. Design your what-if worksheet and select the changing cells in the worksheet.

2. Select Scenarios from the Tools menu; then click Add in the Scenario Manager dialog box.

3. Type the scenario name, verify the contents of the Changing Cells text box, select a protection option if desired, and click OK.

4. Enter the changing cell values; click Add to add another scenario if desired.

5. Repeat steps 3 and 4 for each scenario. Click OK when you're done.

View Scenarios ➡ p. 254

1. Select Scenarios from the Tools menu.

2. Click the name of the scenario you want to display.

3. Click Show.

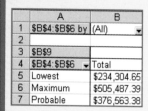

Create Scenario Summaries and Pivot Tables ➡ pp. 254–256

1. Select Scenarios from the Tools menu.

2. Click Summary or Pivot Table.

3. Enter or select the result cells in the Result Cells text box.

4. Select the report type: Scenario Summary or Scenario Pivot Table.

5. Click OK.

Protect Scenarios ➡ p. 256

1. Pull down the Tools menu, choose Protection, and select Protect Sheet.
2. Select the Scenarios check box if it is not already selected; click OK.

Use Solver ➡ pp. 257–261

1. Create the what-if project and click the target cell.
2. Select Solver from the Tools menu.
3. In the Solver Parameters dialog box, choose Max, Min, or Value Of and enter a specific value. Enter or drag over the changing cells, or click Guess. Click Add to add a constraint.
4. In the Add Constraint dialog box, enter or click the cell reference, select an operator, and enter the constraint value. Click Add to add another constraint if desired.
5. Repeat step 4 for each constraint. Click OK when you're done.
6. Back in the Solver Parameters dialog box, click Solve.
7. In the Solver Results dialog box, choose to keep the results that Solver found or to restore the original values. You can also select one or more report types. If you want to save your results as a scenario, click Save Scenario, enter a scenario name, and click OK.

Spreadsheets allow us to manipulate factors such as time, and variables such as interest rate, letting us imagine "What if I had *more* time to pay off this debt? How much *lower* would my payment be?" or "If the interest rate continues to rise, how much sooner can I earn back my investment?" In Excel, projected outcomes based on variable data, are called *scenarios*.

In this chapter, you'll learn how to generate reports on your scenarios with Scenario Summaries and Pivot Tables. Then you'll look at Excel's Solver feature, which lets you pick one desirable outcome and then prompts you to specify how much or how little other factors can drift in an effort to reach this outcome.

Keeping Track of Changing Variables

Spreadsheet data is composed of intricate pieces, and together the pieces form a whole picture, usually a financial one. However, the currency itself is only part of what's important. We must also factor in time, interest rate, and other constraints that affect the spreadsheet's overall message.

What Is a Scenario?

Imagine that you are looking at a spreadsheet that calculates an amount borrowed, the interest rate, and the years allowed to pay off a loan, as well as the monthly payment amount. In Excel's terminology, each time you manipulate *one* of these factors, you are creating a scenario. For example, raising the monthly payment on this loan by $50 dollars represents one scenario, and lowering the payment while extending the time to pay it back represents another scenario.

What Is Scenario Manager?

Rather than making you flip through lots of scenarios and risk forgetting the important conclusions associated with each set of changes, Excel provides Scenario Manager, which is a dialog box that saves the scenarios you generate, along with meaningful titles. Its purpose is to keep track of all your scenarios, giving you more freedom to play with the data without worrying about losing the thread. Later, you can use Scenario Manager to determine which set of figures turned out to be the most flattering to your viewpoint.

Scenario Manager saves all your "what ifs" along with your spreadsheet data, so you can have a permanent record of these slightly different (or more than slightly different) takes on your figures. This way, when you save your spreadsheet, you're also saving a set of contingencies, or projections, and their possible outcomes.

How Scenarios Work

Scenario Manager requires that your spreadsheet have at least one formula. Scenarios require that you allow one factor to remain unchanged (for example, the number of payments per year, or the interest rate), while you allow the other factors to drift up or down and the program calculates possible outcomes. For example, you might pose the question: "If I allowed the interest rate to go up a little, and the payments to grow by a few dollars, how much more could I borrow?" That would be one scenario. Another scenario might be, "If the interest rate is left unchanged, and I were to borrow less money, how much would my payments drop?" Scenario Manager then saves these several possible twists on the spreadsheet, along with your data, and allows you to scroll among them with a couple of mouse clicks.

Starting with Good Data

Before diving into Excel's Scenario and Solver features, look at your what-if worksheet carefully. Make certain that you've included all of the variables—the changing cells—that affect the results. And make sure that there aren't any stray cell references in formulas or functions that can affect the results without your being aware of the changes. Use the auditing tools discussed in Chapter 14 to make sure.

Also, locating the variables and answer cells cleverly can save you time and frustration. The answer to your what-if problem will be values in one or more cells. These are called result or target cells, and they must contain formulas or functions that reference the changing cells. If you place these close to the changing cells, you won't have to spend too much time scrolling around the worksheet to see your results.

Creating a Scenario

	A	B
1	Mortgage Analyzer	
2		
3	Income	$85,000
4	Loan Amount	$125,000
5	Interest Rate	9.2%
6	Term	30
7	Payment	$1,024
8		
9	Total Paid	$368,575

To create a scenario, you need a worksheet containing your what-if problem. As an example, let's use the simple mortgage analyzer shown here.

To perform a what-if analysis, you would change one or more of the values in cells B4, B5, and B6. What if the interest rate goes down to 8-percent, or you take out a 15-year loan, or you borrow less money? How would that affect your monthly mortgage payment and the amount that you pay? There are an awful lot of combinations that you can try—too many to trust your memory. Instead, just create a set of scenarios. Follow these steps, which use the same cells for all three scenarios (cells B4, B5, and B6):

1. Choose which cells you want to change (you don't have to use the same ones with every scenario).

2. Select Scenarios from the Tools menu to see the Scenario Manager dialog box, which will list your scenarios. Right now, nothing is listed because you haven't yet created a scenario.

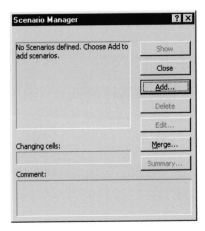

3. Click Add to see the Add Scenario dialog box. This is where you name the scenario and choose which cells you want to change.

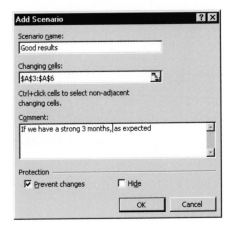

4. Enter a name for the scenario that explains how it fits into the scheme of things. For example, I entered **Good Results**, because this first scenario assumes that all will go well for the business in question. The current active or selected cells are listed in the Changing Cells text box.

5. Click the get-out-of-the-way button at the right side of the Changing Cells text box, so you can see the cells you want to change as part of the scenario.

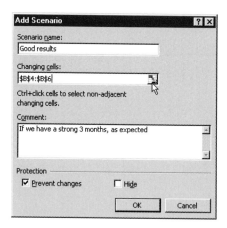

6. Select the cells you want to change. If you're following along with this Mortgage Analyzer example, choose B4, B5, and B6.

7. Click the come-back-now button at the right side of the field when you've selected the cells on the worksheet.

8. Add a comment if you wish. This comment will be visible whenever you access this scenario. When Scenario Manager starts to display lots of scenarios, you'll appreciate an identifying comment to jog your memory.

9. Click OK. You'll see a dialog box showing the changing cells and their current contents.

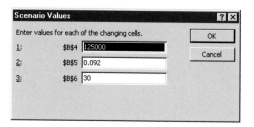

10. To add more scenarios, click Add in the Scenario Manager dialog box. The Add Scenario dialog box appears, so you can name a new scenario, verify the changing cells, and pick protection options. If you're following along with this Mortgage Analyzer example, type **Minimum** as the scenario name. Then click OK.

11. In the Scenario Values dialog box, enter the following values in the changing cells to create another scenario:

    Cell B4   7500
    Cell B5   .05
    Cell B6   35

12. Click Add for one more scenario. Name it Hopeful, click OK, and then enter the following values:

    Cell B4   8000
    Cell B5   .006
    Cell B6   25

13. After entering this last set of numbers, click OK in the Scenario Values dialog box to display the Scenario Manager dialog box again, this time listing the three scenarios:

Viewing Scenarios

Scenarios are saved along with the worksheet, so you can view them any time you want. Whenever you want to see how the changing cells affect the results, follow these steps:

1. Select Scenarios from the Tools menu. The Scenario Manager dialog box appears, listing the scenarios you have created.

2. Drag the dialog box out of the way so you can see the result cells (in this example, cells B7 and B9).

3. Click the scenario you want to see and click the Show button. Each time you do, Excel changes the values in the changing cells to match those entered in the scenario, so you can see their effects immediately.

4. When you're done, click Close. The worksheet displays the values from the last scenario viewed.

Creating Scenario Summaries

Summary reports allow you to compare the changing cells and the results, side-by-side, in a separate worksheet.

To create a Scenario Summary report, use these steps:

1. Select Scenarios from the Tools menu. The Scenario Manager dialog box appears, listing the scenarios you have created.

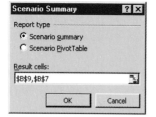

2. Click Summary to see a dialog box like the one shown here.

3. Drag or click the result cells to display those cell references in the Result Cells text box. For example, in the mortgage analysis, click cell B7 (the monthly payment) and then CTRL-click cell B9 (the total paid). You can also just type the cell references in the Result Cells text box. Either way, the report will show the effects of the changing variables on those two cells.

4. Select Scenario Summary as the report type and then click OK. Excel creates a new Scenario Summary worksheet, as shown here. It shows the values applied by each scenario and the results. You can print this summary for a recap of each combination in the what-if analysis.

Scenario Summary				
	Current Values:	Maximum	Minimum	Hopeful
Changing Cells:				
$B$4	$125,000.00	$125,000.00	$7,500.00	$8,000.00
$B$5	9.2%	9.2%	5.0%	6.0%
$B$6	30	30	35	25
Result Cells:				
$B$7	$1,024.00	$1,024.00	$1,024.00	$1,024.00
$B$9	$368,640.00	$368,640.00	$430,080.00	$307,200.00

Notes: Current Values column represents values of changing cells at time Scenario Summary Report was created. Changing cells for each scenario are highlighted in gray.

Creating Scenario Pivot Tables

With pivot tables, you can look at different data sets on a single spreadsheet. Change your view of a data segment by clicking a drop-down menu revealing more choices. To experiment with this feature, from the Data menu select Pivot Table and Pivot Chart Report. A wizard will guide you through the creation of a pivot table and chart. The details of this feature are beyond the scope of this book, but the best way to get your feet wet with pivot tables is to create one from a set of scenarios.

To create a pivot table from a scenario, click Summary in the Scenario Manager dialog box, and when the Scenario Summary dialog box appears, check the Scenario Pivot Table option button. You'll see a labeled table with drop-down menus, as shown here.

	A	B	C
1	$B$4:$B$6 by	(All)	
2			
3		Result Cells	
4	$B$4:$B$6	$B$7	$B$9
5	Hopeful	1024	307200
6	Maximum	1024	368640
7	Minimum	1024	430080

The drop-down menu lets you determine which data set (scenario) you want to view. When you've created complex scenarios with many variables and parameters, the ability to click and see a single set of results can be very helpful.

Changing Scenarios

If you want to see other combinations of variables, you can create additional scenarios. You can also return to existing scenarios to modify the name, the changing cells, and the values of the variables. Either way, try these steps:

1. Make sure you're back in your original sheet with the formulas and not the Scenario Summary sheet.

2. Choose Tools | Scenarios, select the scenario name, and then click Edit to see the Edit Scenario dialog box—an almost identical twin to the Add Scenario dialog box.

3. Edit the name, changing cells, description, and protection, as appropriate. Then click OK to display the values.

4. When the values are as you want them, click OK (there is no Add option this time around).

Protecting Scenarios

The Add Scenario and Edit Scenario dialog boxes contain protection options—but they don't do the job completely. To implement reliable protection, you have to protect the entire worksheet. Here's how:

1. Close the Scenario Manager and then pull down the Tools menu.

2. Point to Protection; then click Protect Sheet to see this dialog box.

3. Select the Scenarios check box, if it is not already selected.

4. Click OK.

Using Solver

Scenario Manager makes it easy for you to keep track of different scenarios, but what if you're looking for a specific result? For example, what if you know the result you want to achieve, but not the combination of variables? Suppose you want to pay $850 a month on a mortgage. How many combinations of loan amounts, interest rates, and terms would you have to enter to yield that payment amount? Do you have the time to add scenarios for every possible value, watching the result cells to see which gives you the answer you want? No way. Instead, you can have Excel find the values for you using Solver. Solver applies values to changing cells until a result cell reaches the maximum, minimum, or specific value that you designate.

Installing and Loading Solver

Solver is an extra feature—an add-in—of Excel. It takes some time and a little disk space to load add-ins, but you need load only those that you want to use.

   If Solver is not listed in your Tools menu and is also not in the Tools | Add-Ins dialog box, you'll need to fish out your Excel CD or disks and install Solver. Use the following procedure:

1. Choose Settings and then Control Panel from the Start menu.

2. Double-click Add/Remove Programs.

3. Click the Office or Excel option (depending on what you purchased) and then click the Add/Remove button. Insert the CD or disk when asked to do so.

4. Click Add/Remove in the Office Setup dialog box; then click the Excel option and click the Change Option button.

5. Click Add-ins; then click the Change Option button.

6. Click to put a check mark beside Solver.

7. Click OK or Continue repeatedly until you've completed the installation and you exit Setup.

After Solver has been installed, you may still have one more step necessary to load it for use. If Solver is not listed in your Tools menu, then it was not one of the add-ins loaded when you started Excel. To make sure Solver—or any other add-in—is loaded, pull down the Tools menu and click Add-Ins to see the following dialog box:

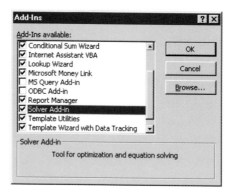

Scroll the list and select the check box for Solver Add-In and for any other features that you want to add. You can also deselect those you don't want to bother loading the next time you start Excel. Then click OK. Excel loads the add-ins that you selected; you do not have to wait until the next time you start Excel.

Solving What-If Problems

Solving what-if problems using Solver is similar to creating scenarios—again, you use the same processes of selecting cells and telling Excel what you want it to do. We'll see how to use Solver, working with the same mortgage analysis worksheet that we used for scenarios.

Selecting the Cells

First you need to select your target cells in your what-if worksheet.

1. Create a what-if worksheet.

2. Click the cell that you want to find the value for (called the target cell in Solver)—in this case, cell B7. The cell must

contain a formula or function that is calculated from other cells in the worksheet.

3. Pull down the Tools menu and click Solver to see the Solver Parameters dialog box. The address of the target cell appears in the Set Target Cell text box. If the address is not the cell you want to calculate, drag the dialog box out of the way (or click the get-out-of-the-way button) and click the target cell on the worksheet.

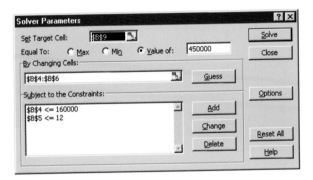

4. Choose the result you want Solver to calculate: the maximum or minimum calculated value or a specific value. For example, if you are trying to find a combination of variables that will give you a monthly payment of $850, select Value Of and enter 850 in the text box.

5. Designate the changing cells (the cells you want Solver to modify to arrive at the result). You could enter the cells yourself in the By Changing Cells text box, but instead click Guess. Excel examines the target cell, identifies the cell references in the formula or function, and then automatically assigns the referenced cells as the changing cells. If the guess is incorrect, enter the cells yourself.

Adding Constraints

So far, so good. But there is one problem. Depending on your worksheet, there may be many combinations of variables that achieve the same result. In most situations, you aren't just interested in the result, but how you get there. For example, Solver could calculate an $850 monthly mortgage payment based on a 1 percent loan. Since it's highly unlikely that you'll find such a loan—unless it's from a very close relative—the solution is invalid. You need to set some ground rules under which Solver will work.

These ground rules are called constraints, and they are restrictions on the values that Solver can apply to changing cells. In brief, constraints tell Solver the realities of life. In our mortgage example, we'll use a few simple constraints:

- The mortgage amount must be at least $80,000 but no more than four times your annual salary.
- The interest rate must be at least 6 percent but no more than 10 percent.
- The length of the loan must be for 30 years or less.

All of your constraints will be listed in the Subject to the Constraints list box in the Solver Parameters dialog box, and you'll use the Add, Change, and Delete buttons to work with them.

1. Click the Add button to create the first constraint and display the Add Constraint dialog box.

There are three elements in the Add Constraint dialog box: the cell reference, the constraint operator, and the constraint value. The cell reference is the address of a changing cell, the constraint operator is a logical operator, and the constraint value is a value or cell reference that limits the changing cell. A constraint is, essentially, an expression that evaluates to either a true or false value, and it can test for only one value.

The limitations on the valid mortgage amount must be formed by two constraints. The first will limit the amount to at least $80,000; the second to no more than four times the annual income.

2. Click cell B4, since the insertion point should be in the Cell Reference box. Excel inserts $B$4 into the box.

3. Point to the arrow next to the operator field to see the list of operators and select >=.

4. Click the Constraint text box and type 80000.

5. Click Add to accept the first constraint and to create the next one.

6. Click B4 again as the cell reference, choose the <= operator, and enter 4*B3 in the Constraint text box.

7. Click OK to accept the constraint and to redisplay the Solver Parameters dialog box listing the two constraints.

8. Now, on your own, add the following additional constraints to the Add Constraint dialog box:

CAUTION

If you click Add and decide not to create another constraint, click Cancel. You'll get an error message if you click OK.

Cell A5	<=	0.1
Cell A5	>=	0.06
Cell A6	<=	30

These should appear in the dialog box like this:

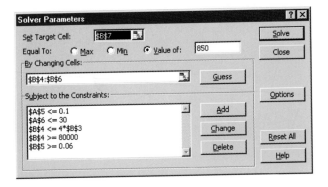

Viewing the Results

Now you're ready to see what Solver can do.

1. When you're done, display the Solver Parameters dialog box and click Solve.

   Solver begins applying values to the changing cells, keeping within the limitations of the constraints and observing the target cell. When it finds a combination, it displays the results on the worksheet, along with the Solver Results dialog box:

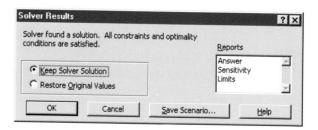

2. In this dialog box, you have two options: Keep Solver Solution or Restore Original Values. If you select Save Scenario, you can enter a scenario name, and Excel will save the values of the changing cells as a scenario; you can then choose to restore the original values, but you can also quickly display the Solver results by viewing the scenario from Scenario Manager.

SHORTCUT
You can CTRL-click on multiple report types, and Excel automatically creates each specified type, one after another.

Generating Reports

At this point, Solver also lets you generate three types of reports:

- An **Answer report** shows the original and final values of the target cell and the changing cells, along with the constraints.
- A **Sensitivity report** explains how sensitive the solution is to small changes in the target cell formula or in the constraints.
- A **Limits report** shows the values and the lower and upper limits of the target and changing cells while satisfying the constraints.

To generate a report, select each type you want (you can select more than one) and then click OK. Excel creates the reports in another worksheet or worksheets.

EXPERT ADVICE

To learn more about Solver, use Excel help and the sample file provided with Excel in the program Files\Microsoft Office\Office\Examples\Solver folder. You'll find examples of the types of problems that Solver can solve in the Solvsamp.xls workbook. Solvsamp includes six worksheets containing typical business what-if problems. After displaying the worksheet and opening Solver, you'll find that the parameters have already been set.

Checkpoint

In this chapter, you've learned about Scenario Manager and Solver, two tools that can help automate your what-if projects. Using these Excel features, you can estimate and calculate just about any scenario you can imagine—from estimating car payments to calculating your grade point average to determining how much to save for retirement.

Finally, in Chapter 12, you'll delve into the exciting world of intranets and the Internet. Here, you'll not only learn about intranets and the Internet, but you'll also learn how to publish your worksheets and charts on these networks.

CHAPTER 12

Excel, the Internet and Intranets

INCLUDES

- Creating links in Excel Documents
- Installing Internet and intranet tools
- Developing Internet-aware Worksheets
- Adding links to worksheets
- Saving worksheets for a Web
- Testing worksheets before publishing
- Publishing worksheets on a Web
- Sharing worksheets

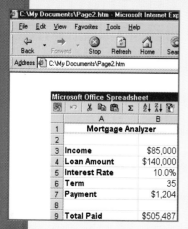

Decide to Publish on a Web ➡ pp. 270–271

1. The Internet is a worldwide network of computers that all speak the same language and can share information.

2. Intranets are very much like the Internet, but they contain only information that is accessible from within a company or organization.

3. HTML is the language used to make information available on a Web—either the World Wide Web or in a similar fashion on an intranet.

4. A Web is a network of information accessible through Internet browsers like Netscape or Internet Explorer.

5. URL (pronounced you-are-ell or Earl) stands for Uniform Resource Locator and is an Internet address.

6. You could put the latest company information on an intranet so everyone in the company can know what's going on, or you can put public information out on the Internet for the benefit of, say, your shareholders.

Load Internet and Intranet Tools ➡ pp. 271–273

1. Put your Office 2000 installation disc in the CD-ROM drive. Quit any programs you are running.

2. A Preparing to Install confirmation dialog box may appear. After a moment, you'll see the Office 2000 Setup screen. If you don't see it, click the My Computer icon, then click your CD-ROM drive icon. When the CD folder appears, click the Setup.exe icon.

3. On the Office 2000 Setup dialog box, click the Add or Remove Features Icon.

4. Click the plus sign next to the Office Tools icon.

5. Click the down-facing arrow on the Office Web Components icon, and chose Run All From My Computer.

6. Click the Update Now button.

7. A blue bar moving rightward indicates the installation progress.

8. When the update is finished, a confirmation screen will appear.

Add Links to Worksheets ➡ pp. 275–277

1. Click a cell and type the text you want to turn into a link.

2. Select Hyperlink from the Insert menu.

3. In the Insert Hyperlink dialog box, enter the URL or browse to the file to which you want to link. Using one of the options at the far left of the dialog box, you can create a document from scratch, and link to that.

4. If this Spreadsheet will be viewed by only the most current browsers (4.0 versions or higher), then you can create a screen tip, which is a short message that appears to the visitor when the mouse rolls over the cell with the link in it.

5. After choosing or creating a linked file, click OK.

Save Worksheets as Web Pages ➡ pp. 278–280

1. Open the worksheet.

2. Select File | Save as Web Page.

3. The Save As dialog box appears, with Web Page already specified as the Save as Type (see the bottom of the dialog box).

4. Determine if you want to save the entire workbook as a Web page, or only one sheet, clicking the appropriate radio buttons. If you choose "Selection: Sheet," you can click the Add Interactivity button, and your visitors will be able to edit the spreadsheet online, without downloading it.

5. Click Change Title to create a title that will be viewed by visitors at the top of the page. Remember that the document's File Name is not the same as the Web Page title.

Test the Worksheets Online ➡ p. 281

1. If necessary, display the Web toolbar by right-clicking on any toolbar, and choosing Web from the list.

2. Choose Go | Open from the Web toolbar.

3. Browse to the file you want to view or type the URL into the address box.

4. Click OK. Alternately, you can chose Web Page Preview from the File menu.

Publish Worksheets to a Website ➜ pp. 281–282

1. Open the worksheet you want to publish as HTML.

2. Select File | Save as Web Page.

3. Follow the onscreen instructions, remembering to select interactivity if you want it, and the cell ranges you want converted to a Web Page.

4. Select an FTP site for the File path.

5. Excel will begin uploading your page to the folder designated for you by your ISP or system administrator. The uploading process could take a few minutes, or even more.

6. When uploading is finished, you'll see a confirmation dialog box indicating that your page is uploaded.

Set up FTP Locations ➜ pp. 282–284

1. Select Save As from the File menu.

2. In the Save in list box, choose Add/Modify FTP Locations.

3. Type in the name of the FTP site provided by your network administrator or ISP support staff.

4. Type in the Username and Password you were given. Make sure your Username is known by Windows. If not recognized, open Control Panel, select Users, and add the required username.

5. Back at the Add FTP dialog box (from step 3), click Add to save the FTP site record.

6. Set up additional FTP sites, or click OK to finish.

Publishing Online with Advanced Options ➜ pp. 284–285

1. After giving your spreadsheet a title, click Publish. The Publish as Web Page dialog box appears.

2. Use the Choose dropdown menu to determine which sheets or cell ranges you want to publish to the Web.

3. If you've selected Add interactivity with, you can chose to publish your spreadsheet with simple spreadsheet functionality, allowing visitors to sort, rearrange, even add to the existing data, or use it as a Pivot Table. This allows visitors to arrange the data along different axes, reconfiguring and filtering the data with dropdown menus.

4. Click Publish, and your spreadsheet will be published as a Web Page in the folder specified in the File name data box.

Excel 97 was designed to be easily used with both the Internet and with corporate intranets. There are many uses for these online publishing features. For example, you can inform the entire company of the latest company sales figures (by publishing to an intranet, a company-wide network), or, put profit projections out on the Internet for the benefit of your shareholders around the world.

This chapter provides you with Internet basics and shows you how to use Internet tools efficiently and effectively. To get the most out of this chapter, you'll need a connection to the Internet (either direct or through your modem and an Internet Service Provider) or to your company intranet. You can use the hyperlink features without the benefit of the Internet or intranets.

Create Editable Online Spreadsheets

This is a rather exciting moment for Excel and Internet users, because with Office 2000, you can post Excel spreadsheets online that are fully editable by others, without having to convert the spreadsheet from a Web page format to an Excel file. If you want someone else to edit your Excel document, if they have Office 2000, all you need to do is upload the spreadsheet as a Web page. It can be edited online by your coworker, no matter where she or he is. When the spreadsheet is accessed, Excel toolbars appear while viewing online. No conversion is necessary. For you to view or further edit this spreadsheet, simply visit the Web page yourself, and build upon the changes your coworker has made. This means that Excel spreadsheets are now fully customizable, online documents that can be easily edited by any number of intranet or Internet-connected coworkers.

Deciding to Use Excel with Networks

Internet technology is becoming more a part of our regular computing day, and here are some reasons why:

- Technical support and other "extras" like free Excel templates and tutorials are readily available on the Web.
- Financial information can be published directly from your worksheets to the Web for everyone to see.
- You and others in your company can easily share information around the office, the city, or the world.

Differences Between the Internet and Intranets

A company-wide intranet is administered by a professional in your company who has deployed a variety of network technologies to make the computers in your company aware of each other. This is done for ease of file transfer, and as a way to publish company-wide information instantaneously. At times, financial data from an Excel spreadsheet will be of interest to everyone (or almost everyone) in your company. Thus, for you to have the tools to deploy your spreadsheets data across a company-wide intranet is a great idea. Here are two points to keep in mind regarding publishing Excel data throughout your company's intranet:

- Everyone can read your data even if they don't have Excel on their computer. Excel makes it easy to publish "standalone" spreadsheets that can be viewed by anyone with a network connection.
- Publishing Excel data across an intranet takes only a couple of minutes, and the process is not intimidating at all.

By contrast, posting information on the World Wide Web (the Internet) means that anyone with Internet access can view it. In some cases, it can even be tampered with. So posting sensitive financial information to the Web should not be done without forethought.

Remember: If you don't want everyone in the world to see it, don't publish it on the Web.

Getting Connected

Standard Internet technologies such as an Internet Service Provider (ISP) connection and a fairly up-to-date web browser are all you need to post Excel documents on the Web (the Internet). Newer versions of America Online and Prodigy will also provide the type of connection necessary to post an Excel document on the Web.

To post Excel documents on a company-wide intranet, your company's System Administrator (the "Network Person") will oversee all your connectivity needs.

If you need more information about actually getting connected to the network and what you can do after you get there, check out *The Internet for Busy People, Second Edition* by Christian Crumlish (Osborne/McGraw-Hill, 1997).

The next section of this chapter discusses the installation of Excel-related Internet tools. Even if you think you did a full installation of Office 2000, its worth reviewing this section, just to make sure you are really ready to go. Regarding intranets, check with your company's computer support group to make sure that your Internet or intranet connection works and that you have all the necessary passwords to use it. Then you'll be ready to roll.

By the way, throughout this chapter we'll just be using Internet as a generic term for Internet or intranet, just as we'll be using Web to describe either the World Wide Web or a corporate Web site.

DEFINITION

Browser:
A browser is a program that allows you to view HTML documents on the Internet or on an intranet. Browsers are used by the worksheet creator (such as yourself), who wants to view and test worksheets before publishing on a Web; browsers are also used by the people who will be viewing or modifying the worksheets you create.

Adding Internet and Intranet Tools

Now that you've decided to use Internet technologies to publish your Excel worksheets, let's make sure your tools are installed. You can get this out of the way quickly, just by seeing if Excel's File menu includes the feature "Save as Web Page." If so, then move on to "Publishing your Worksheets on a Web."

If you don't have the Save as Web Page option, you'll need to do some setup work before you can continue. Just follow these steps:

1. Put your Office 2000 installation CD in the CD-ROM drive. Quit any programs you are running, including the Office toolbar.

2. After a moment or two, you'll see the Office 2000 Setup screen. If you don't see it, click the My Computer icon, then click your CD-ROM drive icon. When the CD folder appears, click the Setup.exe icon.

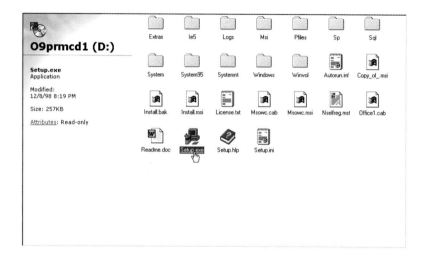

3. On the Office 2000 Setup dialog box, click the Add or Remove Features Icon.

4. Click the plus sign next to the Office Tools icon.

5. Click the down-facing arrow on the Office Web Components icon, and chose Run All From My Computer. The Description area should read "Components for publishing interactive web pages from Excel and Access."

6. Click the Update Now button. You'll see the Office 2000 Installation screen.

7. A blue bar moving rightward indicates the installation progress. A "percentage complete" progress indicator is also displayed.

8. When the update is finished, a confirmation screen will appear, indicating all went well.

Internet Explorer 5.0 is installed as part of the Office 2000 setup process. However, if you'd rather use Netscape, you can download the Netscape Navigator web browser for free from www.netscape.com. Once you've opened to Netscape's home page, click "Browsers."

If Internet Explorer 5.0 was not included in your installation, and you'd like to install it now, place your Office 2000 CD in your CD-ROM drive, and click the Ie5 folder. Open the folder labeled En, and then click the Ie5Setup.exe icon. Clicking this icon begins the process of installing Internet Explorer 5.0.

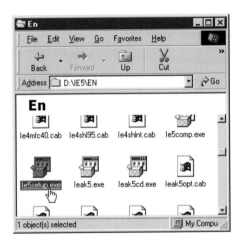

Publishing Your Worksheets on a Web

Putting your worksheets on a Web is basically a four-step process. You need to do the following:

1. Prepare your worksheets for publishing on a Web.
2. Save your worksheets in the proper format.
3. Test your worksheets.
4. Publish your worksheets.

The following sections will walk you through the process.

Step 1: Prepare Worksheets

Sometimes you'll develop worksheets with the express intent of publishing them on the Internet or an intranet. If you have the luxury of planning ahead, you can do some things to make the conversion go more smoothly or to make the information more useful to your readers. Specifically, keeping it simple, minimizing Excel graphics, and making links for your readers will ease the process.

Simple Spreadsheets Work Better

A good way to help your worksheets look good in a browser is to keep them simple. Although the Internet Assistant Wizard does a pretty impressive job converting worksheets, some features just don't convert well at all. Avoid using more than a few fonts. Don't throw in too many text formatting tricks. The less complex your spreadsheet is, the less chance there is of Excel running into a snag when it is converted to a Web page.

Use Minimal Graphics

Paying special attention to graphics is another good way to help your worksheets convert to HTML. In particular, liberal use of graphic objects (like OfficeArt), PivotTables, and AutoFilters have the potential to cause conversion problems. Charts convert just fine, though. Still, when you realize that a particular spreadsheet is bound for the Web, minimize your dependence on elaborate features. This does not mean you have to exclude them, but merely use them less.

Alternatives to Converting an Entire Workbook

If your project is very complex, consider saving charts in sheets by themselves, and uploading them one sheet at a time. Occasionally, the conversion process has problems with sheets that mix charts with tabular data, so it's better to just generate the charts as objects within a new sheet or to move the charts to individual sheets. (See Chapter 8 for the specifics about generating charts.)

Finally, you can help improve the usability of your worksheets on a network by dividing it into smaller pieces and linking them together. Using several small files that link together makes navigating through the information much easier. Think of it this way: when a browser loads a big file, it can take a long time. Similarly, scrolling through a big file can also take a long time. Providing smaller files with links minimizes loading time and can eliminate at least some of that dreaded scrolling. For example, create one spreadsheet called "Reports," and save it as an individual Web page. Next, save another spreadsheet related to the same project, perhaps a Price List or an Inventory Sheet. Save them as separate Web pages, even though they are part of the same project. You can link them together by creating hyperlinks that the visitor can use to navigate between the pages you've created.

Adding Links to Your Worksheets

If your worksheet logically relates to other worksheets, to other Office documents, or to specific Web sites on the Internet, you can create links between them. For example, if you are putting information about sales on a Web site, you might consider adding a link to information about the company itself. Or, if you've broken your worksheet into smaller pieces, you'll need to link the pieces together. You can also create links to other sheets in the same workbook.

For the following example, we'll put a text link to an HTML document on the Web (See Figure 12.1). You can also create a link to another file on your computer, or a link to an E-mail address.

1. Click the cell you want to turn into a link, and type text into it.

2. Click the Insert Hyperlink button on the standard toolbar. The Hyperlink dialog box appears.

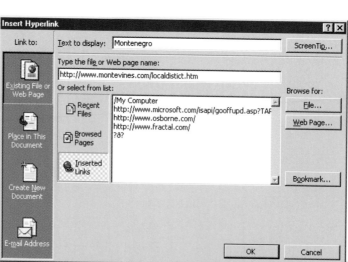

Figure 12.1: Creating a link from an Excel cell to a Web document

3. In the Insert Hyperlink dialog box, enter the URL (Uniform Resource Locator) or use the Browse button to browse to the file you want to link to. You can also chose from a list of recently opened files, or create a new file to link to.

4. If you are sure that only visitors who use the most updated browsers will visit this site, then include a screen tip, which is a short message that pops up when the visitor rolls the mouse over the link.

5. When linking to a file or site, try to be sure that the file or site will not be moved. The link you create will not be able to "follow" the target to a new location.

6. After you've created your link, click OK.

Now you can verify your link by clicking on it from the worksheet. Here are three points to keep in mind:

- If the object is on the Internet and you're not already connected, you may have to open your Internet connection first.
- If your web browser is properly installed, clicking the link should open the link target.
- If it's a file you've linked to, then the program associated with the file should open.

CAUTION

When creating links to Internet sites, go online yourself and double-check that the links you are including are still valid. Also, when creating a link to a file, make sure the visitor will truly be able to access that file. Does the file require a particular software program for the visitor to view it? Will the visitor have administrative rights to view the file? These questions need to be explored before you post your spreadsheet online for the world to see.

After viewing the site or file, you've verified that the link is correct. Simply close the browser or program whenever you like. Excel is still open, by the way. Verifying a link does not alter your spreadsheet or close Excel. Feel free to make more links. Unlike graphics or Excel formatting, creating links will not significantly increase the file size of your Excel document, nor will it make it more cumbersome to handle online.

Saving Along the Way

Adding links is time-consuming because each link must be verified. To make sure you don't lose your work, click the Save button every once in a while. Saving your document in this manner does not ready it for Web viewing, but it does preserve the changes you've made in your spreadsheet.

Editing Your Link

If you need to make changes to the hyperlink later, don't just click on it (that will just open it again). Rather, right-click on the cell with the link, then select Hyperlink, then Edit Hyperlink from the shortcut menu. This same menu contains the command to delete the link as well.

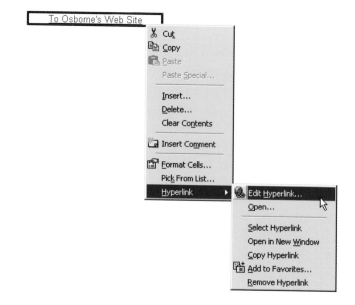

After you've developed your worksheet, you'll need to save the document for use on a Web.

Step 2: Save Worksheets

The first step in publishing your worksheets on a Web is to save them in the right file format. So far, you've been saving your worksheets as Excel files—with the .xls extension. When you want to publish your worksheets on a Web, you need to save them as web pages, using the .htm or .html extension.

HTML (which stands for HyperText Markup Language) is the language of Web technologies. By saving your worksheets as HTML documents, anyone using a Web browser will have to access your worksheets. In this release of Excel, Microsoft has added new functionality to spreadsheets for online use. As mentioned earlier, spreadsheets saved with Excel 2000 are fully interactive online, and can be edited by anyone with Internet Explorer 5, and the Web Office Components that are standard Office 2000 features. So it's best not to think of Excel 2000 spreadsheets that you've prepared for the web as simple HTML documents.

Let's briefly walk through the process of saving a spreadsheet as HTML (See Figure 12.2), and then check the results.

1. Open the worksheet you want to Save as Web Page.

2. Select File | Save as Web Page. A special Save As dialog box appears. It contains additional Web-aware options such as a Title field (for adding a Web page title to your spreadsheet), and options to save limited portions of your workbook as Web pages.

3. You may select only a segment of a spreadsheet, and save only that portion as a web page. If you do, then a "Selection" option appears in this dialog box, indicating that you can chose to not

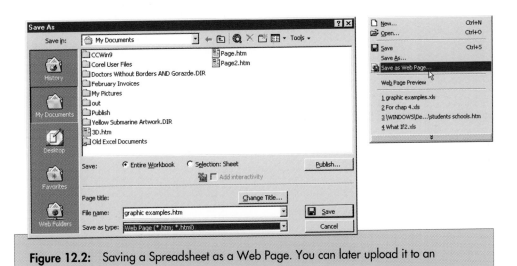

Figure 12.2: Saving a Spreadsheet as a Web Page. You can later upload it to an online location.

save the whole page, or workbook, but rather, just the cells you've previously selected.

4. In the Save In area, you can choose to save your Web-aware spreadsheet in one of four areas. However, it is highly recommended that you store all files related to Web pages in the same folder. Additionally, it's a good idea not to save Web data in folders that are used to save other file types as well. The best action to take is to create a new folder, and allow Excel to store all Web-related files there, when prompted. This assures that all your internal Hypertext links will still be accurate, after you've uploaded your page to its online location.

5. Provide a title and other descriptive information about the document. The information you provide here is the primary information your readers will see about your HTML document, so make it good.

6. After choosing a location, picking save options, and typing a title for your page, click Next.

CAUTION

Whatever you do, don't make a typo in your e-mail address. Excel automatically formats your email address as a hyperlink, with which visitors can generate an e-mail. Make sure this information is correct.

Step 3: Testing Worksheets

Testing your worksheets is highly important. In particular, you'll need
to make sure that they look the way you want and that the information
is accurate and complete. Even if you saved your Excel document
without interactivity, there will still be some variance in appearance
from browser to browser. To quickly check (approximately) how the
pages will look in a Web Browser, click Preview Web Page from the
File menu. To more thoroughly verify how the page will appear and
function online, do the following:

1. If it's not already available, display the Web toolbar by clicking
   the Web Toolbar button on the standard toolbar.

2. Choose Go | Open from the Web toolbar.

3. Browse to the file you want to view.

4. Click OK.

If your Web page does not appear as you thought it would, do not
try to go back and directly edit out the errors. For example, if a font
looks the wrong size, such a situation is rarely resolved by going back
into Excel and making it the right size. The problem is not the feature
itself. The problem is an error in the conversion process. If such an
error is suspected, consider implementing some of the steps discussed
above regarding simplifying your spreadsheet, removing unnecessary
graphics, and saving one sheet at a time. If you are happy with the way
your Web page looks and operates, proceed to the next step.

Step 4: Publish Worksheets

Well, now that you've created, saved, and tested your worksheets, it's
time to publish them. A technology exists solely for the purpose of
transferring files from your personal computer to an intranet or Internet
location. Not surprisingly, this procedure is called *File Transfer Protocol*

Who determines where you get to store your intranet or Internet-bound files? If you're posting your files to a company-wide intranet, your company's System Administrator will provide you with the Username, Password, and any other instructions you need. If the World Wide Web is your destination, then the technical support staff at your ISP will supply you with instructions.

(FTP). The process of uploading your files to your final intranet or Internet site will seem just like transferring a file from one folder to another using Windows Explorer. Actually, what you are doing is transferring a file from your computer to a remote location, meaning, another computer. In this case, the computer is managed by the ISP you do business with, or your system administrator.

Office 2000 makes it easy to upload files. You will not need any additional "FTP software" to make this happen. As you'll see in the next section, what you will need from the Web Gurus who are in charge of your uploading space, includes:

- An open Internet or intranet connection
- The location of the FTP site (for example ftp.mycompany.com)
- A Username
- A Password
- The path to the online folder where you have rights to store files

With these tools, you can implement a File Transfer Protocol session and begin uploading your spreadsheets. Once you've posted (uploaded) your files to the designated location, visitors are free to view and enjoy your work. After uploading the files correctly, you are officially "on the Web."

Setting Up FTP Locations

Before you can put your files on a server, you need to set up the FTP locations in Excel. To tell Excel about the FTP sites you have access to, do the following:

1. Select Save As from the File menu, which opens the Save As dialog box.

2. In the Save In list box, scroll way down and choose Add/Modify FTP Locations. The Add/Modify FTP Locations dialog box appears.

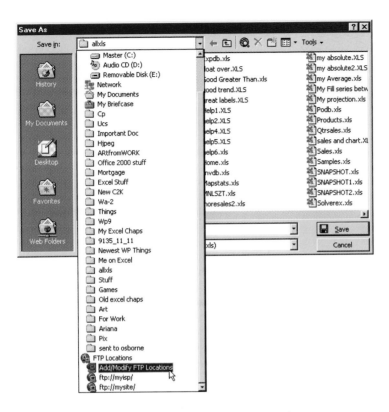

3. Type in the name of the FTP site (for example ftp.mysite.com), as provided by your administrator or ISP support staff.

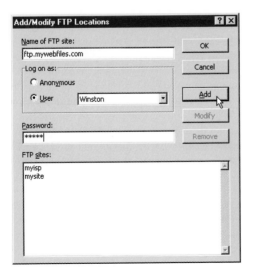

4. Supply the User name and passwords provided for you. The Username will have to be one that Windows is familiar with. If you type in a Username, and the Add button of this dialog box does not appear, you will have to open the Windows Control Panel and click User. Follow the steps provided to add the new Username to the list that Windows recognizes.

5. After providing all the necessary information, click Add. The FTP site will be saved as one of your standard Save As Location choices. This makes saving to FTP just as easy as saving to a standard hard drive location.

6. Click OK to finish.

EXPERT ADVICE

If you have to browse through several levels of directories to get to the location on the server that you have rights to, be patient. You'll only need to do this once, because once you've set up your FTP program to locate your designated FTP directory, the program will remember that location for you.

Publish Your Worksheets as HTML

Now that you have your FTP sites established, you can go ahead and publish your worksheets. Just follow these steps:

1. Open the worksheet you want to save as a Web page.

2. Select File | Save as Web Page. Type in a file name. Change the name to eight characters or less, so that other browsers will not have trouble opening the sheet.

3. Indicate if you want to upload a single sheet, or a workbook. If a single sheet is selected, then the Add Interactivity option is available. Adding interactivity allows others to edit your spreadsheet online. If you want to add interactivity to an entire

workbook, select Workbook now, then, in the next dialog box, you'll be able to add interactivity.

4. After making filename, location, interactivity, and save option choices, click Publish.

5. You'll see a dialog box with more publishing options, including the ability to choose Interactivity type: Spreadsheet or Pivot Table. (Saving with Pivot Table functionality lets visitors click the dropdown menus of a Pivot Table and see a variety of data results).

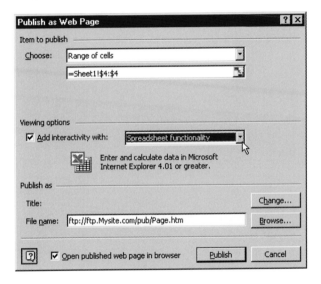

6. It is at this point that you can opt to save your workbook with Interactivity selected, rather than just a single sheet.

7. Click the Browse menu to select a location. Remember that your FTP site is also one of the choices for saving. Chose this site to post your spreadsheet online.

8. This dialog box also has a Publish button. Click it to finally begin uploading your sheet or workbook to its online destination.

Sharing Documents on the Internet

Saving an Excel worksheet (files with the .xls extension) on an FTP site allows others who have Excel to view, change, and print your actual worksheet. Saving a worksheet as a Web page and putting it on the Internet allows more people to see it—anyone with a Web browser could look at it. If you've added interactivity to the worksheet, then visitors can also edit it. Figure 12.3 shows a Worksheet in a Web Browser with interactivity added.

Sharing Worksheets with People Who Don't Have Excel

If you need to share a worksheet in its original form with someone who doesn't have Excel, direct them to the Excel Viewer. For

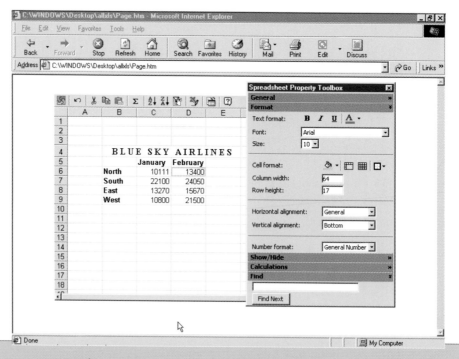

Figure 12.3: When you specify Interactivity, then visitors with more advanced browsers can edit your spreadsheet without downloading it.

coworkers without online access or Excel, the Excel Viewer allows them to join in the fun as well.

You'll just save your worksheet as usual, and make your worksheet available to your coworker as you normally would, via mail, floppy disk, or network, for example. Your designated reviewers must download the Excel viewer from the Microsoft Web site. Have them follow this link:

http://www.microsoft.com/isapi/gooffupd.asp?TARGET=/ downloadCatalog/dldExcel.htm?ShowType=Viewer

If this link is no longer accurate, instruct them to log on to the Microsoft web page (www.microsoft.com), click Downloads, then Miscellaneous Viewers, and then select the Excel Viewer, when it appears. They'll need to follow the links in the Web pages to get to Downloads and the Microsoft Excel viewer. After your colleagues have downloaded and installed the viewer, they can download and view (but not edit) your worksheet. Below is Microsoft's Excel Download page. Note that the Excel Viewer is checked for download. The viewer is free, and, by Microsoft's explicit permission, can be distributed to anyone.

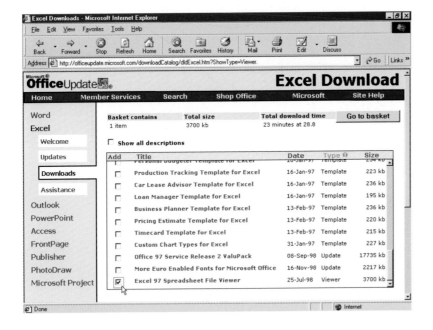

Checkpoint

In this chapter, you've learned a little bit about the Internet and corporate intranets and, more importantly, you've learned how to use Excel to publish your work on these networks. You can publish your spreadsheets so that other people—around the world—can work on the same spreadsheet, or you can post your spreadsheets so that the information is available for people to see.

Whew! Well, that's all folks. You are officially an Excel whiz!

Index

#

overflow, 118
#NUM! error, 163

A

Absolute cell references, 98-100
Actions, macros as, 234
Active cells
    defined, 13
    listing most recent, 18
Add-and-Repeat labels, 67-68
Adding numbers, 94-95
Add-ins, steps for adding, 165-166
Add-Ins dialog box, 165, 258
Align or Distribute (graphics), 221-222
Alignment tab (Format cells dialog box), 122
Alphabetization, 63
Analysis ToolPak, adding, 165-166
Answer report (Solver), 262
Arguments (function), 159, 164
Arithmetic operators, 85

Arrows
    adding to spreadsheets, 209-211
    drawing on charts, 189-190
Ascending sort, 63
Assign Macro dialog box, 241
AutoFilter, 144-146
AutoFilter top ten, 145-146
AutoFormat, 112-114
Automatic recalculation, 98
AutoShapes, 211-215
AVEDEV() function, 172
Axes (chart), 179, 193-194

B

Background color, 110
Background images, 223-224
Banner with text, 212
Billing spreadsheet, iv
Bold fonts, using, 110
Border tab, Format Cells dialog box, 126
Borders, 110-111, 125-126

Brochures, ii
Button icons (toolbar), 49
Buttons (toolbar)
    adding, 48-50
    adding icons to, 49
    assigning macros to, 238-241
    removing, 50

C

Calculations, 94-97. *See also* Formulas; Numbers
Callouts, adding to spreadsheets, 211
Category axis (chart), 179-180
Category names (chart), 182
Cell address, 6-7
Cell contents, 8
    adding while selecting cells, 66-67
    clearing, 65-66
    erasing, 20-21
Cell ranges, selecting, 13. *See also* Named ranges
Cell references, 86-88, 98-100
Cells (worksheet), 4. *See also* Columns
  (worksheet); Rows (worksheet); Worksheets
  (sheets)
    adding to sheets, 63
    automatically filled, 19-21
    borders around, 125
    currently active, 7
    cut-and-paste, 59
    fitting text into, 119
    formatting within, 121
    inserting in sheets, 64-65
    listing most recent active, 18
    moving, 57-62
    moving among, 16
    moving to a new sheet, 59
    organization of, 6
    protecting, 23-24
    selecting, 13-16, 57
    selecting and adding content, 66-67
    selecting with a keyboard, 15-16
    selecting with a mouse, 13-15
    sorting, 62-63
    too narrow for numbers, 118
    typing in, 19
Centering text across columns, 123
Chart axes, 179
Chart axis default, changing, 193-194
Chart data series, 181
Chart data series markers, 182
Chart data series names, 181
Chart data series ranges, 181
Chart defaults, changing, 193-194
Chart elements, editing, 185-186
Chart toolbar buttons, 185
Chart type default, changing, 194
Chart Wizard, 182-184
Charts, ix, 175-199
    creating, 182-184
    deleting, 198
    drawing arrows on, 189-190
    modifying, 184-193
    overlay, 192-193
    parts of, 180
    printing, 197-198
    publishing on the Internet, 198
    resizing and moving, 186-187
    terminology, 179-182
    text boxes for, 187-189
    3D, 180
    trendlines, 191-192
    2D, 180
CLEAN() function, 173
Clipart, 206, 217-218
Clipart Gallery, 218

College Expense table, viii
Colors
    background, 110
    fill, 126-127, 213
    font, 126-127
    line, 213
    picture, 226-227
Column headers, 14, 111
Column width, changing, 118
Columns (worksheet), 6
    adding to sheets, 63
    centering text across, 123
    deleting, 66
    freezing, 147-149
    hiding temporarily, 118
    inserting in sheets, 64-65
    maximum per sheet, 5
    modifying, 117-119
    moving, 57-62
    resizing, 118
    selecting, 14
    sorting, 62-63
Command, adding to a menu, 51
Comparison operators, 86
Constraints, using in Solver, 259-261
CONVERT() function, 158, 168
Copy-and-paste
    for images, 225-226
    multiple, 60-62
Copying, 56-62, 225-226
Currently active cell, 7
Custom AutoFilter dialog box, 147
Custom Lists tab, Options dialog box, 69
Customize dialog box, 51
Cut-and-paste, 58-60

D

Data patterns, creating, 68-69
Data series (chart), 181-182
Database functions, 167
Date sequence/series, 19, 68
Date and time functions, 166-167
Dates and times in cells, 78-79
DAVERAGE() function, 167
DAYS360() function, 166
DCOUNT() function, 167
Deleting charts, 198
Descending sort, 63
Documents. *See also* Files
    linking cells to, 276
    opening, 12
    reusable, 32
    sharing on the Internet, 286-287
DOLLAR() function, 160, 173
Drawing toolbar, 210
Drawings (simple), 207

E

Edit menu, navigating with, 17-18
Engineering functions, 167-168
Excel Viewer, 286-287
Expense template, vii
Expert selecting, 66-70

F

Files
    assigning passwords to, 23
    finding, 10-11
    protecting, 23
Fill Color, 126-127, 213
Filling in a list, 67-70

Fills, 126-127, 213-214
Filters, using to view data, 143-147
Financial functions, 168-170
Financial templates, 32
Find command, 17, 38
Fitting text, 122
Flow chart tools, 208
Flyers, ii
Folders, templates in, 37
Font Color, 126-127
Font options, 120-121
Font size or type, 120-121
Force-fitting text, 122
Format AutoShape, 190, 214
Format AutoShape dialog box, 190
Format cells dialog box
    Alignment tab, 122
    Border tab, 126
    Number tab, 79
Format Line, 214
Format Painter, 112, 116-117
Format Text dialog box, 189
Formats, creating, 117-127
Formatting, 103-128
    examples of, 108-111
    purpose of, 108
    removing, 128
    special, 124
Formatting number cells, 78-80
Formatting numbers, 123-124
Formatting text, 119-123
Formula bar, 7, 9
Formula cell, 7, 75-76
Formula entries, 164
Formula operators, 85-88
Formula references, and moving cells, 100

Formulas, 6. *See also* Functions
    absolute references in, 99-100
    advanced techniques with, 89-100
    applying to new cells, 83-84
    with cell ranges as arguments, 137-141
    copying, 83-84
    creating, 81-82
    equal sign with, 81
    moving, 84
    order of operations in, 82-83
    referencing cells in, 82, 86-88
    template, 33
    testing, 94
    with text triggers, 89-94
    verifying, 93
    viewing all in a worksheet, 81
    working with, 75-77, 80-94
Freezing rows and columns, 147-149
FTP (File Transfer Protocol), 281-284
FTP locations, setting up, 282-284
Function arguments, 159, 164
Function error messages, 163-164
Function operators, 159
Functions, 90, 155-173. *See also* Formulas
    as built-in formulas, 158
    parts of, 159
    pasting, 161-163
    that require add-ins, 165-166
    types of, 166-173
FV() function, 159

G

Go To, 18
Graphics, 201-229. *See also* Images
    adding to spreadsheets, 209-220

assigning macros to, 241-242
cut-and-paste, 58, 60
editing, 220-227
imported, 208-209
insertion methods, 227-228
showing restraint with, 205
types of, 206-208
Grid lines (chart), 181
Grouping images, 224
Groups of cells
border around, 125
cut-and-paste, 59

H

Headers (column and row), 14, 110-111
Hidden windows, viewing, 244
History button, 11
HTML (hypertext markup language), 278
publishing worksheets as, 284-285
saving worksheets as, 275, 278-280
Hyperlinks, 275-278

I

IF formula dialog box, 92
IF formulas, 76, 89-94, 171
Images. *See also* Graphics
aligning, 220-222
copying and pasting, 225-226
grouping and layering, 223-224
moving, 220-221
nudging, 220-221
from outside sources, 219-220
using repeating, 228
Imported pictures, 208-209
INFO() function, 170
Information functions, 170

Insert Picture dialog box, 219
Instant calculations, 94-97
Internet, 265-288
getting connected, 271
vs. intranets, 270
publishing charts on, 198
sharing documents on, 286-287
tools for, 271-273
Intranets (corporate), 265-288
getting connected, 271
vs. the Internet, 270
tools for, 271-273
Invoice template example, 41-46
Invoice toolbar, 44-45
ISEVEN() function, 170
ISNONTEXT() function, 158

K

Keyboard selection tricks, 15-16

L

Label patterns, creating, 68-69
Labels
cut-and-paste, 58, 60
making stand out, 110
Layering images, 223-224
Leasing template, 46
Limits report (Solver), 262
Line Color, 213
Lines, drawing, 125, 209-211
Links
adding to worksheets, 275-278
cell to Web document, 276
editing later, 278
verifying, 277

Lists
 avoiding data growth in, 69-70
 filling in, 67-70
Loan payment calculator, iii, 169, 252-253
Logical functions, 170-171
Lookup functions, 171-172
Lookup tables, 87-88
LOWER() function, 158

M

Macros, 231-244
 assigning to graphic objects, 241-242
 assigning to toolbar buttons, 238-241
 deleting, 243
 recording, 235-237
 running, 237-242
 sample, 237
Maps, annotated, v, 195-197
Math functions, 172
Menus, customizing, 47-48, 51
Microsoft Map, 195-197
Mixed cell references, 98
Mortgage Analyzer example scenario, 252-253
Moving cells, formula references and, 100
Moving cells to a new sheet, 59
Moving data, 56-57
Multiple cells, selecting, 13, 57
Multiple worksheets, working with, 149-152
My documents folder, 10

N

Named ranges, 133-134
 as arguments in formulas, 137-141
 creating, 135-137
 listing all, 140
 updating and deleting, 140-141
Naming worksheets, 149-150

Navigating, 16-18
 with the Edit menu, 17-18
 with the keyboard, 17
Navigation keys, table of, 17
Networks
 Excel with, 270-271
 getting connected, 271
NOW() function, 166
Number formats, 78-80
Number series, filling, 96-99
Number tab, Format Cells dialog box, 79
Numbers (numeric data), 6
 adding, 94-95
 entering, 19-21, 77
 formatting, 123-124
 replaced with pound signs (####), 118
 special symbols for use with, 77
 treated as text, 79-80
 working with, 71-100

O

Office 2000 CD templates, 39
Online editable spreadsheets, creating, 269
Open dialog box, 11
Opening a document, 12
Opening a worksheet, 10
Operator (function), 159
Outlines, 213-215
Overlay charts, 192-193

P

Page Break Preview, 128
Page breaks
 inserting and removing, 127
 moving, 127
 viewing, 127-128
Password, assigning to a file, 23

Paste Function, 161-163
Paste Function dialog box, 162-163
Paste Name dialog box Paste List, 140
Paste Special, for images, 225-226
Personal Macro Workbook, 243-244
PI() function, 172
Pictures. *See also* Graphics; Images
    color and depth, 226-227
    imported, 208-209
Pivot Chart Report, 255
Pivot tables, creating, 255-256
Placeholders, 33
Planner template, 46
PMT() function, 169
Point and click, 19
Precedence in formula operations, 82-83
Printing charts, 197-198
Projecting data, 95-97
Protecting scenarios, 256
Protecting your files, 23
Protecting your work, 22-24
Protecting your workbooks/sheets/cells, 23-24
Publishing charts on the Internet, 198
Publishing worksheets on a web, 273-285
    adding links, 275-278
    as HTML, 284-285
    preparing, 274-278
    saving as HTML, 275, 278-280
    testing, 281
    using FTP, 281-284

Q

Quitting Excel, 24

R

RAND() function, 172
Range names, 133-141. *See also* Named ranges

Range reference, 87
Recalculation, automatic, 98
Record Macro dialog box, 236
Recording macros, 235-237
Redo arrow, 21
Reference functions, 171-172
Reference operators, 86
Referencing cells, 86-88, 98-100
Relative cell references, 98
Repeating image, using, 228
Replace command, 17
Retirement Planner, vi
Rotating text, 122
ROUND() function, 160
Row headers, 14, 111
Row height, changing, 117
Rows (worksheet), 6
    adding to sheets, 63
    deleting, 66
    freezing, 147-149
    hiding temporarily, 118
    inserting in sheets, 65
    maximum per sheet, 5
    modifying, 117-119
    moving, 57-62
    resizing, 117
    selecting, 14
    sorting, 62-63
Running a macro, 237-242

S

Sales projections, creating, 96
Save as HTML option, 275, 278-280
Save As option, 21-22
Save as Web Page option, 21, 271-272
Save option, 21
Save Workspace option, 22

Saving worksheets, 21-22
Scenario Manager, 249, 253
Scenario Manager dialog box, 253
Scenario pivot tables, creating, 255-256
Scenario summaries, creating, 254-255
Scenarios
        changing, 256
        creating, 250-256
        explained, 248
        how they work, 249
        Mortgage Analyzer example, 252-253
        protecting, 256
        viewing, 254
Segments (sheet), expanding/collapsing, 141-147
Select All, 15
Selecting cells, 13-16, 57, 66-70
Send to Back (layering images), 223
Sensitivity report (Solver), 262
Series axis (chart), 179-180
Series of dates, filling, 19, 68
Series of numbers, filling, 96-99
Shading, 126
Shapes (complex), adding to spreadsheets,
    211-214
Shapes (simple), adding to spreadsheets, 209-211
Sharing documents on the Internet, 286-287
Sheet 1, 5
Sheets. *See* Worksheets (sheets)
Shortcut key combinations, 236. *See also* Macros
Single-cell reference, 87
Solver add-in
        generating reports, 262
        installing and loading, 257-258
        Parameters dialog box, 259
        Results dialog box, 262
        using, 257-263
Sorting cells/rows/columns, 62-63

Spreadsheet Solutions, 33, 36
Spreadsheet Solutions folder, 36
Spreadsheets, 4. *See also* Worksheets (sheets)
SQRT() function, 159-160, 162-164, 172
Starbursts, adding to spreadsheets, 211
Starting Excel, 4-5, 9-10
Statistical functions, 172-173
Style dialog box, 115
Styles, 112, 114-116
SUM() function, 172
Symbols, for use with numbers, 77

T

Template file, identifying, 37-39
Template formulas, 33
Templates, 30-47
        for business, 31-32, 35
        common features of, 32-33
        in folders, 37
        free, 31-32, 35
        included with Excel, 30-31
        invoice example, 41-46
        locating and opening, 34-35, 38
        Microsoft, 32, 35
        naming conventions for, 40
        Office 2000 CD, 39
        Osborne/McGraw-Hill, 31-32, 35
        personalizing, 42-44
        renaming, 40
        steps for using, 39
        types of, 46-47
        unzipping, 35
Testing worksheets before publishing, 281
Text, 8
        centering across columns, 123
        entering, 19-21
        fitting into cells, 119

formatting, 119-123
   inside a banner shape, 212
   numbers treated as, 79-80
   rotating/wrapping/force-fitting, 122
   that spills into an adjacent cell, 118
   truncated, 118
Text alignment, changing, 121
Text attributes, customizing, 120
Text boxes, 187-189, 215
Text functions, 173
Text operator, 86
Text triggers, formulas with, 89-94
Three-criteria sorting, 63
3D charts, 180
Tick marks (chart), 181
Titles, 110-111
Toolbar buttons
   adding, 48-50
   adding icons to, 49
   assigning macros to, 238-241
   removing, 50
Toolbars
   adding buttons to, 48-50
   customizing, 47-50
   removing buttons from, 50
   restoring, 50
   useful additions to, 50
Totals, 111
Trendlines (chart), 191-192
Trigonometry functions, 172
2D charts, 180
Typing in a cell, 19

U

Undo arrow, 21
Undoing any action, 21

Units of measurement, 111
Unprotecting your work, 24
Updating, 56
UPPER() function, 173

V

Value axis (chart), 179-180
ValuPack folder, 39
Variables, tracking changing, 248-250
Verifying formulas, 93
Verifying links, 277
Viewing data, using filters for, 143-147
VLOOKUP() function, 172

W

Web, publishing worksheets on, 273-285
Web document, linking a cell to, 276
Web page, worksheet as, x, 275, 278-280
What-if projects, 245-263. *See also* Scenarios
Word art, 207-208, 216-217
Workbooks, 5
   converting, 274-275
   copying worksheets within, 151
   moving worksheets within, 150-151
   moving/copying worksheets to, 152
   previewing, 12
   protecting, 23
   when to create, 5
Worksheet functions. *See* Functions
Worksheet segments, expanding/collapsing, 141-147
Worksheets (sheets), 4. *See also* Columns (worksheet); Rows (worksheet)
   changing the look of, 108
   copying within a workbook, 151

maximum rows and columns, 5
moving and copying, 150-152
moving within a workbook, 150-151
moving/copying to a workbook, 152
naming, 149-150
opening, 10
protecting, 23-24
rearranging, 53-70
saving, 21-22
from scratch, 9
types of information in, 6
when to create, 5
working with multiple, 149-152
Wrapping text, 122

X axis (chart), 179-180

Y axis (chart), 179-180

Z

Z axis (chart), 179
ZTEST() function, 172-173